De Gaulle:

Statesmanship, Grandeur, and Modern Democracy

De Gaulle:
Statesmanship, Grandeur, and Modern Democracy

Daniel J. Mahoney

with a new introduction by the author and a foreword by
Pierre Manent

Transaction Publishers
New Brunswick (U.S.A.) and London (U.K.)

New material this edition copyright © 2000 by Transaction Publishers, New Brunswick, New Jersey. Originally published in 1996 by Praeger Publishers.

Copyright Acknowledgments
The author and publisher gratefully acknowledge permission for use of the following material:
De Gaulle, Charles. Excerpts from *The Call to Honour*. Translated by Jonathan Griffin. London: Weidenfeld & Nicolson, 1955.
De Gaulle, Charles. Excerpts from *The Complete War Memoirs of Charles De Gaulle*. Copyright © 1955, 1956 and 1959 by Librairie Plon. Reprinted by permission of Georges Borchardt, Inc.
De Gaulle, Charles. Excerpts from *The Edge of the Sword*. London: Faber and Faber Ltd, 1960.
De Gaulle, Charles. Excerpts from *Salvation*. Translated by Richard Howard. London: Weidenfeld & Nicolson, 1960.

This book is printed on acid-free paper that meets the American National Standard for Permanence of Paper for Printed Library Materials.

Library of Congress Catalog Number: 00-023489
ISBN: 0-7658-0689-4
Printed in the United States of America

Library of Congress Cataloging-in-Publication Data

Mahoney, Daniel J.
    De Gaulle : statesmanship, grandeur, and modern democracy / Daniel J. Mahoney ; foreword by Pierre Manent.
        p. cm.
    Includes bibliographical references and index.
    ISBN 0-7658-0689-4 (pbk. : alk. paper)
    1. Gaulle, Charles de, 1890-1970—Philosophy. 2. Gaulle, Charles de, 1890-1970—Views on France. 3. Gaulle, Charles de, 1890-1970—Political and social views. I. Title.
DC420.M325 2000
944.083'6' 092—dc21   00-023489

Contents

Introduction to the Transaction Edition

When I began work on this book in the early 1990's I set out with several tasks in mind. To begin with, I wanted to respond to certain misconceptions about de Gaulle that had become nearly routine in Anglo-American discussions about him: that he was best understood as a modern day representative of a "Bonapartist" tradition in French politics, that his defense of the "grandeur" of France reflected a romantic and deeply anachronistic approach to politics, and that he was imbued with an irrational but quite French disdain for all things American. In addition, I had read enough of de Gaulle's principal writings as well as the secondary literature to be impressed by his remarkable thoughtfulness not only about matters concerning France and her history, but also in regard to politics and political philosophy simply. As I proceeded, these initial impressions were only confirmed. The result is this book about the thought and action of Charles de Gaulle which perhaps emphasizes his thought even more than his action.

The first chapter of the most famous of Charles de Gaulle's pre-World War II writings, *The Edge of the Sword*, is preceded by an epigram from Goethe's *Faust* that is intended to clarify the essentially contingent nature of political action: "In the beginning was the Word? No! In the beginning was action!" De Gaulle certainly remained committed to the understanding that political and military leaders could be guided by abstract or a priori principles only at their own peril. Politics, especially war, is always a matter of circumstances. But de Gaulle also believed that politics must never lose sight of fundamental principles, especially a sense of the broad limits imposed by "the natural order of things." Beginning with his very first book on the reasons for the German defeat in the First World War, de Gaulle emphasized that action must respect the sense of measure "which alone renders durable and fecund works of energy." All of his thought and action were a response to Germanic or Nietzschean modernity with its exaltation of the "will to power" and its denial of a natural order, which establishes the limits of all political action.[1] His hortatory rhetoric about national and political "grandeur" is in no way intended as a substitute for classical restraint or political moderation. Rather it is best understood, as I argue in this book, as a call for the French to overcome the ideological divisions that have especially plagued them since the Revolution of 1789 severed the unity of "eternal France." It is just as fundamentally a corrective to the lack of civic-mindedness and the preoccupation with material well-being characteristic of the modern democratic regime.[2]

De Gaulle was a quintessentially *French* statesmen and his practical vision always remained tightly focused on France. His appeal to the glory and greatness of France was, in some sense, an end in itself, since he fully appreciated honor as a self-subsisting motive of political life. But it also aimed at overcoming the debilitating divisions characteristic of post-revolutionary French politics, as I have suggested. And yet de Gaulle understood, as keenly as any modern statesman, the nature of democratic politics within which the drama of modern French politics unfolds. I remain struck by the profound affinities between de Gaulle's analysis of modern democracy and that of a great French predecessor whose work he did not know or at least know well: Tocqueville. Both Tocqueville and de Gaulle feared the enervation of modern individuals resulting from a private and apolitical understanding of liberty. Tocqueville even flirted with a Gaullist-style politics of grandeur to correct "the natural vices" inherent in the democratic "social state," including its practical materialism and its tendency to encourage individualism or apathetic withdrawal from public life. It is important to stress that de Gaulle's emphasis on grandeur did not entail, anymore than Tocqueville's, a rejection of democracy. It is rather an effort to correct or mitigate the natural tendencies of democracy while preserving its strengths and accepting its undeniable justice.

But, in order to understand truly the nature of democracy, it is necessary to turn to political philosophy. This, de Gaulle did with remarkable competence. I am not suggesting that de Gaulle was a political philosopher in any conventional understanding of that term, especially as he remained squarely focused on the pressing requirements of practical life. But as I emphasize in the book, his account of the problem of democracy is in some cases informed by and is broadly congruent with the analyses of a wide range of nineteenth and twentieth century conservative and conservative-liberal thinkers including Tocqueville, Burckhardt, and Ortega y Gasset. In my view, it is as profound a perspective on the possibilities and limits of the democratic enterprise as is available today.

De Gaulle's critique of 'Nietzschean' modernity and his 'Tocquevillean' appreciation of the problem of democracy come together in his important discussion of "the crisis of civilization" in his Oxford speech of November 25, 1941. That speech is subjected to detailed exegesis and analysis in Chapter 5 of this book. I have little to add here to the analysis that I have already provided of what remains one of de Gaulle's most searching analyses of modern politics. But a penetrating lecture by the political philosopher Leo Strauss on "German Nihilism," delivered in February 1941 but only recently published,[3] helps confirm the depth of de Gaulle's lucidity and the self-conscious character of his moderation.

Strauss points out that German nihilism, in both its deepest intellectual sources and its popular manifestations, was guided by an initially non-nihilistic motive, by a deep revulsion against the bourgeois reduction of human life to "civilization," to an inordinate concern for material provision and self-preservation. German nihilists could not imagine anything worse than bourgeois society and so turned to a radicalized form of militarism as an alternative to the morality of self-interest since "courage is the only unambiguously non-utilitarian value." But in the process they rejected not only modern or Anglo-French "civilization" in the name of "culture" but also "the eternal principles of civilization" rooted in science and morals. As Strauss correctly notes, they threw out "the baby with the bath" and failed to see (as the less theoretically-minded English clearly did) that modern civilization was, at some level, "a reasonable adaptation of the old and eternal ideal of decency, of rule of law, and of that liberty which is not license, to changed circumstances." Whatever his quarrel with "perfidious Albion" this is a truth that de Gaulle unhesitatingly affirmed. He insisted on the common Christian and liberal roots of *modern* civilization. De Gaulle was a forceful critic of democratic individualism, of the passivity and mediocrity of a merely bourgeois existence, but he defended democratic liberties as, in part, a precious acquisition of the West's pre-modern past. He did so *en pleine connaissance de cause*, knowing that modern civilization, at its best, embodied "the eternal principles of civilization." In his Oxford speech and elsewhere, de Gaulle spoke eloquently in opposition to all forms of racialist and nationalist collectivism as well as against the temptation of ideological or personal despotism, *even his own.* Claude Guy's recently published record of his conversations with de Gaulle during the period immediately after World War II, *En Écoutant de Gaulle*, contains a particularly revealing formulation of de Gaulle's principled rejection of dictatorship:

In the short run, dictatorship sometimes embarks upon great things. But it *always* finishes badly, because, in order to make people accept the weights of constraint and moral oppression, it is soon necessary for it to drag the country along in some exaggerated enterprises, to obtain for it successes as a result of external adventures which will necessarily finish poorly. I would say that this is why I am opposed to dictatorship (emphasis mine).[4]

Charles de Gaulle was indebted to spiritual and intellectual traditions that predated philosophic modernity but he accepted the modern liberal regime and tried to correct its excesses through prudent statesmanship. It is difficult for contemporary social science to appreciate de Gaulle since it has little place for statesmanship in its science. The closest it comes is the rich Weberian notion of "charismatic leadership." This notion certainly illuminates multiple dimensions of political life. And de Gaulle himself approximates some aspects of this concept in his own rich discussion in Chapter 3 of *The Edge of the Sword* of the need for the man of action to cultivate "prestige." But the concept of charismatic leadership fails to distinguish adequately the public-spirited statesman or "man of character" as de Gaulle called him, from the despot and the unscrupulous politician and hence obscures as much as enlightens the understanding of political phenomena. One major purpose of this book is to remind social scientists that any articulation of "charismatic leadership" must confront the self-understanding of the "magnanimous statesman" such as Churchill or de Gaulle, who is remarkably self-conscious about his nature and activity. Social scientific discussions of leadership must come to terms with the Aristotelian analysis of magnanimity.

If I were writing this book today, I might emphasize a few things differently, but I am convinced that it remains an essentially solid because equitable account of the Gaullist self-understanding. In emphasizing that de Gaulle was not irrationally anti-American, I may have understated his deep aversion to American hegemony in Europe and interventionism in the Third World during the 1960's, an aversion not incompatible, in de Gaulle's view, with a deeper commitment to the West in its struggle with Soviet totalitarianism.[5] Today, I would also place more emphasis on the fragility of the constitution of the Fifth

Republic. DeGaulle's constitutional re-founding overcame the institutional and moral weaknesses of the two previous French constitutional orders, but in the process, created new, and quite serious, problems of its own. It is an open question whether the General's constitution can permanently survive "cohabitation" since its presence fundamentally weakens the power of the executive and unwittingly makes him preside over a cabinet consisting of representatives of the *opposition*. One critic has astutely observed that such an arrangement is at odds with the very logic of representative government; representative government depends, as Montesquieu first noted, "on a firm distinction between government and opposition, on the reciprocal exclusion of the majority and the opposition".[6] Whether or not this profound structural problem can be mitigated by a reduction of the French President's term to five as opposed to seven years, as some have proposed, is still very much an open question.

Let me conclude. This book, while broadly sympathetic to de Gaulle, should not be mistaken as a brief for Gaullism. Many inveterate Gaullists ignore the deeper intellectual reflection of their hero and have transformed his inspiration into an ideology. In addition, Gaullism, or at least the neo-Gaullism of Jacques Chirac, appears moribund. Contemporary neo-Gaullists are unable or unwilling to defend de Gaulle's unflagging insight that the European community, if it is to amount to something significant, must have a political character drawn from the coordinated activities of states that were to be its essential "pillars." A Gaullism that forgets this is hardly worthy of its name.

Undoubtedly, it is one task of scholarship to "banalize" de Gaulle, to see beyond the heroic mythology of his self-presentation. But at the end of this process of demythologization one is still left with the irreducible greatness of an extraordinary statesman. De Gaulle continues to inspire through the memory of his actions and, perhaps even more importantly as time goes by, through his eloquent and often profound reflections on the political condition of modern man.

Daniel J. Mahoney
Worcester, MA
August, 1999

NOTES

1. English-language readers will be able to appreciate more fully this aspect of de Gaulle's thought with the publication of Robert Eden's excellent translation and introduction to de Gaulle's first and previously untranslated book, *La Discorde Chez L'Ennemi*, to appear as *The Enemy's House Divided* from The University of North Carolina Press in 2001.

2. An earlier scholarly analysis has come to my attention which nicely highlights the "domestic" purposes served by de Gaulle's emphasis on grandeur and recognizes the link between greatness and measure in his thought. See Philip G. Cerny, *The Politics of Grandeur: Ideological Aspects of de Gaulle's Foreign Policy* (Cambridge University Press, 1980). My book differs significantly from Cerny's in placing much greater emphasis on de Gaulle's debt to Charles Péguy for the idea of a "mystique" of the greatness of France that could overcome its division into two great ideological parties of the Left and Right and in recognizing that the "politics of grandeur" addresses the problem of democracy and not merely divisions inherent in French politics and history.

3. See Leo Strauss's lecture entitled "German Nihilism," delivered at the Graduate Faculty of Political and Social Science, The New School for Social Research, February 26, 1941. The text appears in *Interpretation: A Journal of Political Philosophy* (Spring 1999, Vol. 26, Number 3), pp. 353-378. All the quotations from Strauss are taken from this text.

4. Claude Guy, *En Écoutant de Gaulle: Journal 1946-1949* (Paris: Grasset, 1996), pp. 79-80. For de Gaulle's fascinating differentiation of the statesman, politician and dictator, see pp. 69-70. For a discussion of these passages, see Nicolas Tenzer, *La face cachée du gaullisme* (Paris: Grasset, 1996), pp. 219-222.

5. On de Gaulle's foreign policy in the 1960's see Maurice Vaisse, *La Grandeur: Politique étrangère du général de Gaulle, 1958-1969* (Paris: Fayard, 1998) as well as the excellent discussion of Vaisse's book by Charles G. Cogan in *French Politics and Society* (Vol. 17, No. 1, Winter 1999), pp. 79-83.

6. See Pierre Manent, "Mesure de la France," *Commentaire* (Printemps 1998, Vol. 21, Numéro 81) pp. 96-98. The quotation is from p. 97.

Foreword

I have two principal reasons for recommending quite heartily the reading of this book. The first is particular and interested: at a time when it seems that the Anglo-Saxon world is turning against France with an incomprehensible aggressiveness, it helps to explain profoundly my country to the American public. The other motive is general and disinterested: through study of the thought and action of an eminent statesman, this book illumines the political condition of modern man. In this brief presentation I will consider only the second point.

When one draws up the list of obstacles that inhibit the progress of political science, one often forgets the main one: the very idea that we have of science. Ordinary political science assigns itself the task of arriving at general laws, or at least "generalizations," based on the greatest possible number of similar, or analogous, cases. This is the method of the common denominator. However, what is most common is the least interesting, the least significant. The consequence is that the normal result of science consists more and more in knowing things ever more certainly and precisely—about objects less and less worthy of interest. On the contrary, it is what first of all vitally interests the citizen that sets in motion true political science. The latter orients itself in political life; it engages itself in relation to what political men say and do. The words and deeds of political men, of statesmen, are the first object of true political science. Daniel Mahoney's book on Charles de Gaulle is a contribution of the first order to this science.

The political career of Charles de Gaulle is one of the richest and most astonishing of the twentieth century. This singular brilliance, however, has

put it at a disadvantage in the eyes of many observers: today, whatever is
unique is very close to being strange or foreign, and what is strange is not
far from being ridiculous. De Gaulle claimed to identify himself with the
French *nation*, that is, with a political form generally judged to be obsolete—after having been harmful—and to a particular nation whose standing fell in the twentieth century. Therefore, he appears as a "curious" figure
for whom one has, eventually, a "romantic" sympathy, or a "reasonable"
antipathy, but in either case he is irrelevant to one who considers "the true
problems of today's world." Daniel Mahoney shows just how far this
widespread belief is removed from the truth.

Politics in the proper sense, in the most elevated sense, is something
quite distinct from the rights and interests of individuals and groups, which
legitimately occupy quotidian social and political life. What is properly
political is what concerns the political body—in this case, the nation as a
whole: it is the honor and sovereignty of the body politic; it is also its
constitution. Therefore, to study the conduct of de Gaulle—who entered
into action in order to preserve the honor and sovereignty of France in
1940, and who re-founded her Constitution in 1958 and 1962—is to study
the very meaning of political life.

Charles de Gaulle wrote a great deal before circumstances gave him the
opportunity to act. And more rarely his action was in conformity with the
reflections that had preceded it. One of Daniel Mahoney's great merits is
to reconstitute, on the basis of de Gaulle's writings, de Gaulle's view of the
whole, of politics and of the human condition in general. He shows in a
convincing manner that, contrary to a reproach often leveled against him,
de Gaulle was not at all "Nietzschean." In his first book devoted to
Germany in the First World War, de Gaulle explains that it was precisely
the "Nietzscheanism" of the German generals that was one of the causes
of that lack of measure which led not only to Germany's military defeat but
also its political decomposition. More generally, Mahoney shows how
self-affirmation and the affirmation of the nation—two affirmations
equally imperative with de Gaulle—are not separable from the recognition
of "an order of things," or from a "nature of things," which is objective and
which obliges men, in the two senses of the verb, to oblige. In short,
Mahoney demonstrates that de Gaulle is fundamentally classical—a conclusion that confounds equally most of his critics and most of his admirers.

With de Gaulle the affirmation of the nation is not the romantic
affirmation of a collective self in which the individual self would lose itself
with pleasure, but rather the self-conscious and obstinate search for a
political means to rise above the almost fated lowering that weighs on

modern democracy, and perhaps on the human condition itself. Without ever making artificially of de Gaulle a political philosopher, Mahoney establishes that de Gaulle expressly shares the fears of those great European thinkers from Tocqueville to Ortega y Gasset who see democratic man menaced by an individualistic retraction, which paradoxically, but necessarily, favors collectivist enterprises. De Gaulle had reflected seriously on "the condition of modern man." One can judge that the national solution he proposes is not satisfactory; at the very least, however, he attempted by its means to respond to the most difficult problem facing us.

It is at this point that we touch on what is most admirable and least noticed about de Gaulle. He who seems to personify a certitude untouched by doubt, he whose hand never trembles, was very acutely aware of the complexity of things, and in particular of the problematic character of the nation, the political form that simultaneously cannot be done without and that must be surpassed. Mahoney shows this perfectly in analyzing the General's European policy. De Gaulle had a divided soul. He knew how much Europe was more than France, and this is why he was also a "good European." But he also knew that the vitality of Europe had always been made up of the vitality of a France fiercely French, of an England intransigently English, of an Italy unabashedly Italian, to say nothing of Germany. This is why he sought uneasily to construct Europe by means of nations. And this is why at the end of his life—with the exaggeration authorized perhaps by old age and services rendered—he considered himself one of the "last Europeans."

Mahoney has not written a hagiography. He does not describe an infallible man. In particular, he shows that the Gaullist analysis of the postwar world suffered from a grave defect: the underestimation of the ideological virulence of communism. Daniel Mahoney judges severely, and I think justly, this period, or this aspect of the General's international action, when he seemed to place France at equal distance from what he called "the two superpowers," the United States and the Soviet Union. In a man as reflective as de Gaulle, this defect derived from a general error of analysis, and not, as is said sometimes, from a sentiment of anti-Americanism, which in fact was foreign to him. It is true that de Gaulle wanted France, or Europe, "to take its destiny in its own hands," and he wished that it would cease "to depend on American protection." As such this ambition was legitimate, even if one can disagree with the manner in which it was formulated and put into practice. As for the wartime difficulties with Roosevelt, Mahoney shows that things are clear enough: the great American president quite simply was mistaken about de Gaulle, whom he took to be an aspiring despot, and this error of judgment was the principal cause of grave political differences that could have been avoided.

I admire the fact that, so young and writing from so far away, Daniel Mahoney—who already has published a remarkable work on Raymond Aron—understands French things so well. I admire even more the power of the work, the fertile passion and the intelligence with which he strives to comprehend the human meaning of politics.

Pierre Manent
École des Hautes Études en Sciences Sociales
Paris, October 1995

Preface

The great German antiliberal political and legal theorist Carl Schmitt famously claimed that there was no such thing as a liberal politics—only a *liberal critique of politics*. The French statesman Charles de Gaulle, a friend of liberty but an ambivalent liberal, understood and experienced the discomforting if partial truth of this claim. He believed that human beings were political animals who naturally desired to live in communities dedicated to shared, noble purposes. Yet he also knew that modern men are *individuals* who resist or ignore these purposes. The individuals of modern democracies are torn: they resist the political realization of their human and civic natures even while crying out to have them fulfilled. The statesman–writer de Gaulle believed that it was the task of statesmanship to articulate and kindle these political purposes by reaching for the summits, for the dazzling, stellar light of national unity and ambition that he called "grandeur." But he also believed that the responsible statesman must limit himself by accepting the human and political limits within which nature and history have placed them. The democratic statesman must aim to correct the corrosive acids of modern individualism even while accepting the idea that a largely decent materialism and individualism set the inescapable boundaries and animate the moral vision of modern liberal democratic societies.

De Gaulle wished to promote the "greatness of France," and this meant attending to the never satisfied requirements of economic growth and social well-being. As president of France from 1958 to 1969, de Gaulle rather successfully attended to these demanding, if not always glorious, tasks. Yet success at stimulating economic development and modernization inevitably strengthens the very individualism and materialism of modern societies which a politics of greatness aims to correct or mitigate.

De Gaulle knew that his dilemma was the dilemma of the public-spirited statesman within modernity: he must improve living standards for the sake of social comity and the power and greatness of the nation even while knowing that this necessary task paradoxically exacerbates the erosion of civic virtues and political instincts that are inherent in modern individualism. De Gaulle never despaired of this fated circle, and despite the pessimism he felt at the end of his tenure as president, he never really thought that this circle was fundamentally tragic or vicious. He did not despair of liberal democracy: he did not succumb to the illusion of the impatient or tyrannical that "anything" is better than democratic mediocrity. He appreciated that there was dignity enough and abundant tasks for the statesman in reminding modern individuals that their humanity could not be fulfilled in the absence of sustained, common political purposes. Such a statesmanship and its accompanying hortatory rhetoric cannot help but humanize and even ennoble our democratic destiny.

When we reflect on the dark twentieth-century experience of totalitarianism and the self-indulgent and dehumanizing "postmodern" radicalization and "deconstruction" of modern individualism, we more fully appreciate the dignified, even noble moderation that underlies de Gaulle's qualified correction of modern democracy. This book, a meditative reflection on the thought and action of Charles de Gaulle, aims to highlight the grounds of his noble but elliptical or elusive moderation. De Gaulle is no Nietzschean or even Bonapartist: but what is he in his moral and political bearing? In attempting to answer this question, we turn primarily to de Gaulle's own writings and speeches which are a guide not only to the history of modern France but also in their own right make a profound contribution to our understanding of the structural and spiritual dilemmas attendant to the regime of modern liberty.

It is a pleasure to express gratitude to those who have aided me on this project. I wish above all to thank my parents whose unflagging encouragement and generous technical help were indispensable to the completion of this book. Generous grants from the Bradley Foundation, the Earhart Foundation, and Assumption College allowed me the time and leisure to pursue research and writing. My friend and colleague, Paul Seaton, read the entire manuscript and made invaluable suggestions for improvement. For this act of friendship, I am particularly grateful. David DesRosiers, Peter Lawler, and Brian Anderson provided deeply appreciated friendship and ongoing intellectual stimulation. Pierre Manent read the entire manuscript and generously provided a foreword to the book. The cheerful and always competent Carmella Murphy typed and retyped the chapters of this work and now knows more about de Gaulle than she ever thought possible or desirable. My secretary Barbara Cichowski helps make my professional life infinitely more efficient than it otherwise would be. To others, especially our summer community at Hatch Lake, and my friends in Norfolk, Massachusetts, I owe the pleasure of a real community of thought and friendship.

Chapter 1

Introduction: The Thought and Action of Charles de Gaulle

Charles de Gaulle has entered into history. In France, he no longer is the subject of intense political debates but is instead claimed by and for all the parties (although, of course, by some more than others). Even the socialist François Mitterrand, an old enemy and the author of a rather undignified polemic against him called *The Permanent Coup d'État*, assumed the Gaullist presidency, with all its quasi-monarchical prerogatives, with ease and self-assurance. In 1990 Mitterrand presided over the huge national commemoration of the one hundredth anniversary of de Gaulle's birth, the fiftieth anniversary of his appeal to resistance, and the twentieth anniversary of his death. "As General de Gaulle, he has entered the pantheon of great national heroes, where he ranks (according to a public opinion poll taken in 1990) ahead of Napoleon and behind only Charlemagne."[1] The old disputes about de Gaulle's person and motives, the fierce polemics centering around his claim to the special contract with France, one forged over the dark abyss of June 1940, the criticism of his alleged authoritarianism—all have given way to a "consensual mythology of General de Gaulle the national savior and liberator"[2] among the public, if not all the scholars and intellectuals.

A voluminous and richly detailed biographical literature, led by Jean Lacouture's acclaimed biography of de Gaulle,[3] now allows us to see beyond the mythological de Gaulle, but it does not refute his undoubted heroism and greatness. This literature instead allows us to understand them. It therefore provides important material for a political science that seeks to understand political phenomena in all their remarkable amplitude. It helps us make sense of the complex relations among de Gaulle's different activities as thinker, writer, officer, rebel, statesman, and politician.

Lacouture's magisterial biography, in particular, with its clear, vigorous prose, its detailed investigation of his writings, discourses, and correspondence, its careful and sympathetic study of the intellectual foundations and unfolding exigencies of his statecraft, and its sheer mastery of all the pertinent sources and issues will remain an indispensable guide for all those wishing to penetrate the mysteries of de Gaulle's soul.

Andrew Shennan's useful book *De Gaulle*[4] chronicles the career of de Gaulle the politician, which is the subject of so many acrimonious political disputes. Yet even Shennan admits that there is something grand, irreducible, and mythological about the reality of the General himself. No account of de Gaulle that wishes to capture the man and his works can simply be a "profile in power" (to quote the title of the series in which Shennan's book appears), for Charles de Gaulle was undoubtedly one of the great human beings of the twentieth century, a member of that distinguished elite of natural aristocrats who deserve the appellation "statesman."

This fact is all the more interesting in that de Gaulle had, as Daniel Chirot put it, the opportunity but not the inclination to become a tyrant.[5] The starting point for understanding the moral foundations of Gaullism is the recognition of the fact that de Gaulle rejected the option of tyranny, both personal and ideological, on intellectual and moral as well as on pragmatic grounds. This spokesman for the grandeur and rank of France was also a considered partisan of political moderation, which in modern circumstances necessarily entails support for some variant of liberal democratic constitutionalism. Yet it is not immediately clear what motivated de Gaulle's unambiguous rejection of the option of tyranny. De Gaulle attempted to assuage the concern of critics at a press conference in May 1958, on the eve of his return to power and the establishment of the Fifth French Republic, by asking if he, who had always respected the basic public liberties, was to begin a career as a dictator at the age of sixty-seven![6] This work aims to help us understand the principled character of de Gaulle's self-limitation, the grounds of his respect for public liberties, and his rejection of various despotic temptations.

It is a commonplace that de Gaulle, however responsible and public-spirited his exercise of political authority may have been, was in his moral and political bearing a Nietzschean and Bonapartist. It is asserted that his politics finally rests on nothing more than self-assertion, even if his more traditionalist and nontotalitarian politics of grandeur was capable of willing moderation or self-restraint for the sake of the nation's unity and integrity. The British diplomat Lord Gladwyn, who admired de Gaulle, called him a "Nietzschean superman beyond good and evil."[7] Emmanuel d'Astier, the resistance leader who served de Gaulle as the commissioner of the Interior in the French Committee of National Liberation in Algiers during the war years, formulated perhaps the most interesting description of this position. According to d'Astier, de Gaulle "was to make of Nietzsche, Charles Maurras and Machiavelli a very personal salad."[8] John Weightman, the literary critic, has called de Gaulle "a committed neo-Nietzschean intellectual" who was as "bleakly convinced as Sartre or Camus that there is no given meaning to existence, and who took it upon himself to create his own meaning by an extraordinary act of will in extremely difficult circumstances."[9]

Support for the thesis of de Gaulle's Nietzscheanism is usually derived, as we shall see, from a cursory reading of two of his prewar writings, *Le Fil de l'épée*[10] and *Vers l'armée de Métier*.[11] (Two other prewar books, which correct an "existentialist" reading of de Gaulle's understanding and intention, are not well known in the United States.)[12] Evidence is found in the thought and action of the prewar de Gaulle, the officer and writer who was known only in limited political, military, and literary circles. Many biographers have looked for antecedents to June 18, 1940, the appeal to resistance and break with the established French military and political authority, in the character, actions, and writings of the pre-1940 de Gaulle.

All of the biographies and commentaries find a man of "monumental self-assurance"[13] who firmly believed in his destiny. Lacouture begins the first volume of his work by recounting the remarkable story of the fifteen-year-old de Gaulle in 1905, then a student at the Jesuit college of the Immaculée-Conception, composing a twenty-page essay describing how "General de Gaulle" would save France in the year 1930 from a German-led invasion of France by a Europe "angered by the [French] government's ill will and insolence."[14] Even at the age of fifteen de Gaulle seemed to have a premonition of and even a supreme confidence in his destiny.

Lacouture emphasizes at great length de Gaulle's bearing as a rebel who delighted in opposing the misguided judgments of his supposed superiors. He regularly found himself in trouble with his superiors at the École de Guerre because of his proud attitude and independent judgment. He delivered a remarkable series of lectures on the nature of military and political leadership, lauding those "men of character" who are not appreciated until the supreme crisis arrives, before an audience at the École de Guerre in 1927 that included officials in the military hierarchy. He later broke with Maréchal Pétain, the hero of Verdun, his first patron and mentor, who had appointed him to his military Cabinet in 1925. Pétain had commissioned de Gaulle to ghostwrite a book on the history of the French army to be entitled *Le Soldat*. When Pétain involved other officers in the project and in effect diluted de Gaulle's carefully constructed work, de Gaulle insisted to Pétain that the work was essentially his own and that he was not willing to share work on the project. In 1938 the book was published under de Gaulle's own name as *La France et son Armée*, and the break with Pétain was complete.[15]

Most importantly, de Gaulle opposed the entire political and military strategy adopted by the various French governments and military command during the interwar period. In 1934 he published his manifesto *Vers l'armée de Métier* (translated into English as *The Army of the Future*), which attacked the exclusively defensive strategy of the French, with its reliance on the so-called Maginot Line. De Gaulle advocated a comprehensive military reform, the creation of an enhanced military organization and authority, and the establishment of dynamic tank divisions reflecting the primacy of offense over defense in the age of the internal combustion engine. He self-consciously attempted "to politicize the debate"[16] over military strategy. He would enlist the support of an impressive group of politicians and intellectuals from the Left and Right, including the future Premier Paul Reynaud; this conservative, Catholic officer even tried, less than successfully, to "convert" the Socialist Léon Blum, the head of the Popular Front government, to the cause of a military "re-founding." De Gaulle's efforts would go unrewarded, and the disastrous Battle of France was an undesired practical vindication of de Gaulle's position. The same men who opposed de Gaulle's strategic ideas would energetically work for the armistice in June of 1940. In his Appeal of June 18, de Gaulle discreetly notes his vindication. De Gaulle continued to play the role of "Cassandra" (as Lacouture correctly notes)[17] even when he knew that, for all intents and purposes, the Battle of France, if not the global or world war, was lost. On January 26, 1940, in a memorandum to eighty prominent French political and military officials, he made his last dramatic effort to educate the French state to its military responsibilities in an age of mechanized warfare.[18] But this was precisely an act of public edification or education, not an act of defiance or self-referential rebellion.

De Gaulle was never a simple-minded conservative or traditionalist (although Lacouture may go too far in stressing his status as rebel). His repeated flouting of established authority had as much to do with his profound appreciation of the decadent character of the French military and political elite and state as it did with his supreme pride and recognition of himself as a "man of character." As Lacouture himself recognizes, there was nothing antinomian about de Gaulle. He did not rebel, in 1940 or 1958 or at any lesser moment, for rebellion's sake.

De Gaulle undoubtedly was a man of the greatest determination and the deepest ambition. For example, Lacouture gives a fascinating account of de Gaulle's indefatigable efforts to escape from German prisons during World War I. There is something extraordinary, and surely metaphorical, about the repeated efforts of this tall and very French-looking officer to escape across Germany so that he could return to France to leave his mark on events and contribute to the national cause. His captivity, while leaving much time for study, reflection, and writing, was the occasion of deep sadness, bordering on despair, for de Gaulle.[19]

In his works *The Edge of the Sword* and *The Army of the Future*, de Gaulle draws a portrait of the "man of character" who is "made for great deeds."[20] (This portrait, so important for grasping de Gaulle's self-understanding, is described and analyzed at length in Chapter 3.) These much misunderstood portraits, which are clearly self-portraits and self-anticipations,[21] may convey, if read carelessly and outside the larger context of de Gaulle's thought and action, a sense of de Gaulle as an existentialist or Nietzschean. The man of character is characterized by depth, singularity, and self-sufficiency. He is "not popular except in critical times."[22] He despises the merely ordinary or routine.

Yet his ambition is neither crude nor narrowly self-serving. He wishes to be of great service to something larger than himself even as he draws on an inner reserve of ambition and fortitude and follows his "star" or "luck" or "fortune."[23] Stanley Hoffmann captures the dual and paradoxical aspect of the Gaullist hero: he is "both his own law *and* the servant of France."[24] De Gaulle once praised Léon Blum to his aide Claude Mauriac as an ambitious man "in the good sense of the term."[25] According to de Gaulle, Blum was so deeply ambivalent about him because he was what Blum admirably wanted to be: the man to whom the nation would owe its salvation. De Gaulle, on that occasion, differentiated ambition in the good sense from the self-seeking that "overlooks essentials."[26] De Gaulle formulated this distinction in the concluding chapter of *The Army of the Future*, where he writes about the "man made for great deeds":

And so he would be condemned to emasculation or corruption, if he lacked the grim impulse of ambition to spur him on. It is not, to be sure, that the passion for rank and honours, which is only careerism, possesses him, but it is, beyond doubt, the hope of playing a great role in great events![27]

There is a widespread belief, based on superficial readings of *The Edge of the Sword* and *The Army of the Future*, which asserts that de Gaulle's Catholicism was in reality nominal and cultural, something that did not penetrate the depths or core of his being. As a Frenchman who worked to transcend the partisan divisions of monarchical and republican France, de Gaulle had no choice but to be a (discreet) Catholic, or so the argument goes. One passage in particular from the chapter "Of Prestige" in *The Edge of the Sword* has become the proof text for the Machiavellian and Nietzschean interpretations of de Gaulle. In the context of describing how the man of character sustains his prestige in an era when the customary sources of obedience have eroded, de Gaulle makes clear that the virtue of the statesman is not a search for evangelical perfection. De Gaulle writes:

It is not at all a question of virtue and evangelical virtue does not lead to empire. The man of action does not conceive himself without a strong dose of egotism, pride, hardness, and cunning. But he is allowed that, indeed, they will be regarded as high qualities, if he can make of them the means to achieve great ends.[28]

De Gaulle certainly had his own rather prodigious dose of egotism, pride, hardness, and cunning. His political persona therefore appears to be a curious synthesis of Aristotelian magnanimity and Machiavellian *virtù*. But it also included a Christian spirit of humane care for one's fellows who are, de Gaulle maintained, beings with souls. He believed in the irreducible dignity of human beings who are souls as well as matter. In his practical politics, he was capable of hardheaded Machiavellianism (as his calibrated disembarkment from French Algeria after 1958 evidences), and in his foreign policy he upheld the moderate Machiavellianism of Richelieu's *raison d'État*[29] in a liberalized and humanized form. (He did not seize his neighbor's provinces but, instead, brought about Franco-German reconciliation.) Nonetheless, de Gaulle was an admirer of the realistic but moderate and limited principle called the *balance of power*.[30]

De Gaulle never separated his evocation of grandeur, his defense of the legitimate role of ambition in political life, and his recognition of the powerful role that necessity plays in the life of nations, from his classical recognition of the necessity, dignity, and indispensability of personal and political measure. His criticism of "thinking" Germany's capitulation to the allure of the Nietzschean "Superman" in *The Discord Among the Enemy* (1924) and his surprisingly critical portrait in *France and Her Army* (1938) of a Napoleon who divorced greatness from all measure are particularly striking examples of de Gaulle's rejection of the fascist temptation of unlimited national and personal self-assertion. Like any thoughtful observer of political life, de Gaulle understood the inescapable Machiavellian dimensions and requirements of political action and the necessity to forego evangelical perfection. But it is wrong to conclude that de Gaulle made of "Nietzsche, Charles Maurras and Machiavelli a very personal salad." De Gaulle's Catholic recognition of moral boundaries and political limits and classical commitment to the life of personal honor enabled him to resist and transcend the Nietzschean critique of moderation and self-limitation. He recognized what according to him Napoleon failed to see, that "souls like matter, have their limits."[31]

As *The Discord Among the Enemy* testifies, de Gaulle admired the energy and determination of the German war chiefs, but he deplored their radical individualism or Nietzscheanism. Their courage was marred by a colossal intellectual and moral failing: they rejected any notion of a common good ratified and directed by public-spirited statesmanship. They were too deeply influenced by Nietzsche's thought about the Superman who ignores the "limits drawn by human experience, by good sense, and by law." Their amoral individualism, their ambition divorced from a sense of limits, their "zest for unbounded enterprises"[32] opened Germany to the discord that fatally wounded its civic spirit and martial courage after July 1918.

The German military leaders showed disdain for the very idea of a legitimate political authority to which the military was necessarily subordinated. De Gaulle makes clear that this intellectual and spiritual corruption began to show its effects from the very beginning of the war. By his failure to abide by the military plan painstakingly designed by the young von Moltke's General Staff, the German Commander von Kluck made possible the French recovery known as the "Miracle on the Marne" in September of 1914.[33] More fundamentally, the German military led first by Admiral Alfred von Tirpitz and then followed by Erich von Ludendorff pushed for a declaration of "unlimited submarine warfare." The moderate Chancellor Theobold von Bethmann-Hollweg who hoped for a peaceful settlement brokered by Woodrow Wilson and the Americans, lost the decisive battle in January of 1917: Germany opted for unlimited warfare and thereby made American intervention in the war all but inevitable.[34] By the middle of 1917 Germany had for all intents and purposes been transformed into a military dictatorship led by Ludendorff. This regime lacked the moral and political confidence that belongs to legitimate civilian authority. It precipitously collapsed in the fall of 1918 after a series of military reversals and the impact of American intervention in the war began making itself felt. Lacking elementary self-knowledge and refusing to accept their political responsibility, Ludendorff and the other military subverters of the German order blamed anyone and anything but their own insubordination for the German tragedy: hence, the subsequent claims of the famous "stab in the back" by anti-German democrats. For de Gaulle, the corruption of the German monarchy and its role in the unfolding German tragedy taught universal lessons that shaped the Gaullist enterprise and helped him resist any "German" or "Nietzschean" political or philosophical temptations. Germany was defeated because its elites ignored the natural or human order of things. De Gaulle draws a philosophical or ontological conclusion: they were finally defeated by "outraged Principles"[35] as well as by the Allied armies. As much as anything else, they were defeated from within through a process of moral and political degeneration caused by the willful displacement of legitimate political authority.

De Gaulle admired the "unbelievable prestige"[36] with which Napoleon surrounded the name and arms of France. Napoleon had made his compatriots truly aware of France's existence. He had cloaked her in a grandeur that the nation had not seen before or would experience after. But he left her bleeding, drained of blood and courage, smaller in size and distinctly vulnerable to foreign invasion. He had also taken away much of her liberty. He had asked too much of fallible and limited men. De Gaulle's judgment on Napoleon's fall is revealing of de Gaulle's own soul, committed to both moderation and grandeur. "Tragic revenge of measure, just correction of reason, but superhuman prestige of genius and marvelous virtue of arms!" "In the presence of such a prodigious career, the judgment remains divided between praise and blame."[37]

De Gaulle admired Napoleon and his evocation of grandeur, but he rejected Bonapartism. Lacouture tells us that de Gaulle was pained and angered by charges of Bonapartism[38] made, most famously, by Raymond Aron in a 1944 article in *La France Libre*, "L'Ombre du Bonapartisme" ("The Shadow of Bonapartism"). Aron later regretted the tone and much of the substance of this article. Despite ongoing disagreement with de Gaulle's policies and reservations about the strident uniformity of the Gaullist movement, Aron genuinely admired de Gaulle and recognized that de Gaulle was an "authentically great man." His mature judgment of de Gaulle's political intention was that he aimed to establish an "absolute and limited" rule—"a parliamentary empire" that attempted to fuse liberalism and constitutional monarchy in a manner befitting the historical requirements of the French people.[39]

Lacouture, in particular, notes how misunderstood the great Gaullist constitutional discourse at Bayeux was at the time it was delivered in June

1946.[40] De Gaulle's pride was confused with the haughty bearing of a tyrant *manqué*. His defense of executive power was misunderstood or distorted. In Lacouture's discussion of Gaullist constitutionalism, we hear the confession of a man of the republican Left who sees and admits his blindness due to a previously distorted view of the nature and requirements of democracy.

Let us try to explain the stubborn inability of dogmatic democrats to understand the constitutional character of de Gaulle's political reflection and action. De Gaulle clearly understood the problems that modern democracy posed for the sustenance of human dignity and liberty. He was a friend, although no obsequious admirer, of democracy. Earlier, while recognizing the thorough corruption of the Third Republic, de Gaulle had refused to abandon democratic principles and institutions or his loyalty to the republican character of contemporary France. He was willing to act as a "Dictator" in the Roman sense, as a "supra constitutional" defender of public order, of the common interest, when the very existence of the state was threatened, first by foreign invasion and occupation after 1940, and later by the dissolution of effective and legitimate authority in 1958. But in 1946 de Gaulle refused the fascist temptation of establishing a national and personal dictatorship to cope with the problems associated with the restoration of the *status quo ante*: a weak, parliamentary regime of parties that lacked an effective executive authority to represent and speak for the nation as a whole and that was incapable of dealing effectively with national emergencies, guiding foreign policy, and protecting national independence. Instead of establishing a dictatorship, de Gaulle offered his blueprint for constitutional reform at Bayeux on June 16, 1946, a blueprint that would serve as the inspiration for the establishment of the *Rassemblement du peuple français* (the RPF), the Gaullist movement that would work for the establishment of a new constitutional order for France. In his Bayeux address de Gaulle made clear that his real enemy was not democracy but confusion or "trouble in the State."[41] He evoked the memory of previous failed French Republics and the specter of weak and failed democracies in Italy, Germany, and Spain, which had given rise to authoritarian and totalitarian dictatorships. De Gaulle presented himself as the true friend of democracy, one who understands the ways in which a weak state can alienate citizens from the government, engender anarchy and moral confusion, and strengthen the temptation of dictatorship. A "semi-presidential" Republic, with an independent and energetic executive authority to speak and act for the unity of the nation, not a weak and sectarian parliamentarianism, was the true alternative to anarchy and totalitarianism. It was this constitutional understanding that would inspire the legislators of the Constitution of the Fifth

French Republic, Michel Debré and the constitutional committee under the architectonic supervision of the General himself. Dictatorship was to be rejected not only on pragmatic, but also on deeply moral grounds.

It is necessary to quote de Gaulle's admirably measured and manly reflection at length:

And yet, what is dictatorship but a great adventure? Its beginning undoubtedly appears advantageous. In the midst of the enthusiasm of some and the resignation of others, in the strict discipline which it imposes, with a brilliant front and with one-sided propaganda, it takes, at first, a dynamic turn in sharp contrast with the anarchy which preceded it. But it is the destiny of dictatorships to indulge in excesses.

As the citizens grow impatient and nostalgic for liberty, it becomes necessary for the dictator to offer them the compensation of increasingly greater successes at any price. The nation becomes a machine which he accelerates without restraint. In both domestic and foreign policy the goals, the risks, and the efforts gradually exceed all measure. With each step a multitude of obstacles arise, both at home and abroad. In the end the spring breaks. The nation again finds itself broken and in a worse condition than it had been before the adventure began.[42]

Few passages better illustrate the notion that de Gaulle's ambition was not that of the tyrannical soul, discussed by the classical philosophers, who identifies his own good, however grasping, unmeasured, and overbearing, with the human or civic good simply. De Gaulle was a *statesman* who serves something greater than himself. He was, to be sure, a fallible man, haughty, stubborn, and not always sufficiently open to compromise or disagreement. But the roughness of his character was an indispensable element of a larger and exceedingly rare political *virtue*, magnanimity, that de Gaulle genuinely embodied, as we argue in Chapter 3.

Let us turn to another standard accusation and assertion made about de Gaulle: that his roots lay in the conservative nationalism of Charles Maurras and *Action Française*. Of course, in some general sense de Gaulle and Maurras belonged to the Right, but to two different and finally incompatible versions of the Right.[43] If the great intellectual and moral failing of the democratic Left in our century has been its propensity to believe *pas d'ennemis à gauche* and to indulge the excesses of so-called progressive regimes however inhuman or totalitarian they might be in practice, the nonfascist but still antidemocratic Right was tempted by a parallel delusion: that the enemy of my enemy is my friend, that fascism and National Socialism belong in some broad if imperfect sense to the forces of civilization because of their systematic anticommunism. De Gaulle was an anticommunist because he was a principled and consistent antitotalitarian. Like Churchill, de Gaulle was an anticommunist who judged Nazism to be the pressing and immediate danger to the liberty and equilibrium of Europe in the 1930s. De Gaulle's statesmanship, after Hitler's accession to power, was dedicated to preparing France for the coming confrontation with National Socialist Germany. De Gaulle never faltered in his opposition to Nazi imperialism and his opposition to all sentiments of disarmament and appeasement. In *The Army of the Future*, de Gaulle wryly observes that democratic France has become the "Penelope" of international politics, weaving her web of parchment agreements as the international dangers multiplied.[44] He worked tirelessly on behalf of a more dynamic military strategy, which took into account France's myriad diplomatic commitments and her intrinsic geographical vulnerability to attack and therefore the inadequacy of a purely defensive strategy. This was not merely the reflexive response of a nationalist to the "eternal ambitions" of the Germans. Lacouture writes in a memorable formulation: "Charles de Gaulle had a clear idea not only of France but also of Western Civilization and in 1939 he was never in any doubt as to his duty to confront the challenge thrown down by totalitarianism."[45] In the late 1930s de Gaulle actively associated himself with a Christian Democratic lay movement, the Friends of *Temps présent* (a pro-republican, anti-Nazi Catholic journal), which rejected the rabid illiberalism, indulgence toward fascism, and unconcealed anti-Semitism of Charles Maurras and his followers.[46] Like Maurras and the partisans of *Action Française*, de Gaulle recognized the decadence of the Third Republic's political institutions. The "national re-founding" that he called for at the end of *The Army of the Future* was ultimately a call for something far more profound than the adoption of a new national military strategy.[47] Even more fundamentally, de Gaulle recognized that liberal civilization was undergoing an unprecedented spiritual and civilizational crisis. Throughout his writings and speeches he called for the revitalization of Western civilization based on a "certain conception of man,"[48] one that rejected all forms of theoretical reductionism and materialism and worked to correct the dehumanizing excesses of mass society. De Gaulle knew that the mass movements of the Right, with their political dictatorships and militarized societies, could not address the deeper threats to human individuality that plague our increasingly de-Christianized and collectivized modern and democratic civilization. His reflections on the social question show that he transcended liberalism with its essentially individualist conception of human beings and the political community without rejecting human liberty or the institutions of liberal constitutionalism. A largely post-Christian world must form new sources of social integration that correct the individualism of liberalism while maintaining the respect for individual and public liberties that are the great achievements of the liberal order. This is the theme of one of de Gaulle's greatest wartime speeches, delivered at Oxford on November 25, 1941. It is arguably the clearest public expression of his hopes for the revitalization of Western civilization. It is examined in detail in Chapter 5.

If de Gaulle was not a Maurrasian, what was the character of his nationalism or, as he would prefer, his patriotism? Charles de Gaulle was the partisan of an idea and principle that he called grandeur. And he did not believe that there could be true grandeur without measure, or that there could be measure without respect for human liberty. As Malraux wrote in *Felled Oaks*, it is wrong to think that de Gaulle believed in some tyrannical way that he owned or had some exclusive right to the exercise or embodiment of greatness. Rather, he understood himself to be its servant or caretaker.[49] He wished to keep democracy and greatness together, and it is clear that the *nation*, in his case the French nation, was the intermediary, the living entity that allowed the possibility of a fruitful synthesis between democracy and greatness.

A major purpose of this book is to show that de Gaulle's efforts to do justice to the sometimes contradictory requirements of democracy and greatness reflect neither romantic nostalgia for a lost world nor idiosyncratic personal or national prejudices. The very French de Gaulle had a deeply considered intellectual framework, with "universalist" implications for all modern and democratic peoples, for considering what must be done to protect human liberty and dignity in modern times. The seemingly parochial and fiercely patriotic de Gaulle was the most reflective and "philosophic" of modern statesmen. His writings and speeches speak to the modern and democratic condition as well as to the situation of modern, democratic France. This conjoining of the particular and the universal makes his thought and action difficult to penetrate and seemingly opaque, even or especially for the French. They often do not understand de Gaulle because they are too confident that they know him. To understand his action, one must enter his thought and discover his principles which are primarily revealed in his writings: particularly in his prewar books but also in his two sets of *Memoirs* as well as in his most important public speeches. An open-minded investigation of de Gaulle's thought leads to some surprising discoveries. This statesman presents highly developed and intellectually coherent analyses of the nature of democracy and of the development of the modern world and of modern France. He also has prescriptions, too often and readily dismissed as merely romantic or nostalgic, for humanizing and energizing a disenchanted and "mediocre" world. The main chapters of this work attempt to uncover these analyses and prescriptions and to reveal their cogency and relevance for an appreciation of the "problem of democracy." This work studies de Gaulle's explicitly political career, particularly during the war years and as president of the Fifth Republic, only to the extent that it can help us illuminate and clarify his thought and the motives of his action. It is neither biography nor history, but rather a work of political reflection.

This book is, on one level, a response to a deep-seated American prejudice about de Gaulle. Only if we free ourselves from that prejudice can we begin to understand and allow ourselves to be educated by the thought and action of de Gaulle. It is tempting for Americans to regard Charles de Gaulle as an alien and even, from time to time, a ridiculous figure, a posturer who ignored the reduced influence and role of France, and an anti-American who deplored our civilization and ignored France's unavoidable dependence on American power. This view, which was the official position of President Roosevelt and his government and which remains a widespread judgment about de Gaulle and the Gaullist enterprise, rests on an almost willful refusal to consider the intellectual foundations of de Gaulle's political project as well as the soul or character of that remarkable man. Roosevelt saw in de Gaulle a ridiculous *poseur* who evoked comparison with Joan of Arc and Clemenceau and who harbored unrestrained political ambitions.[50] This book aims to contribute to the necessary task of demythologizing and de-ridiculizing Charles de Gaulle. Contrary to the assumptions of a dogmatic, positivistic social science, the result of such a process of demythologization leaves us with the reality of a man who is no mere power-seeker and certainly no aspiring despot. His ambition is informed by deep historical insight and a level of philosophic reflection that is rarely present in even the most thoughtful statesman. His is a *moralized ambition*, an example of "ambition in the good sense." His passion for France seems slightly unreal and unaccessibly heroic in an age when passions fluctuate between the petty and the ideological. His politics of grandeur may have aimed too far and high, but de Gaulle was acutely aware, despite a sometimes overblown exhortatory rhetoric, of those limits inherent in the human condition that mark or constrain even a politics of grandeur. This statesman will be remembered for two principal moments when his moral will, his passionate but humane sense of honor, and his love of country led him to permanently leave his mark on the century. In 1940 de Gaulle saved France from complete humiliation and self-disgust. In 1958 he assumed the part of Legislator and helped endow France with a modern, effective, energetic, and liberal constitutional order. He thereby allowed the French to regain self-respect, if not their rank of former times. It ought to be a central task of a political science that wishes to comprehend the phenomenon of politics in its heights and depths to investigate the thought and action of a statesman such as Charles de Gaulle.

Chapter 2

De Gaulle's Idea of France

INTRODUCTION: GRANDEUR AND THE MYSTIQUE OF FRANCE

The thought and action of Charles de Gaulle are inseparable from the destiny of France and from de Gaulle's understanding of that destiny.

No words of de Gaulle are better known and worthy of sustained reflection than the opening words of his *Mémoires de Guerre*. "All my life I have had a certain idea of France."[1] This chapter investigates the relationship between de Gaulle's idea of France and the historical "reality" of that enduring people and nation.

As we have argued in Chapter 1, it is tempting but mistaken to regard de Gaulle as a political mystic or an archaic nationalist. In this chapter, we establish the grounds of that judgment. De Gaulle shared the fundamental insight of Charles Péguy: a people must be shaped by a "mystique" if it is to maintain solidity and constancy, if it is to partake of great human works.[2] To recognize the mystique of the nation—that vision of the past that defines and makes a people a living organism and that entails the call to unity in the present and the defense of the nation's place within the order of nations—is not to partake of political irrationalism or archaism. Rather, it is to recognize a fundamental and irreducible political "reality." De Gaulle, of course, knew that the consciousness of the nation's reality and moral substance was largely unintelligible to what Péguy called the "intellectual party." These are political "atheists" who believe in nothing and who partake of the distinctive "sterility" of a purely modern or reductive rationalism.[3]

At this point it is necessary to allow de Gaulle to speak in his own voice. Let us attentively consider the opening lines of the *Mémoires de Guerre*:

All my life I have had a certain idea of France. This is inspired by sentiment as much as by reason. The emotional side of me naturally imagines France, like the princess in the fairy stories or the Madonna in the frescoes, as dedicated to an exalted and exceptional destiny. Instinctively I have the feeling that Providence has created her either for complete successes or for exemplary misfortunes. If, in spite of this, mediocrity shows in her acts and deeds, it strikes me as an absurd anomaly, to be imputed to the faults of Frenchmen, not to the genius of the land. But the positive side of my mind also assures me that France is not really herself unless in the front rank; that only vast enterprises are capable of counterbalancing the ferments of dispersal which are inherent in her people; that our country, as it is, surrounded by the others, as they are, must aim high and hold itself straight, on pain of mortal danger. In short, to my mind, France cannot be France without greatness.[4]

De Gaulle's France is called to greatness; it is dedicated to an exalted and exceptional destiny. De Gaulle follows Péguy: France is an "elected" people or race whose destiny is of universal significance.[5] The selection is both a selection by Providence and a necessity of national survival. The French are certainly capable of mediocrity, but such mediocrity arises when they lose consciousness of *la France*, when they fall back upon their petty selves. The history of France is the history of a movement or an oscillation between the requirements of grandeur and "the ferments of dispersal which are inherent" in the French people. As de Gaulle emphasizes in the first chapter of *The Army of the Future*, a commitment to greatness is a practical imperative if France is to compensate for the military and geographical vulnerability of the French hexagon, especially her untenable border in the northeast and the resulting exposure of Paris.[6] But it is also a moral necessity. Without a statesmanship imbued with a passion for the greatness and rank of France, the country is destined to be undone by her passionate but unsettled political temperament and afflicted by a series of partisan divisions deeply rooted in her national and revolutionary past. The opening paragraph of the *Mémoires de Guerre* leads up to the Gaullist affirmation par excellence: France cannot be France without greatness.

Grandeur is a concept at the center of de Gaulle's thought and action. But de Gaulle never explicitly defines it. Students of his statecraft must infer its meaning by unpacking the implications and context of his hortatory rhetoric. Stanley Hoffmann is right to observe that grandeur does not entail an ideology because it is "not unalterably tied to any specific policies or forms of power."[7] The commentators agree that grandeur implies the will to be a "player" and not a "stake," and to be an "ambitious," "universal," and "inventive" actor on the world scene.[8] Grandeur involves the self-conscious defense of the independence, honor, and rank of the nation. Many commentators see in a politics of grandeur, the unrelenting commitment to the independence and rank of France, the affirmation of an absolute primacy of foreign over domestic policy. But this is to ignore the fact that it is grandeur which allows this nation, France, to be herself. Will Morrisey more accurately states de Gaulle's understanding of the nuanced relations between domestic policy and foreign policy. Grandeur requires the "subordination of that part of the domestic which is self-indulgent to that part of foreign policy which is responsible, that is, humanly virtuous."[9] Gaullist grandeur cultivates an attitude of solicitude for national unity and self-respect, and not the exercise of unlimited imperial ambitions. The concern for rank is a means toward national flourishing and not an end in itself. It is an indispensable precondition for sustaining the moral and political unity of France. Unity is a precondition of grandeur, but grandeur makes possible national coherence and flourishing.

We have suggested that for de Gaulle, the pursuit of greatness is an indispensable means of promoting the moral and political unity of France. De Gaulle's hortatory rhetoric about the greatness of France both during the Second World War and throughout his subsequent political career aimed to heal the deep divisions characteristic of the French nation and to restore her confidence and self-respect after the debacle of May and June 1940. A foreign policy grounded in a concern for the independence, rank, and greatness of the nation is linked to and necessarily entails an attitude of honorable self-regard. It is for this reason that de Gaulle repeatedly attacked the "farcical" unity promoted by Vichy and its partisans. Vichy promoted a cult of national unity even as it compromised the sovereignty and undermined the self-respect of the nation in the name of a "shameful" but in fact illusory "neutrality."[10] To preserve "national unity in the disgrace of the armistice," the Vichy regime was forced to rely on an increasingly comprehensive system of police oppression.[11] For de Gaulle, in the context of the great world crisis that he called the Thirty Years' War (1914–1945), "national unity is to be found only in combat, self-respect, and in victory."[12]

In an important sense, unity no more than grandeur can be an unqualified end in itself. The character or quality of national unity is as important as the character or quality of greatness. Grandeur, if it is to produce lasting works, and if it is to be at the service of man, must be rooted in an appreciation of the place of measure, balance, and proportion in the "natural order of things." Grandeur can only be productive of durable and humane works if it is guided by an articulated sense of the possible. However, measure itself needs to be balanced by the imperatives of grandeur if it is not to degenerate into mere mediocrity and a national passivity that erode the integrity of the nation. Reasonable statesmanship requires the proper conjugation, the moral weighing and balancing of grandeur, measure, and liberty. The proper conjugation of these goods depends largely on the particular circumstances, character, and history of a people.

Just as there can be no solid and sustainable grandeur without measure, so grandeur needs to respect human and political liberty if it is to avoid degenerating into a crude Machiavellianism. De Gaulle's address of July 27, 1943 on the occasion of the fall of Mussolini's fascist regime takes aim at the self-destructive grandeur of totalitarianism:

The fall of Mussolini is the glaring sign of the certain defeat of the Axis. It is, at the same time, the proof of the failure of the political, social and moral system called totalitarianism, which claims to purchase greatness at the price of liberty.[13]

For de Gaulle, true greatness is possible only in regimes that respect human liberty, but in modern times these regimes, called democracies, are in fact constituted by their commitment to a prosaic and "mediocre" individualism. His recognition of this insoluble predicament leads some to confuse de Gaulle's statesmanship with illiberal forms of political romanticism or with theoretical currents such as Nietzscheanism and Machiavellianism that de Gaulle self-consciously rejected.

Luckily, students of de Gaulle's statesmanship are not left with de Gaulle's poetic evocation of greatness and the destiny of France in the opening page of his *Mémoires*. In 1938 de Gaulle published a book *France and Her Army*, which is a Gaullist history of France and her armed forces.[14] This book contains a historical narrative, but it is also a nuanced reflection on the idea of France and the role of the state and the country's army in shaping that idea. To understand de Gaulle's "political philosophy," we must, of course, understand that most "particular" of entities, France. An understanding of the mystique of France, of France's destiny as an elected people, provides access to de Gaulle's understanding of the "natural order of things," of the political nature of man. De Gaulle, without explicitly referring to Aristotle, understood the sublime task of statesmanship in a largely "Aristotelean" way: the statesman must be a partisan of the whole; he must be a partisan of the common good and not of a particular and narrow conception of justice. But as de Gaulle's book on France illustrates, because of the forces of dispersal from her past which weigh her down, because of the bitter and ideological character of her partisan divisions, de Gaulle must speak, like Barrès and Péguy, of that "eternal France" which is above the conflict of regimes. In Chapter 6, we examine the ways in which the Fifth French Republic was self-consciously intended to transcend the fundamental ideological chasm between the Old Regime and the Revolution which blocks the formation of a politics of *rassemblement*, of the common good.

But it is not only the legacy of the French Revolution that makes a politics which evokes the organic unity of eternal France a pressing necessity. It is also the banal, sterile, commonplace character of the "modern world"[15] or of modern mass society. The modern world oscillates between a stultifying apolitical individualism and totalitarian nationalisms and collectivisms which proffer illegitimate mystiques to the European peoples. De Gaulle instead speaks for the mystique of the nation as the true alternative to depoliticized liberal society and irrational or hyperrational totalitarian mysticisms (i.e., fascism and communism).

In the first pages of his *Mémoires de Guerres*, de Gaulle speaks of the culture, patriotism, and piety of his mother and father. They were living bridges between the old and the new France and imparted to their children "a certain anxious pride in [their] country" which "came as a second nature."[16] They imparted to their children not only pride in national successes but also the patriots' pain at those "weaknesses" and "misfortunes" that wound France. The weaknesses and misfortunes that afflicted the nation included national reversals (e.g., the surrender of Fashoda) but especially sources and reflections of national disunity: the Dreyfus case, social conflicts, religious strife. De Gaulle's parents were conservative and Catholic, and belonged in some broad sense to the Right, but they were not rightist sectarians and they placed the unity of France and commitment to the truth above hostility to the Republic or nostalgia for monarchy. Henri de Gaulle was convinced of the innocence of Dreyfus, for example. He was an uneasy republican, loyal to republican institutions but opposed to republican demagoguery and anti-Catholicism. His parents' spirit of decent patriotism deeply marked de Gaulle. It was France's propensity toward profound partisan and ideological strife, the waste of political and intellectual talents in "political confusion" and "national disunity," which particularly pained de Gaulle as he came to political consciousness during adolescence. He instinctively understood how the clash of "hollow ideologies" undermined the "moral balance" of the nation and left her vulnerable to her hereditary enemies and to the new threats arising from transnational totalitarian movements and enterprises.[17] In *The Army of the Future* de Gaulle identifies the *Union Sacrée* of 1914, the reconciliation of Catholics and republicans with the "national instinct" and the old national divisions with "sophistry."[18] *France and Her Army* can be seen as a manifestation of de Gaulle's statesmanship on behalf of a politics of grandeur and national reconciliation. It is an example of that higher partisanship that unifies the public career of the pre- and antebellum de Gaulle.

FRANCE AND HER ARMY: CLASSICISM AND ROMANTICISM

France and Her Army, like *The Edge of the Sword* and *The Army of the Future*, begins with an evocation of the moral and unifying role of the "sword" in political life. De Gaulle had no time or respect for pacifist illusions.[19] As we stress repeatedly throughout this book, de Gaulle did not celebrate the sword or its exercise for its own sake. Rather, he feared that France, in reaction to the ferocious bloodletting of the First World War, was succumbing to "dreams" and "pieties" about an international order where the role of force would be reduced to an almost invisible minimum. This liberal understanding ignored the stubborn "egotism of nations" and, as is evidenced by the Kellogg-Briand Pact, "declare(d) that war should be outlawed and affected to efface the power of the sword from History."[20] Meanwhile, the totalitarians declared the value of force in darkly atavistic tones. De Gaulle's criticisms of the liberal partisanship on behalf of the permanent pacification of international politics was an act of statesmanship aimed at protecting the liberal polities from the spirit of appeasement.

For de Gaulle, politics and war are intimately and dialectically intertwined. The army is the most powerful and revealing sign of the character of society and the handmaiden of the state itself. In fact, the reality of France as a nation is coextensive with the union of a strong government and a powerful army. De Gaulle writes of the place of the sword in the formation of France as a nation:

France was fashioned by blows of the sword. Our fathers made their entry in History with the sword of Brennus. The Roman armies brought them civilization. After the fall of the Empire the country regained consciousness of itself, thanks to the axe of Clovis. The fleur-de-lys, the symbol of national unity, is only the image of the three-pronged javelin.[21]

As France and her army are inseparable, so the art of war must be part of a more comprehensive *politique* or art of politics. But although a state may be created by force of arms, the waging of war is worth something only in virtue of a *politique*. A dominant theme of de Gaulle's prewar writings is the great theme of Clausewitz's *On War*: "War is the continuation of politics by other means." There are not only rhetorical similarities between de Gaulle's and Clausewitz's respective treatments of the art of war and the place of that art within the larger political world. There is also a substantial common intellectual and spiritual ground: a shared recognition of the primacy of political judgment, a similar reflection on the dialectic between ends and means in the military art, a common emphasis on political moderation and the limitation of violence, a mutual recognition of the moral and political wisdom inherent in the European system of the balance of power.[22] We will return to these themes as we analyze de Gaulle's discussions of the Old Regime, the Revolution, and Napoleon. De Gaulle and Clausewitz share in common a neoclassical political sensibility and an aversion to the unbridled emancipation of popular and ideological enthusiasms. They are *neo*classical in that neither believed that a simple return to the exemplary moderation of the European system of the balance of power was possible. The French Revolution and the wars of the Revolution and Empire had unleashed violent and semitotal war, ferocious national passions, and new forms of ideological and mass politics. Neoclassical statecraft must henceforth operate judiciously within that new "ideological" context.

The fruitful coexistence of neoclassical and romantic styles and approaches to political life is a characteristic feature of de Gaulle's "political philosophy." This coexistence is not merely a biographical idiosyncrasy or a reflection of the diverse influences on de Gaulle during his intellectual formation in the Belle Époque. Rather, it is a recognition of an antinomy that is at the heart of political life as well as a response to the particular characteristics of the French people and their history.

Stanley Hoffmann accurately describes the centrality of this fundamental polarity of romanticism and classicism in de Gaulle's thought and action:

Another set of polarities was the General's romanticism and classicism. (His admiration for Chateaubriand, who assured the transition between the two, is no surprise.) It was the romantic who proclaimed "me and history," asserted his unprecedented character, saw the world as a turmoil in which the man of action, occasionally, discreetly, discontinuously "decides and prescribes . . . and then, after action has been launched, seizes again by spurts the system of his means which facts relentlessly put out of shape." . . . It was the classicist who insisted on measure and balance, saw the leader as a kind of grand entrepreneur, the function of whose investments and innovations was to preserve the continuity and flow of history, who ruled like a Cornelian Emperor, and knew that in this century "no man can be the people's substitute." Romanticism and classicism also blended in de Gaulle's military programs and use of technological innovations. He put the radio, during the war, and television, after 1958, at the service of *le caractère*. His old hostility to the "system of armed masses," which inspired his design for a professional army and later his reconversion of the French Army to the atomic age, reflected a romantic fondness for mobility, decisiveness, lightning action, which made him admire Hoche, Foch, and Clemenceau, and a classic concern for maximum efficiency in the use of limited resources which made him celebrate Louvois and Turenne, Carnot and Pétain.[23]

This polarity and antinomy can best be described in Péguyist language as the effort to do justice to the requirements of both *politique* and *mystique*.

De Gaulle, for all his indebtedness to what he describes in *France and Her Army* as the "spiritual radiance"[24] of Péguy is a far more political thinker than his teacher and inspiration. Péguy tends to dismiss politique as being far less important than mystique and almost inevitably corrupt and corrupting. Politique is of human interest above all because a profound tendency of the social order is the degradation of a mystique into a politique that devours its inspiration and foundation.[25] Politique, for Péguy, is something to be resisted, to be hemmed in. What gives any *politique* its dignity is its all too rare faithfulness to its original, primordial mystique.

Péguy is not finally a political thinker because he is *au fond* morally revolted by periods of quiescence, especially bourgeois quiescence. His soul longs for the excitement and moral challenge of grand epochs whose turmoil and conflict demand and bring forth great acts of human devotion. De Gaulle, on the other hand, admires the skill that statecraft requires in even the most ordinary of times. He admires, as we will see, the "classical" statecraft of Louis XIV and the ancien regime whose wars were an instrument of a calibrated statesmanship that weighed ends and means and respected the integrity of civil society. If de Gaulle also rejects bourgeois quiescence, he is more sympathetic to the restrained mystique of the ancien regime which is neither Christendom with its total way of life, its profound and universal human communion nor the revolutionary devotion to the "rights of man."

In this context, it is necessary to turn to the foreword to de Gaulle's first book, *The Discord Among the Enemy*. At the conclusion of his foreword, de Gaulle announces that a practical aim of his book is to contribute in a "modest way" to the formation of the minds and character of French military leaders "in accordance with the rules of classical order."[26] De Gaulle aims to educate in moderation. In the rules of classical order, one can draw "the sense of equilibrium, of possibilities, of measure, which alone render the works of energy durable and fruitful."[27]

Probably no sentence in all of de Gaulle's weighty corpus better captures his moral and political intention. He wishes to teach others, first and foremost the military elite who were his immediate audience in the 1920s, but also the broader French public, and finally students and followers of the writer–statesman de Gaulle, the valuable human and civic lesson about the necessary moral complementarity of measure and energy, the recognition of limits and the possibility of grandeur, and of politique and mystique. The oft-noted Nietzschean elements of his thought are much better understood in Péguyist or Bergsonian terms. Any healthy politique must remain true to an underlying source of national purpose and cohesion. And human works are not simply "rational constructions" but are the products of creative impulses, unanalyzable intuitions, and of primordial energies that are not the product of a priori rules or doctrines. But the human self needs to be ruled. Happily for the cohesion of social life, there are principles or general rules of measured human conduct which can be ignored only at our peril.

Yet *France and Her Army* is preceded by a quotation from Péguy which is strikingly romantic in character. The quotation reads "Mère, voyez vos fils, qui se sont tant battus!"[28] ("Mother, see your sons, who have fought so hard!") It is fitting to begin a book that treats the history of France and her army with an evocation of those who have fought and died for the country. But we must analyze the quotation more closely. It is characteristically Péguyist and Gaullist. France is not an abstraction or a mere historical entity or the social "system" that is so dear to the social scientists of our time. France is rather a Mother, providential in her care and status (like the Mother of God or de Gaulle's "Madonna in the frescoes") who watches over and spurs her children to greatness. Péguy's language is inseparably theological and political. As Pierre Manent notes, Péguy appeals to that civic sacredness which the pagans knew, that sense of the city as a human communion—a sense of civic sacredness that was eroded under the successive assaults of the Christian separation of the two realms or cities, liberalism's depoliticization and demystification of the social order, and of totalitarianism's perversion and transvaluation of the human quest for community.[29]

De Gaulle, then, begins his book with an appeal to mystique—to civic sacredness and civic communion. He wishes to inculcate a profound love of France, the civic equivalent of pious devotion to the cult of the Mother of God. That theological-political devotion, embodied in the French tradition, by the simple heroism, piety, and patriotism of Joan of Arc (the great subject of Péguy's art), is the mystical ground of any French patriotism capable of withstanding what Walter Lippmann called the "acids of modernity." De Gaulle does not believe that the rationally grounded "rights of man" can provide the civic cohesion for a national community in the fullest and deepest senses of those terms. The democracies, in his mind, survive as viable communities in large part because they are nourished on the moral and political capital of a world that precedes the "modern world."

During his great wartime speeches as well as in his *War Memoirs*, de Gaulle will appeal to that premodern theological and political understanding. He does not hesitate to use explicitly theological language. The final volume of the *War Memoirs* is entitled *Salut* (*Salvation*), and, for de Gaulle, nothing less than the civic salvation of France was at stake in his efforts to re-found the nation's institutions after the Liberation. De Gaulle closes the first volume of his *War Memoirs*, *L'Appel*, by giving a dramatic account of his Péguy-inspired address to ten thousand French people in London at Albert Hall on June 18, 1942 to commemorate the second anniversary of his great "Appeal." De Gaulle's speech, an effort to define the spiritual purposes, so to speak, of Fighting France, attempts to define his own relationship to "eternal France." De Gaulle, in his own self-presentation, is the servant of France, her "son" who calls Frenchmen to climb the slope toward liberty, honor, and undiminished national sovereignty.[30] De Gaulle closes his June 18, 1942 Albert Hall address by quoting the same epigram from Péguy which begins *France and Her Army*. In that same spirit the soaring peroration of *L'Appel* evokes France as a Mother, the Madonna of Joan of Arc and Péguy. De Gaulle writes:

A truce to doubts! Pouring over the gulf into which the country has fallen, I am her son, calling her, holding the light for her, showing her the way of rescue. Many have joined me already. Others will come, I am sure! I can hear France now, answering me. In the depths of the abyss she is rising up again, she is on the march, she is climbing the slope. Ah! mother, such as we are, we are here to serve you.[31]

THE ORIGINS OF FRANCE

But to descend from mystique to politique, there can be no France without a state. The history of France, according to de Gaulle, is the history of the search for a legitimate and authoritative state. The theme of the state, the source of legitimate political authority and of the moral unity of the nation is ever present in de Gaulle's writings and discourses. De Gaulle speaks of the state in quasi-Hegelian terms as that extrajuridical entity that envelops and protects but does not engulf civil society. The state is in an overarching theme in de Gaulle's thought precisely because the absence or weakness or abdication of the state historically is at the source of France's travails.

France can only be said to have consolidated a fully constituted state during the period of absolute monarchy or the Old Regime. This is why de Gaulle treats the entire period from the Roman imposition of order in Gaul through the Christianization of France, the establishment of the feudal order, and the establishment of national monarchy in theory and over many centuries in practice, in one succinct chapter of *France and Her Army*, entitled "Origins."[32]

Rome had originally broken the "fury of the Gauls" with the military arts of the Legions. The Roman conquest was "to impress upon our laws and mores, as in our language, our monuments, our roads and our artistic creations the mark of her rule and authority, while manifesting to a score of generations the spirit of military might."[33]

It was Rome and Roman authority that provided the ideal and "nostalgic desire" for "a centralized state and a regular army, an ideal which survived all the Barbarian invasions."[34] The eclipse of Roman authority meant the eclipse of an authoritative, centralized unitary political community, that is, a state. But Rome would act as a historical image of the possibility of a centralized political order, and that possibility would gain new allure as an alternative to a disintegrating feudalism during the so-called Renaissance. The weaknesses of the medieval monarchy and the inadequate feudal institutions and practices during the Hundred Years' War would gradually lead to the strengthening of national monarchy and to the formation of a small but historically revolutionary *national army*—that is, to the establishment of institutions and an army that could really claim to speak in the name of France. The French monarchy, beginning with Henry IV, would respond to the wars of religion by establishing a sovereignty that is above the corporate particularities of feudalism and independent of the clash of religious opinions. If Rome was to provide the reflection of the possibilities of political universality, Christianity was to provide Europe and France with the vision of moral universality. As de Gaulle writes elsewhere, Christianity shaped France by giving her a "single morality."[35] And despite the disintegrative and centrifugal forces and the unrestrained warrior ardor that characterized the social order of feudalism, de Gaulle recognizes that it produced "certain beneficial effects in the moral order." Chivalric honor coexisted with Christian morality and was undoubtedly shaped by its moralization and spiritualization of the social sphere. Like a superb flower growing on the "thorns" of battle, chivalry "ennobled" the works of force even if it was not capable of "softening" them.[36]

During many centuries of feudalism and countering its disintegrative effects, the monarchy acted as a force for "unity."[37] In the period of the late Renaissance, France began to have a functioning state and the strongest army in the world. "In the military sphere, as in the others, the Renaissance has prepared the way for the classical epoch,"[38] that is, the so-called Old Regime. Of all the periods in French history, this is the one for which de Gaulle seems to evince what Pierre Manent calls a "discreet preference."[39] It is therefore necessary to closely scrutinize his analysis of the Old Regime and in the process to raise the following important questions: how does this preference relate to de Gaulle's partisanship for eternal France, that France which simultaneously transcends and incorporates all her regimes? How does de Gaulle understand the phenomenon of the political regime and the problem of fundamental regime change?

DE GAULLE AND THE OLD REGIME

The second chapter of *France and Her Army* is entitled "Ancien Régime."[40] This was the "classical" period for de Gaulle. It is classical because of its taste for reality, its eschewing of abstractions, its preference for the empirical, for facts and the substance of social life, over theoretical and ideological schemes.[41] It is classical above all because of the subordination of the military art to the political art, a subordination that allowed the Old Regime to maintain a real equilibrium between the works of energy and a respect for the requirements of *measure*. The Old Regime "manifests and embodies the just proportion between self-affirmation and moderation."[42]

Classicism for de Gaulle entails a sense of balance or proportion. The proportion of the Old Regime was above all a "just proportion between the end pursued and the forces of the state."[43] The statecraft of the Old Regime is radically anti-ideological or, more precisely, pre-ideological. It is a politics and policy of "circumstances." Its balance is not the balance or moderation of classical philosophical ethics. Its moderation is not the mean between vicious excesses or extremes that Aristotle called virtue in his *Nicomachean Ethics*. Rather, it is a modernized form of classicism, which partakes of a distinctively modern political ethic, what Richelieu in his *Political Testa-*

ment called "raison d'État" and what Raymond Aron has called "moderate Machiavellianism."

Moderate Machiavellianism has not fully broken with classical and Christian moralities, but it partakes of a peculiarly post-Machiavellian latitudinarianism regarding the means available to political actors. The old regard for the universality of Christendom with the superintendence of the Catholic Church and Catholic morality is replaced by a respect for that framework or limit known as the European balance of power. This attenuation of Christian morality, this partial liberation of the nation with its absolute monarch as the sovereign embodiment of the political will—the *partial* de-universalization of political morality is also a kind of renaissance or return to authentic classicism. The qualified liberation of the politique of the sovereign state, what would later come to be called the national interest, entailed a partial return to the classical world with its affirmation of the independence and autonomy of the political art. But the neoclassicism of the Old Regime is unmistakably marked both by Christian universalism and by Machiavelli's transvaluation of the meaning of political virtù. "Though little scrupulous as to the means employed, it showed its greatness by keeping a just proportion between the end in view and the forces of the state."[44] The paradoxical marriage of unscrupulosity regarding political means with genuine moderation regarding the ultimate ends of statecraft is the defining mark of the political ethic of the Old Regime.

De Gaulle illustrates the "empiricism" of the Old Regime through an analysis of its "instrument," the army.[45] Facts and not theories guided its discipline and code of honor and shaped its strategy and tactics.

The Old Regime was almost continually at war. "But the wars of the period rarely aroused great national passions."[46] None of the conflicts of the period—and de Gaulle lists them in order to illustrate the omnipresent realities of political conflict and the incessant use of the military instrument—justified disturbing the ordinary rhythm, integrity, and continuity of the social order. De Gaulle unobtrusively illustrates the relative liberalism of the Old Regime, or at least its respect for the concrete liberties of ordinary Frenchmen:

But none of the resulting struggles seemed to provide justification for tearing peasants away from their fields, craftsmen from their trades, or bourgeoisie from their businesses or public offices. Saint-Germain was accurately expressing the general sentiment when he wrote: "It is not necessary to destroy the nation in order to form armies." The majority of Frenchmen, therefore, were to be allowed to live their lives peacefully. Only a few of them would be required to make war.[47]

But de Gaulle goes on to ask, which ones were to be required to fight? In the answer to this question we see the empiricism and unscrupulousness of the Old Regime writ large. The society of the Old Regime was characterized by a multitude of privileges, contracts, and traditions that "limited, complicated and modified" the rights of classes, provinces, townships, corporations, and so on. One would not have been able to impose military service on any of the bodies of society without "tearing up this framework." As a result, recruits were drawn in a manner least likely to disturb the integrity of the social order. They were drawn from those on the edges of society: the down and out, from the lot of questionable characters who had little choice between the army and the gallows, the restless young looking for "adventure and a uniform." Each colonel was responsible for finding recruits for his own regiment. There were no professional guidelines determining such recruitment, and crude tactics, including drunken manipulation, were permitted. But, de Gaulle adds, abuses were expected not to be too patent. De Gaulle cites the minister of war Louvois: "small irregularities should be overlooked and only violence and kidnapping from fairgrounds and markets are forbidden."[48] As Will Morrisey has written, this is empiricism indeed![49]

Even the toleration of such irregularities and these most "empirical" and "circumstantial" methods of recruitment were not sufficient to form an army of adequate size to carry out the politique of the Old Regime. The regime was forced to rely on foreign mercenaries and on arrangements with allies and weaker and subordinate neighboring powers. More than a third of the army were not French nationals during the reign of Louis XIV. The army was therefore discreetly referred to as the Army of France in due respect for its cosmopolitan composition.[50]

De Gaulle also stresses the "empirical" approach of the Old Regime concerning the selection of French officers. They were drawn from the nobility because the nobility had a taste and tradition for war, because it had extensive financial resources that were of much value to the state, and because a nobility that fought for the king of France was a nobility whose loyalties were likely to become increasingly national rather than provincial. Everything involving the army, of course, was not so circumstantial and haphazard. After all, the Old Regime was, as Tocqueville shows, a modernizing monarchy. De Gaulle shows how Louvois and his successors built a national army, increasingly efficient, standardized, and professionalized. During his thirty-year tenure as minister of war, Louvois used "will and discernment," intelligence, and knowledge of men and society to build an increasingly disciplined and organized national force. This minister of the Old Regime was "disdainful of theories" but "amourous of the real," and he was persistent in his efforts to reform and ameliorate conditions. "At the same time daring and patient, active and prudent, rigorous and practical, Louvois was the Minister of War who suited, *par excellence*, the Old Regime."[51] He was, as Will Morrisey notes, a Gaullist "man of character"—a man who combined respect for the real with tireless energy and the firm exercise of authority.[52] Largely because of Louvois, the Old Regime provided France with an army that was truly a national "instrument."

De Gaulle also provides portraits of great French commanders and generals such as Condé and Turenne who fruitfully combined the virtues and ethic of the old aristocracy with loyalty and service to the new national order.[53] But our interest lies decidedly elsewhere. Besides its ability to react to circumstances, to respond to and to build on facts, what was the moral and political strength of this Old Regime? How was it able to synthesize self-affirmation and moderation, energy and limits, grandeur and respect for the order determined by the European balance of power?

De Gaulle shows how the strategy and tactics of the Old Regime were imbued with the spirit that animated the regime. This was a period in which the military art, and strategy more broadly, were truly "instruments" of the political art. It was the classical period of balanced statecraft par excellence. "At no other period of History was war more strictly subordinated to *politique*."[54] This was a politique that combined, as we have already noted, a genuine flexibility and even opportunism in regard to means with a measured sense of the necessarily limited ends or purposes of statecraft. The political authorities did not hesitate to unleash war, but they carefully defined its objectives and limited its scope.

The moral boundaries of the Old Regime did not include a place for total war or the unleashing of unlimited violence. "Governments were careful to limit the objectives at which they arrived."[55] De Gaulle suggests that the Wars of Religion, with their unleashing of disorder and a self-destructive fanaticism, had taught the French an invaluable lesson about the need for *la règle*, for rule and order and restraint in domestic and foreign relations.[56] This *règle* so aptly reflected in the moderate Machiavellian statecraft of the Old Regime would be ignored by the Revolutionaries who unleashed unprecedented societal disorders and the furies of secular religion.

The "rule" of the Old Regime was not only embodied in the national monarchy, illiberal or "absolutist" in its principles, tolerably liberal in its practice. It was more fully embodied in the European system of the balance of power, a self-regulating and self-limiting order of nations who rejected, in principle, the notion of universal empire or unchallenged national hegemony. The governments of the Old Regime "strove incessantly to increase their territory, to support their allies and to weaken their rivals, but they avoided great jolts, ruptures of the equilibrium and upheavals."[57] They were conscious of the nation's limited resources and hence rejected the option or temptation of hegemony. De Gaulle makes eminently clear that they recognized the *material* and *moral* limits inherent in statecraft. Without being particularly highminded or moralistic, the statesmen of the Old Regime had a concrete or pragmatic appreciation of the material and spiritual limits that provided the broad contours of an acceptable politique. It is an insight, an empiricism, a respect for the facts of social life, that both the French Revolutionaries and Napoleon, in their different ways, would forget to the peril of France.

The system of the European balance of power would not allow the complete destruction of an adversary. Nor would it tolerate the rise of a continental tyrant or hegemon. Its spirit eschewed "furious ambitions" and "inexpiable hatreds," in a word either sectarian or ideological fanaticism. These "poison the relations between nations and menace the order of the world."[58]

The Old Regime sought to increase the unity, extend the power, and cultivate the glory of France. But it had neither the material means nor the ideological inclination to pursue a foreign policy of unlimited self-asser-tion. Its strategy was determined by the restrained political ends of the regime and the self-limiting nature of the European balance of power. It was also marked by the inherently limited material means and the stubborn independence and self-absorption of civil society. As a result, the strategy of the ancien regime "avoided gigantic shocks, total destruction of the enemy, invasion on a grand scale, as well as the desperate resistance of the nation."[59]

De Gaulle paints the statecraft of the Old Regime, reaching its lumines-cent peak during the reign of Louis XIV, in sparkling and sympathetic strokes. His portrait is an idealization; this French patriot says little about the imperialism of Louis XIV's regime and how he was perceived through-out the continent at the time as a threatening, incipient tyrant. De Gaulle would probably respond by saying that even the imperial pursuits of that regime (i.e., the seizure of Palatinate, the systematic expansion of France's frontiers) were essentially limited in aim and scope. France wished to protect herself, maximize her security, contribute to her glory, and become the most powerful nation on the continent.

Even the great liberal Montesquieu, who feared the despotic propensities of the centralized monarchy established by the Old Regime, defended Louis

XIV on this score. "The enemies of a great prince who has long reigned have accused him a thousand times, *more from fears than from reasons*, I believe, of having formed and pursued the project of universal monarchy."[60] (emphasis mine). Yet there is no doubt that de Gaulle exaggerates the moderation and sense of proportion inherent in the politique of the Old Regime. De Gaulle presents the statecraft of Frederick the Great as the perfection of the proportion and moderation of the Old Regime. "He did not for one moment dream of destroying his neighbors, any more than they wished to annihilate Prussia." He avoided ambitious plans, large-scale operations, devastating attacks, or relentless pursuits. He recognized the limits of his means and scrupulously avoided "arousing national passions." His politique, strategy, and tactics were "vigorous with measure, exploiting circumstances without abusing them" and "formed a harmonious and solid whole."[61] The portrait is largely true as far as it goes. But de Gaulle underestimates the immoderation lurking in the ceaseless resorting to war by a Louis XIV or Frederick the Great. These ambitious princes of the Old Regime made the nation radically subservient to their own designs and engaged in an "intensive exploitation of her capabilities."[62] Their moderation was grounded in a finally illiberal relation of authority to society. But de Gaulle does not directly address the problem of the absolutist or despotic political character of the Old Regime—the orthodox or republican evaluation of that order since 1789. Yet he does suggest this regime was far from tyrannical in practice. Its ministers, such as Louvois, succeeded by persuasion and diplomacy as much as by force or war. And society remained remarkably resistant to the pressures of an increasingly confident but still essentially limited central power.

Several other points about de Gaulle's account of the politique of the ancien regime need to be made. The first is to distinguish de Gaulle's defense of the moderation of the Old Regime and his endorsement of the European balance of power from the standard position of social science "realism" in academic International Relations theory. De Gaulle does not see the balance of power as a cybernetic or mechanical system of impersonal, material inputs and outputs which has eternal truth and efficacy in a world characterized by international anarchy. He understands the historical specificity and the moral and cultural underpinnings of that order even as he sees it reflecting a harmony, balance, or sense of proportion rooted in the natural order of things. In his evaluation of the moderate statecraft of the European order of the balance of power, de Gaulle is closest to historically minded American statesmen—theorists such as George Kennan and Henry Kissinger. But there is a moral dimension to de Gaulle's evaluation of the subordination of the military art to *politique* which is sometimes lacking in the American realists. The realists emphasize the self-interestness, the resort to unscrupulous if limited means which characterizes the system of *raison d'État* which he praises. They fail to sufficiently appreciate how dependent that order was on premodern and Christian moral categories and presumptions that infused Europe with a common political consciousness and a respect for moral universality.[63] Nor do the realists sufficiently appreciate Clausewitz's (and de Gaulle's) insight that the subordination of war to politics/policy is a moral principle as well as a practical imperative that guarantees a place for architectonic and sovereign political judgment. The idea of absolute war, the logic of war as an undirected duel of wills, must be restrained "by the influence of political objectives, by the rationality of political understanding."[64] Only then can human beings determine their destinies and resist being the playthings of nonhuman necessity.

DE GAULLE AND THE FRENCH REVOLUTION

Let us turn to the complex subject of de Gaulle's analysis and judgment of the French Revolution. We have already seen de Gaulle's favorable analysis and discreet preference for the Old Regime. But as de Gaulle stated in his speech at the Place de la Concorde on September 4, 1958, the ancient monarchy, the Old Regime and the Revolution, and the subsequent French regimes all contributed to the building or making of modern France.[65] What then is de Gaulle's judgment about the Revolution, its works and its principles? And how does de Gaulle understand the place, role, and reality of the regime in French history and in political life generally?

De Gaulle certainly recognized the "revolutionary" character of 1789. The Revolution transformed the traditional European political and social order and unleashed radical innovations, "boiling passions," and a readiness to shed blood that "alarmed the consciousness of the masses and the prudence of governments."[66] It involved no mere rebellion but a revolutionary upheaval of traditions, institutions, laws, and mores.

While the Old Regime wished to avoid the radical disruption of society, the Revolution attempted no less than what Burke called a "revolution in the minds of men." This revolution pushed Europeans to war because, de Gaulle notes, for centuries Europeans had feared French power and were "involuntarily imbued with French thought and . . . to that extent the more disturbed by the path it was taking."[67]

Europe was impelled as "by an elemental force"[68] to go to war. But this was a new kind of war, lacking proportion, restraint, or any sense of principled or practical limits. The politique of the Old Regime affirmed the necessity of self-restraint and saw nothing but the poisoning of the order of domestic society and the European balance of power in the unleashing of "inexpiable hatred." It believed that ideological passions poison the "order of the world." Without expressly criticizing the politique of the revolutionary regime, we can infer de Gaulle's displeasure and reservations about its thoughtless and untempered display of ideological and national passions.

The moderation inherent in the European balance of power was replaced by the fury of ideological and total war.

This time it was not a war of interests fought for a province, a local right, a succession, but a war of principles, national wars—and correspondingly ferocious. To carry on a war of this nature France had to demand of herself a gigantic and unprecedented effort. [69]

De Gaulle does not approve of the politique of the various revolutionary regimes. But he does admire the "greatness" of its mystique—its proud affirmations of the liberty of the nation and of the revolutionary rights of man. The Revolution partakes of a genuine "greatness," albeit a greatness marred by "confusion" and corrupted by ideological fanaticisms.[70] De Gaulle clearly detests Jacobinism, the work of the "extremists" who sowed disorder and undiscipline among troops, paralyzed the political life of the nation (France had nine ministers of war between 1792 and 1793!), and divided Frenchmen from each other and undermined capable, energetic, and public-spirited commanders such as Dumouriez, Carnot, and Hoche.[71] The extremists with their political passions threw away the advantages of prudent command and firmness of purpose that "a man of character" such as Dumouriez contributed to the army and cause of France. For example, the Jacobins for all intents and purposes forced Dumouriez to commit treason by going over to the Austrian side.[72] They could not respect professional competence or military genius but instead were preoccupied with the purity of revolutionary intentions. The "political" frenzy of the Jacobins "took away prestige, often life, sometimes honor."[73] Despite everything, de Gaulle gives an account of a revolutionary army that managed, at least by the period of the Directorate, to restore its contact with reality and to submit to "the eternal laws of action,"[74] which include forming an effective hierarchy and observing military discipline.

It was an army built on the fusion of the experience and "authority" of the remnants of the old army of France and on the "enthusiastic" base of mass recruits made possible by the *levée en masse*—the mass conscription and mobilization of society decreed by the Convention in 1792.[75] De Gaulle undoubtedly recognized something glorious, a source of national energy and superiority, in the citizen army mobilized for the sake of the nation and of liberty, but his emphasis is decidedly on the army as an instrument of France, of eternal France, not of the Revolution per se.

In judging the Revolution, de Gaulle is most discreet. His comment about the "complex situation" in the Vendée is neither revolutionary nor counterrevolutionary in tone or thrust:[76] de Gaulle refuses to exacerbate the already overly heated memories and passions of French partisans. Elsewhere, de Gaulle criticizes the amateurism and fanaticism of revolutionary ideologues who "flung the France of the 'Rights of Man' into the struggle against Europe at the worst moment of our military disorganization."[77] Yet the revolutionary armies are, if even by default, the armies of France, and de Gaulle celebrates their victories and achievements and is wounded, like a patriot, by their weaknesses and reversals.

On the order of principle, de Gaulle prefers the moderation of the Old Regime to the impolitic and inordinate manipulation of passions characteristic of the revolutionary period. Yet the romantic side of de Gaulle's political antinomy admires the self-affirmation of revolutionary France and the glory of the revolutionary armies.

Let us return to our earlier question. Does the regime finally matter for de Gaulle? The answer must be an unqualified affirmation. De Gaulle agrees with Péguy that "there are infinitely deeper forces and realities" than regimes and that it is the people or race "who are the strength or weaknesses of régimes."[78] But de Gaulle will not go as far as Péguy in deprecating the importance or causal efficacy of regimes. De Gaulle is not neutral about regimes; they are not all finally indistinguishable from each other. On the moral and political plane, he genuinely if unostentatiously prefers the politique of the ancien regime to that of the Revolution. Undoubtedly, he admires the "greatness," the "energy" of the Revolution for much the same romantic reasons that the equally anti-Jacobin Tocqueville expressed in the preface of *The Old Regime and the Revolution*: Whatever the political errors of the Revolution, it "was an era of youth, of enthusiasm, of pride, of generous and heartfelt passions . . . men will remember it long, and for many a day to come it will disturb the slumber of those who seek to corrupt or to enslave the French."[79] There is a "greatness" to the Revolution which compares favorably with the feeble materialism of a bourgeois era. At times, both Tocqueville and de Gaulle succumbed, like Péguy, to an exaggerated disdain of the bourgeois world which colored their ultimate judgment of the French Revolution.

As a *thinker*, de Gaulle recognizes the need to maintain an equilibrium between romanticism and classicism. As a human being, patriot, soldier, and statesman, he sometimes admires grandeur even when it is severed from measure. Nonetheless, if all regimes have contributed to the formation of France, some such as the Jacobin Republic caused inestimable damage to her substance and integrity. Others such as the Third Republic lacked adequate constitutional arrangements and were devoid of sufficient political vitality. At the end of *The Army of the Future*, de Gaulle calls for a national re-founding beginning with the formation of a professional army—the first step of the road to a national reconstruction. There de Gaulle celebrates the unknown (?) legislator of the new order or regime:

In order to bring into being the professional army, and in order that that army should be provided with the material and with the new spirit without which it will never be more than a willo'-the-wisp, a leader will have to appear whose judgment is independent, whose orders are irresistible, and who is well thought of by public opinion. He must be in the service of only the State, free from prejudices, disdaining patronage. He must be firmly committed to his task, absorbed in far-reaching plans, well-informed about the men and things to be dealt with. He must be a leader who is at one with the army, devoted to those he commands, eager for responsibility; a man strong enough to compel, clever enough to persuade and great enough to carry through a great task. Such will be the minister, soldier or politician, to whom the nation will owe the next reconstruction of its forces.[80]

In his *War Memoirs*, de Gaulle criticizes the regime established in 1946, the Fourth Republic, as that "bad regime"[81] incapable of combining authority and liberty, energy and moderation, poisoned by a corrupt oligarchic party system.

My point is a simple one. The regime mattered profoundly for de Gaulle. His position on the regime is literally halfway between Aristotle, for whom the regime is the decisive factor in the determination of human and political life, and Péguy, for whom regimes are of decidedly secondary importance compared to the role of "peoples" and "races." One should not underestimate de Gaulle's self-consciousness as a "classical" Founder, a legislator of a new regime—a self-understanding most fully delineated in the Bayeux address and in the *Memoirs of Hope: Renewal and Endeavor*. We will explore these themes in greater detail during our subsequent evaluation of de Gaulle's constitutionalism. De Gaulle's political purpose after 1940 included the gargantuan task of healing, if not overcoming, the enduring divide between the rightist "patriots," who identified France with "the alliance of monarchy and Catholicism," and "leftist patriots or nationalists," for whom "France was first of all the revolutionary republic."[82] This legislator of a new French Republic had to deemphasize the importance of the regime in order to paradoxically create a new regime drawing on and synthesizing the two sides of the national divide. A one-sided public or rhetorical emphasis on the mystique of the nation became a powerful political instrument in the hands of this modern legislator.

NAPOLEON: GRANDEUR WITHOUT MEASURE

Let us turn to de Gaulle's analysis and evaluation of Napoleon. The anarchy and confusion of the Revolution led to a "natural reaction" on the part of society and the army. They welcomed Napoleon's imposition of order and discipline. Napoleon established an "absolute power" that "existed only by virtue of military glory." Even today, the sight of Napoleon's tomb, de Gaulle writes, fills visitors to the Invalides with the "thrill of greatness."[83] Napoleon, as few men before or after, left his mark on events and pursued nearly unparalleled heights of personal and national glory.

But Napoleon's resplendent grandeur lacked proportion and an adequate sense of limits. It severed grandeur, the works of energy, from a recognition of the possible. It lacked measure and therefore coherence. "The nature of imperial power pushed France into an infernal cycle of battles."[84] Napoleon built the most effective and energetic fighting force the world had ever seen. He endowed it with a remarkable *esprit de corps* and a loyalty to his person and deeds. Until his agreement with Tsar Aleksandr at Tilsit in 1807, Napoleon did not ask this force to carry out tasks that were unreasonable or beyond its means. But after Tilsit, Napoleon's political projects increasingly surpassed any measured equilibrium of ends and means "at the very moment when the military instrument began to lose its quality."[85] Napoleon's immoderate pursuit of imperial expansion led to colossal losses of material and human resources. The wastage was all the more "deplorable" because France's opponents were able to put forward larger armies as their peoples became inspired by national passions.[86] In response to the arousal of anti-Napoleonic and anti-French sentiment throughout the continent, Napoleon had to redouble his efforts. He had to even more thoroughly and intensively militarize French society and to unleash the dogs of total war. He drew on millions of recruits throughout France and her sprawling and artificial empire, which stretched from Poland and Piedmont to Spain to

Santo Domingo. He engaged in a mobilization of men and resources, which as Bertrand de Jouvenel puts it, "smacked of barbarism" at least to the older European sensibility. "From September 1805 to November 1813 he took from France 2,100,000 men in addition to the soldiers of the Republic who had been kept with colors."[87]

His officers and soldiers began to lose their spirit as Napoleon continually asked for new and more strenuous sacrifices after 1809. He promised but never delivered on his claims that these exertions would be followed by a cessation of hostilities and imperial pursuits and by a return to "normal life." Napoleon asked too much of an already exhausted nation and thereby "broke the sword of France." He never appreciated this fundamental moral and political principle: "Les âmes, comme la matiére, ont des limites." (Souls, like matter, have their limits.)[88]

We have noted, in a previous chapter, the mixed or ambiguous character of de Gaulle's evaluation of Napoleon. Napoleon's fall was inevitable in that he ignored the limits that constitute the matrix or framework of human and political life. The natural order of human life struck back at Napoleon's insolence and punished him for his contempt for moral and political limits; his fall was then simultaneously "tragic" and "just." But as a soldier de Gaulle admires his "superhuman prestige" and his "marvelous virtue of arms."[89] He left France with poor and ill-defined borders and exposed the country to the mistrust of Europe. These ills still afflicted France as de Gaulle wrote and contributed to the necessity of de Gaulle's partisanship on behalf of *l'armée de métier*.

In *France and Her Army*, despite his admiration for Napoleon's military feats, de Gaulle strongly emphasized the abuse of trust inherent in the Napoleonic divorce of self-affirmation and moderation. Elsewhere, he speaks more admiringly of Napoleon, stressing his grandeur more than the overreaching that undid his works and left France bleeding. This is the case of de Gaulle's conversations with Malraux, *Felled Oaks*. Napoleon made the French "mad with ambition." De Gaulle told Malraux that Napoleon inspired the French to attempt the unthinkable. "In 1940, he was behind me when I told the French they were not what they seemed to be."[90] In an age of bourgeois "individualism," Napoleon provides a "romantic" correction to the pettiness of a civil society that is in constant danger of forgetting the reality and requirements of national existence. Yet even Malraux's de Gaulle, far more romantic than classical because seen through the eyes of the romantic Malraux, affirms the inadequacy of Napoleonic grandeur:

But Napoleon always tried to force fate. Yet, souls have their limits like everything else. From 1813 on, by dent of striking with it, he had broken the sword of France. Once the ratio between the end and the means is snapped, the maneuvers of a genius are in vain.[91]

De Gaulle is finally no Bonapartist, even if Napoleon is a monumental player in the drama of "eternal France."

CONCLUSION

The final chapters of France and Her Army include informative discussions of French history and the French army from the Restoration through the end of the First World War. From our perspective, the most revealing chapters are the final two, "Towards the Revanche" and "The Great War." Let us stop briefly to note several revealing features of the final chapters. De Gaulle pays tribute to the national renaissance that occurred under the intellectual, spiritual, and literary influences of Boutroux, Bergson, Péguy, and Barrès at the beginning of the twentieth century. Thinkers such as Péguy and Barrès "rendered to the elite consciousness of the national eternity by discovering for them the ties which attach them to their forebears."[92] De Gaulle was, of course, profoundly marked by the renaissance of national consciousness and by the theoreticians of French spirituality and national eternity and continuity. They were the formulators and inspirations, avant la lettre, of the Union Sacrée of the old and new France which de Gaulle applauded and in many ways would come to incarnate.

One must also note de Gaulle's generous praise and admiration for Joffre, and especially for Poincaré ("the reason of France"), Clemenceau (the "rage" of France), and Pétain.[93] Pétain, the hero of Verdun, is presented as a man of both authority and humanity. He restored discipline and self-respect to an army plagued by mutinies as a result of deteriorating morale, an army debilitated by the fierce inhumanity and stifling immobility of trench warfare. As a kind of military statesman, he restored the integrity of the army.[94] This sympathetic portrait tellingly highlights the pathos present in de Gaulle's famous remark about the Pétain of collaboration in his Mémoires de Guerre: old age is a shipwreck. The moral deterioration of Pétain was truly a personal, national, and even a European tragedy.[95]

Let us conclude. De Gaulle repeatedly recalls that France was built by the sword. It is the sword which is the indispensable instrument of the political art and the guarantee of national sovereignty. It is this elemental truth which was forgotten by the appeasers and pacifists during the 1930s and by the partisans of Vichy after June of 1940. As we shall see, de Gaulle could not accept the delusions of those "realists who know nothing of reality,"[96] as he called those who accepted the diminished and decapitated sovereignty and status of a "slave-Prince" beholden to an imperial and totalitarian invader. For de Gaulle, the reality of France was too substantial to be obliterated at a stroke. Somebody must speak for France, for her honor and her undiminished and undivided national sovereignty. And it was not sufficient to do so as a mere auxiliary or "foreign legion" of England and the Allies. It is in his appeal to resistance and his controversial "assumption" of the sovereignty of free and fighting France that the classicism and romanticism of de Gaulle and his idea of France meet.

Chapter 3

"The Man of Character" as "Born Protector": Magnanimity, Justice, and Moderation in de Gaulle's *The Edge of the Sword*

If we wish to uncover the authentic or fuller de Gaulle, the man who lay behind the public de Gaulle who burst on the political scene on June 18, 1940, we must scrutinize closely de Gaulle's own anticipatory self-portrait of the man of character, a portrait sketched, as we have noted, in *The Edge of the Sword* and limned briefly in the conclusion of *Vers l'armée de Métier*.

Almost all the commentators, biographers, and de Gaulle specialists have made the obligatory references to this self-portrait, but only a few have made a serious effort to understand it, to explicate it in the broadest and deepest manner.[1] Such a "textual" explication is necessary if we are to understand de Gaulle as he understood himself, if we are to appreciate and evaluate his own self-understanding. At the conclusion of such a rendering of de Gaulle's portrait of the political leader and the political art, we may legitimately quarrel with his understanding of the political condition of man or with the adequacy of his own self-understanding. But the road to understanding de Gaulle must begin in a critically sympathetic confrontation with de Gaulle's self-presentation.

De Gaulle designed and described the public de Gaulle years before he became a national and international figure. He knew what he was before he publicly displayed his "character." So many of the misunderstandings and caricatures of de Gaulle and the Gaullist enterprise have their origin in the failure to confront and accurately digest the earlier Gaullist account of the man of character.[2] The man of character is explicitly described in *The Edge of the Sword* as "the good Prince"[3] who comes to the fore in a time of crisis. What exactly does de Gaulle mean by the good prince? What human, angelic, or diabolic traits and talents does he exercise or display? What is his relationship to the political community, to democracy and the common good? What is his nature and the character of his "virtue"? These are all questions which are addressed in a somewhat ambiguous, at times remarkably direct, but always elegant and penetrating way in Chapters 2 and 3 of *The Edge of the Sword*.

The core of our examination is an explication of Section II of the chapter "Of Character" and Sections I and II of the chapter "Of Prestige" from *The Edge of the Sword* in order to see how de Gaulle combined self-portraiture, and an analysis of the nature of military and political leadership in a democratic age, with what can only be described as a prophetic self-antici-pation, the accurate rendering of his political and personal biography before the events described occurred. Is his anticipatory self-portrait any-thing more than a prediction of the effects that a sufficiently assertive self can produce? Or, rather, does de Gaulle anticipate in a Europe marked by political and spiritual crisis the just and natural role that a magnanimous statesman can play in channeling the torrent "that is carrying all of us toward an apparently measureless, and, in any event, unprecedented fate?"[4]

THE LIMITS OF DOCTRINE

The Edge of the Sword originated as three lectures on the "philosophy" of military leadership, delivered at the École de Guerre in Paris in 1927. In 1932 it was published as a significantly expanded and reworked essay consisting of five chapters and a foreword. This work emphasizes many of de Gaulle's enduring themes: the permanence of conflict in human and international affairs, the consequent need to cultivate the virtue and dignity of the soldier's art, and the interaction with but ultimate subordi-nation of the soldier's art to political judgment and authority. Above all these, de Gaulle relentlessly criticized a priori military doctrines that tended to dominate the thinking of the French military and political elite. In Chapter 1 of *The Edge of the Sword*, "The Conduct of War," de Gaulle articulates an understanding of the conduct of military leadership which synthesizes and integrates "instinct" and "intelligence." De Gaulle devel-ops a Bergsonian account of the integration of instinct and intelligence as the portal or access that human beings have to the mix of flux and constancy which is the human world. Here de Gaulle reveals his profound indebtedness to Bergson's critique of positivistic rationalism. He does not deny that there is an "order of things," but he notes its obscurity and recognizes the limited access that merely theoretical or abstract knowledge can provide to it. This is an insight into the requirements of action but also a theoretical conclusion about the nature of reality and the proper manner of approaching it. De Gaulle writes:

It is Bergson, also, who has shown that the only way in which the human mind can make direct contact with reality is by intuition, by combining his instinct with his intelligence. Our intelligence can furnish us with the theoretic, general abstract knowledge of what is, but only instinct can give the practical, particular, and concrete feel of it. Without the cooperation of the intelligence there can be no logical reasoning, no informed judgment. But without the reinforcement of instinct there can be no profundity of perception and no creative urge. Instinct is the faculty in our make-up which brings us into closest contact with nature. Thanks to it, we can strike deeply into the order of things, and participate in whatever obscure harmony may be found there. It is by instinct that man discerns the reality of the conditions which surround him, and feels a corresponding impulsion.[5]

In the practical sphere, the great military commanders have always been aware of the "limits of reason," the limits of a priori or merely planned responses to unfolding political and military events. De Gaulle points out that Alexander spoke of his "hope," Caesar of his "luck," and Napoleon of his "star."[6] They knew that their political and military greatness were aided by indecipherable gifts of nature. They knew that "they had a particular gift of making contact with realities sufficiently closely to dominate them."[7] De Gaulle does not deny the role that education, training, habits, planning, or military doctrine ought to play in the preparation for or conduct of war. He also certainly recognizes the raw, dangerous, and potentially self-destructive character of untrained instinct.

But he insists on the essentially "contingent" character of warfare as of the entire realm of action. He therefore recognizes the indispensable place of flexibility in planning and the need for that dynamic element of military and political virtue that he calls character. "War is an activity in which the contingent plays an essential role. . . . This contingent element inseparable from the waging of war gives to that activity both its difficulty and grandeur."[8]

THE BACKGROUND

Let us begin by sketching the larger political context within which de Gaulle's analysis of character must be placed. De Gaulle's public activity beginning with the publication of *Vers l'armée de Métier* in 1934 centered around active partisanship on behalf of a professional army. He proposed a specialized supplement to France's republican army, a corps of one hundred thousand men who would form a mobile army of maneuver and attack, motorized and partially armored and capable of taking the offensive if war were to arrive.[9] Such an army would supplement the large-scale units composed of conscripts. This army would capitalize on the revolution in technology and the nature of warfare brought about by the internal-combustion engine. For de Gaulle, this was the instrument that restores the elements of speed and initiative to warfare whose obsolescence the trench warfare of the First World War had seemingly irrevocably established.[10]

De Gaulle's partisanship on behalf of a new strategy and reformed armed forces for France was formulated in opposition to the dogmatic insistence of the French military hierarchy on the superiority of defense over offense, of the static over the dynamic. The established political and military organs and institutions continued obstinately to deny the revolutionary impact of tanks on modern warfare. They also feared that a professionalized army would challenge the republican dogma of a citizen army, a cherished postrevolutionary inheritance. Established authorities insisted, against all evidence, on the solidity of France's border fortifications, and declared that an invasion of France was beyond the realm of the possible.[11] The root of this blindness undoubtedly lay in large part in the quite understandable spiritual exhaustion that overcame France after her victory in 1918. But it had theoretical roots in the *doctrinairism* of the established French military thought. De Gaulle exposes the theoretical untenability of this position in *The Edge of the Sword*.

The Edge of the Sword is de Gaulle's first salvo in his public campaign to alert France to the dangers of current established military doctrine and strategy. This work provides the theoretical underpinnings on which his partisanship for a mechanized professional army rested. Yet Hitler's ascendancy as master of the Reich in January of 1933 would change everything.[12] It would give the greatest political urgency to de Gaulle's efforts to influence public opinion and to change the consensus shared by France's military and political establishments.

De Gaulle lamented the failure of the leadership of the Third Republic to come to grips with the "dynamic" and contingent character of political and military affairs. In practical terms, the attachment of the regime to the panacea of the fixed and continuous front, to the so-called Maginot line of border fortifications, and the accompanying failure to recognize the revolutionary character of those offensive weapons such as tanks, aircraft, and mobile and revolving guns which had already displayed their effects in the final stages of World War I, unfortunately reflected the decadent character of the Third Republic. De Gaulle believed that France was in need of a comprehensive national re-founding. He would state so openly at the conclusion of *Vers l'armée de Métier* (1934).[13]

Near the beginning of his *War Memoirs* de Gaulle discusses the specific character of this decadence, one tied to the regime's inability to carry out the state's primordial responsibility to act responsibly in the world. Already by the time de Gaulle published *The Edge of the Sword* in 1932 the French "state" was undergoing a kind of senescent debilitation brought out by its failure to recognize those contingencies confronting it (new and grave foreign threats, the emergence of revolutionary military instruments), and a lack of appreciation of the means that are necessary to carry out a great nation's moral and political obligations. The regime had lost that confidence which is inseparable from the capacity *to act politically* in the world. De Gaulle writes in particular about the decadence of the regime's dominant conception of war in a striking passage at the beginning of his *War Memoirs*:

Such a conception of war suited the spirit of the regime. Condemned by governmental weakness and political cleavages to stagnation, it was bound to espouse a static system of this kind. But, in addition, this reassuring panacea corresponded too well to the country's state of mind for anyone desirous of being elected, applauded, or given space in print not to be tempted to approve it. Public opinion did not care for offensives, yielding to the illusion that by making war against war the bellicose would be prevented from making war, remembering many ruinous attacks, and failing to discern the revolution in military strength produced since then by the internal-combustion engine. In short, everything converged to make passivity the very principle of our national defense.[14]

The portrait of the man of character and the leader who cultivates prestige, two inseparable facets of de Gaulle's self-portrait and his portrait of politics and military leadership, is developed precisely within this larger context. The French regime had been undergoing a profound spiritual, and moral, as well as a political and military, crisis. The regime clung to discredited doctrines, it was incapable of confronting new threats, and it was seemingly bereft of statesmen or statesmanship. Its rigid hierarchies solicited and rewarded mediocrity and bureaucratic complacency and punished or repelled those men of character who were as a rule "rough," "disagreeable," even "aggressive."[15] A corrupt and decadent parliamentary regime reinforced the mediocrity of democracy itself. "When it comes to choosing men for high positions, the lot usually falls on the pleasing and docile rather than the meritorious."[16] The crisis of the Third Republic therefore exacerbated and reinforced the crisis of authority afflicting modern and democratic civilization. De Gaulle, who earlier warned against the temptation of lawlessness, of contempt for legitimate political authority, of theoretical and practical extremism ("Nietzscheanism") in his first book published in 1924, now encourages those willful and disagreeable men to challenge corrupt democratic and bureaucratic hierarchies and to willfully master contingencies. *The Edge of the Sword* affirms the efficacy and grandeur of the political will.

We must begin with an element of confusion present in de Gaulle's discussion of the "man of character." It stems from his failure to clearly differentiate between the nature and requirements of military and political leadership. In de Gaulle's detailed description of the man of character in Part II of Chapter II of *The Edge of the Sword*, the man of character appears to be a military man who becomes a statesman during a moment of profound crisis. But some of the particular historical examples of character that de Gaulle provides are simply military figures (e.g., Pelissier, Lanrezac, Lyautey), others are statesmen (e.g., Richelieu, Bismarck, Clemenceau), and still others are scientists, discoverers, and adventurers (e.g., Galileo, Columbus, Lesseps).[17] None of these figures simply or fully matches the Gaullist description of the man of character as a "born protector" and "good Prince." They all embody his passion of acting by himself, but they fall short of his liberality and magnanimity. And many were not political figures at all or do not embody de Gaulle's criteria for the "good Prince" (e.g., Napoleon, Alexander). What accounts for de Gaulle's rather atypical display of imprecision and ambiguity? It is, I think, deliberate. In his prewar books de Gaulle, an established if unorthodox military officer, is primarily discussing the "philosophy" of the soldier, of military and state relations, and of the strategy and character of the armed forces appropriate to the French nation.[18] An element of self-limitation is present in all of these books. De Gaulle never fully or directly addresses the question of statecraft or political philosophy. He speaks not only as a soldier, but also as a future re-founder and statesman. There is a discreet dimension to de Gaulle's discussion of leadership which is related to the fact that his self-portrait anticipates his future political role but within a larger and necessarily limited discussion of the philosophy proper to the soldier. Nonetheless, contained within an examination of that philosophy which can restore the "edge to the sword" is a remarkable phenomenology of political magnanimity within a democratic age. The preeminent example of this political magnanimity will turn out to be de Gaulle himself. But the most appropriate example of character cannot yet be an example—he has not had an opportunity to display his soul on the public stage.

And yet this military man who already discerns his future role as "national savior" and even "Prince-President" follows a different path from those paths blazed by Bonaparte and Nietzsche or even articulated by Aristotle or Machiavelli. He traces an account of political magnanimity, of a man "made for great deeds" who has "the hope of playing a great role in great events." This man bears some resemblance to Aristotle's magnanimous man. He is not free from all of the vices, and he possesses some of the virtù of Machiavelli's Prince, but he is also deeply marked by the influence of Christianity and democracy. A Christianized and democratized magnanimous man! Surely one might object that this is a portrait beyond the realm of the historically or humanly plausible.[19] Perhaps. But de Gaulle's man of character is undeniably influenced by Christianity and democracy in his explicit concern for justice and the common good. He markedly differs from Aristotle's canonical presentation of the magnanimous man, not to mention Nietzsche's "Superman," in his refusal to display or even feel contempt or disdain for his subordinates. His proud insubordination and his radical self-reliance coexist with a recognition of both an order of justice and of "common humanity." Let us now turn to a careful examination of de Gaulle's text.

CHARACTER—"THE VIRTUE OF DIFFICULT TIMES"

De Gaulle begins Chapter II of *The Edge of the Sword*, "Of Character," with an historical survey of the various "ideals" drawn from or compatible with the dominant sentiments of the various epochs of French national life which have given the French army its strength and inspiration. Section I of Chapter II presents a kind of encapsulation of the central theme of *La France et son Armée*: the French army is a mirror of the nature and fortunes of the political order in France. It has and must adjust to the vicissitudes of both the regime and the epoch if it is to continue to serve as the sword and shield as well as a moral inspiration of the French nation. As de Gaulle states in his *Memoirs*, "the soul and fate of the nation were constantly reflected in the mirror of its Army."[20] This indicates the immense political responsibility of those charged with the formation and education of the army, a responsibility powerfully felt by a Louvois or Bonaparte but not adequately grasped by those whom de Gaulle contemptuously calls "the figureheads of the hierarchy"[21] who hide behind merely traditional military doctrines and bureaucratic procedures. Here de Gaulle displays what Raymond Aron calls his "higher pragmatism," which allows him to accept and face the eternal challenge of "modernization," the necessity for constant adjustment to circumstances in the material, military, as well as political and spiritual realms, if France is to remain a vital political force in the world.[22] As a lover and partisan of eternal France, de Gaulle is not inordinately attached to any regime or epoch, whether it be of the Old Regime or the Republic. The task for France and her army at the end of the First World War, a war that has exacerbated the crisis of authority in Europe and France, is nothing less than the momentous one of "recreating itself."[23] This renewal must proceed not abstractly, from preordained doctrines or assumptions but concretely and historically "in accordance with the conditions of the moment."[24] But an institutional, material, and even doctrinal renewal of the French army is not sufficient. In accord with the essential requirements of social life, nothing less than a "moral renaissance" of the French army is demanded.

The soldiers of today, like their fathers before them, require a cult which reassembles them, kindles their enthusiasm, and gives them greater stature. It is necessary that a virtue provide for the military order a rejuvenated ideal, conferring to it, through the elite, the unity of its divergent tendencies and provoking ardor and fructifying talents.[25]

Only such a renewed ideal can maintain the confidence of the army against an unfriendly or apathetic public opinion unfortunately but understandably wallowing in the pacifist reaction that almost naturally follows periods of great and destructive conflict.[26] Only an ideal can sustain the spirit of the armed forces through the trials that undoubtedly lie ahead. De Gaulle gives a name to this military and political virtue which will be the center of the moral renaissance of France and her army. He calls it "character." "Character will be this ferment—character the virtue of difficult times."[27] De Gaulle does not give this virtue an unusual or unfamiliar name, but he does provide it with a new and original description and content.

Section II of Chapter II provides a remarkable description of the man of character. One is initially struck by the proud self-sufficiency of this figure, his radical individuality. One is tempted to say that he is like those gods described by Aristotle at the beginning of the *Politics*, who are said to be outside of the city by nature.[28] But if the man of character draws on and from himself, he is not simply for himself.

De Gaulle begins, as we said, by highlighting his individuality. "When faced with events, the man of character has recourse to himself."[29] He shares the self-sufficiency of Aristotle's magnanimous man or of Nietzsche's Superman, but his stance toward events and his attitude toward the community is in some ways preeminently moral. He wishes "to leave his mark on action, to take responsibility for it, to make it his own business."[30] Nietzsche's Superman takes responsibility in the sense that he wills the eternal consequences of his action—he is serious because he wills the "eternal return of the same." But he finally affirms the will as the sole criterion for human action or judgment. On the other hand, action is largely beneath the dignity of Aristotle's haughty magnanimous man. His consciousness of his individuality is so radical that he believes himself to be almost a whole unto himself. He even strives to imitate the immobility and self-sufficiency of a god. Aristotle describes the radical self-sufficiency of the magnanimous man in Book 4, Chapter 3 of his *Ethics*. To understand the original sense of magnanimity, it is necessary to quote from Aristotle's description at some length:

Magnanimity seems even from its name to be concerned with great things; what sort of great things, is the first question we must try to answer. . . . Now the man is thought to be magnanimous who thinks himself worthy of great things, being worthy of them; for he who does so beyond his deserts is a fool, but no virtuous man is foolish or silly.

. . . Now the magnanimous man, since he deserves most, must be good in the highest degree; for the better man always deserves more, and the best man most. Therefore the truly magnanimous man must be good. And greatness in every virtue would seem to be characteristic of a proud man. And it would be most unbecoming for a proud man to fly from danger, swinging his arms by his sides, or to wrong another; for to what end should he do disgraceful acts, he to whom nothing is great?

. . . The magnanimous man does not run into trifling dangers, nor is he fond of danger, because he honours few things; but he will face great dangers, and when he is in danger he is unsparing of his life, knowing that there are conditions on which life is not worth having. And he is the sort of man to confer benefits, but he is ashamed of receiving them; for the one is the mark of a superior, the other of an inferior. . . . It is a mark of the magnanimous man also to ask for nothing or scarcely anything, but to give help readily, and to be dignified towards people who enjoy high position and good fortune, but unassuming towards those of the middle class; for it is a difficult and lofty thing to be superior to the former, but easy to be so to the latter, and a lofty bearing over the former is no mark of ill-breeding, but among humble people it is as vulgar as a display of strength against the weak. Again, it is characteristic of the magnanimous man not to aim at the things commonly held in honour, or the things in which others excel; to be sluggish and to hold back except where great honour or a great work is at stake, and to be a man of few deeds, but of great and notable ones. He must also be open in his hate and in his love (for to conceal one's feelings, i.e. to care less for truth than for what people will think, is a coward's part), and must speak and act openly; for he is free of speech because he is contemptuous, and he is given to telling the truth, except when he speaks in irony to the vulgar. . . . Nor is he mindful of wrongs; for it is not the part of a magnanimous man to have a long memory, especially for wrongs, but rather to overlook them. . . .

. . . Further, a slow step is thought proper to the proud man, a deep voice, and a level utterance; for the man who takes few things seriously is not likely to be hurried, nor the man who thinks nothing great to be excited, while a shrill voice and a rapid gait are the results of hurry and excitement.[31]

The man of character is not self-sufficient in this sense. He is what we could call a socialized and politicized version of magnanimity. He draws from his remarkable natural gifts in order to act. Unlike the magnanimous man, he is powerfully driven to a life of continuous action. He is in some ways above but not against law or convention.

He embraces action with the "pride of a master."[32] But his mastery is not like that described and applauded by Nietzsche in *Beyond Good and Evil*. For Nietzsche, true masters see their subordinates as wholly instrumental to themselves and therefore dispensable. This is true of his spiritualized Superman as well as of the new planetary nobility or aristocracy which Nietzsche envisions to replace the base reign of the "last man."[33] A true aristocracy must believe that it is like those resplendent vines on trees in Java and that these trees exist solely for the well-being of itself, the crown of humanity.[34] Everything else is without human significance, everything else, apart from itself, is deprived or bereft of dignity.

The essential characteristic of a good and healthy aristocracy, however, is that it experiences itself *not* as a function (whether of the monarchy or the common-wealth) but as their *meaning* and highest justification—that it therefore accepts with a good conscience the sacrifice of untold human beings who, *for its sake*, must be reduced and lowered to incomplete human beings, to slaves, to instruments.[35]

In contrast to these perhaps sublime and certainly dangerous Nietzschean heights, the mastery which the man of character displays is rooted in what he has done and what is legitimately "due to him." He is measured by his deeds and by his unique capacity for service. He is, unlike Nietzsche's Superman and in a much more substantial sense than the magnanimous man, a "born protector."[36] He wishes to be given his due for what he has legitimately given to the community. He desires to be "recognized" for his greatness in playing a great role in great events. Yet he is not bereft of self-knowledge and is not unwilling to face his limitations or his failures in his risky confrontation with the torrent of events.

The event, the action, and the man of character with his instinctive and natural gifts form a dynamic triad, a kind of primordial unity in the moral economy of men and nations. The man of character "pays his debts with his own money" and "lends nobility to action."[37] His self-sufficiency is both less haughty in its bearing and superior in self-knowledge to the magnanimous man. He does not attempt to imitate in gait and speech the immobility of the gods. He is filled with zeal for deciding and acting, but he powerfully feels his responsibility for the consequences of his deeds. His claim on the community is not that of a would-be god but rather is an extraordinary claim within the order of human justice. He provides the singular and exceedingly rare form of energy necessary to give order to the human world. He puts his mark on events and thus enables men to master the conditions of their collective existence. In a very concrete manner he allows human beings to live well rather than to merely live—he allows humble souls to experience the majesty of grandeur. Neither a tyrannical soul nor a being in search of apotheosis, de Gaulle gives him an appropriate name. He is a "hero." He provides an "empire over souls"[38] while recognizing that all men, however humble, are souls as well as matter.

MAGNANIMITY AND MODERATION

The paradoxical character of the individuality of de Gaulle's hero has been well formulated by Stanley Hoffmann in a remark that was previously cited: "the hero is both his own law and the servant of France." The man of character draws on his own inner resources, to be sure, but he confronts difficulty not only for the sake of mastering events and himself, but because he is loyal to and is solicitous toward his political community. According to de Gaulle, human beings are naturally political. He does not argue from the Aristotelean claim that the unique human capacity for speech and reason makes deliberation about the advantageous and the just both necessary and possible[39] but instead from the human need for authority, for order and for leaders. "Men, in their hearts, can no more do without being led than they can live without food, drink and sleep. These political animals have the need for organization, that is to say for an order and for leaders."[40] In some real sense the man of character is indispensable to the political community. He allows it to master the conditions of its existence, and his action helps provide it with a sense of purpose, elevation, and grandeur. "He must aim high, see grandly, judge largely," if he is to "establish his authority over the generality of men who splash in shallow water."[41]

By providing his unique brand of political and human artistry, he allows ordinary souls to identify with a mystique that is greater than themselves and that makes them better than they would be otherwise. He even elevates, humanizes, and transfigures the political order and thereby contributes to the development of a common good. But he cannot develop or exercise his singular virtue outside of a political community. In that crucial sense he is not self-sufficient. He cannot carry out his purposes without others. Of course, he clearly needs subordinates who "give of their best when carrying out his orders."[42] When he comes to sight as a ruler, he is the chief within a hierarchy, but that hierarchy must also include "theoreticians" and "counselors" who are more than mere subordinates.[43]

One thinks, of course, of de Gaulle's longtime relationship with André Malraux, the famous novelist who became minister of culture under de Gaulle, and, in effect, the literary and political theorist of Gaullism and French grandeur.[44] De Gaulle and Malraux had a reciprocal need for each other. Malraux provided de Gaulle with the opportunity for genuine intellectual dialogue about his reflection on his "certain idea of France." It is in the realm of ideas that the man of action clearly recognizes his equals or even superiors. One also thinks of de Gaulle's evocation of and admiration for Péguy, Chateaubriand, and Bergson.[45] De Gaulle also embodied the answer to Malraux's search for a new romantic and "existentialist" hero, a search that led him far and wide from explorations of China, India, and Indochina to the battlefields of Civil War Spain. He would sometimes identify his hero with less than great men such as Nehru and with a cruel and bloodthirsty ideological tyrant such as Mao. In de Gaulle, almost by accident, he stumbled on the real article. On his part, the political artist needed the artist and theoretician to give public sustenance and private reinforcement to his self-proclaimed mission and his idea of France.

De Gaulle insists that the "supreme element" in human affairs comes from the "initiative" of the man of character.[46] The man of character is a kind of political artist. He is not an aesthete who tries to remake human beings according to some abstract vision of how the world ought to look. He does not try to change human nature, but rather to bring out its possibilities for "greatness." He provides that element of inspiration and initiative which gives the life of action its "dynamic quality . . . just as the talent of the artist breathes life into matter."[47]

De Gaulle, as political artist and theoretician of action, rejects all theoretical and practical fatalisms and determinisms as well as any cult or irrationalist philosophy of the human will. The political artist, the heroic man of action, the statesman, and founder are all capable of "adding the weight of a singular virtue to the known procedures of any situation."[48] It is largely *because* of the reality of great-souled human beings that human beings are not playthings of the gods, fate, or History. Human and political responsibility for the character of collective existence is possible and necessary. Human beings cannot simply stop the torrent of events that sometimes have the appearance of an abyss, but they are free in their responses to them. They are never completely free to become masters and possessors of nature, certainly not of human and social nature. But the ambition of the few to leave a mark on events helps to guarantee the self-respect of the human race. The man of character vivifies human undertakings through his energetic human artfulness. He is by no means "beyond good and evil," but he accepts and is animated by the "harsh" and solitary "joy of being *responsible*"[49] (emphasis mine). His lonely confrontation with the exigencies of action, and his desire to face difficulties and leave his mark on events are the psychological underpinnings of his artistry. De Gaulle writes:

The man of character finds an attractiveness in difficulty, since it is only by coming to grips with difficulty that he realizes himself. Whether or not he defeats it is an affair between it and him. He is a jealous lover and will share with no one the prizes or the pains that may be his as a result of trying to overcome obstacles.[50]

De Gaulle's great-souled man has both a passion for acting and a "passion for acting by himself." This twofold passion is "accompanied by some roughness in his effort. The man of character incorporates in his own person the severity inherent in his effort."[51] His subordinates feel this severity and "groan under it." They complain about his "haughtiness" and "the demands he makes."[52] We have freely identified de Gaulle's self-understanding with his portrait of the man of character. This phenomenology is largely, but not only, a self-portrait. De Gaulle had a remarkable self-knowledge and was free of the great delusion of the tyrannical soul that he would be loved and "recognized" by all despite what he was and had to do. As we argue at greater length later in this chapter, de Gaulle believed that distance and aloofness were both elements of what it meant to be a man of character, as well as requirements for cultivating the prestige necessary for the exercise of authority.

But this distance, mistaken for mere haughtiness and a requirement of his political artistry, does not prevent the man of character from providing leadership or being a powerful source of political cohesion. If character is the virtue of difficult times, the man of character needs the challenge of difficult times in order to manifest himself. He needs genuine opportunities to be a statesman and Legislator in the fundamental and comprehensive senses of those terms.

At a time of crisis, the true worth of the man of character is or can be recognized. At that moment, "matters are seen in a different light and justice appears."[53] The relationship of the man of character to the community displayed during a time of crisis is one of *justice*, a preeminently natural and political relationship. De Gaulle richly articulates this relationship in the following passages:

When the crisis comes, it is him they follow, it is he who carries the burden on his shoulders, even though they collapse under it. On the other hand, the knowledge that the lesser men have confidence in him exalts the man of character. He feels himself obliged by the humble justice that they render to him. . . .

But when events become serious, when the peril is pressing, when the common salvation immediately demands leaders with initiative who can be relied upon, and are willing to take risks, then matters are seen in a very different light, and justice appears. A sort of ground swell brings the man of character to the surface. His advice is listened to, his abilities are praised, and one trusts oneself to his worth.[54]

A national crisis allows one to see beyond the limits of what Max Weber called "rational-legal" and "bureaucratic" justifications of legitimacy and political authority. But de Gaulle's man of character is not merely or even primarily a charismatic leader. He is not a "value-free" construction of social science. He is a reality of and within the political world. He draws on gifts of nature and not the mysterious *fatum* of the human self. He is expressly part of the natural world, and he is followed and praised *justly* because his judgment and his efforts are truly "great," that is, genuinely superior, beneficent, and praiseworthy. De Gaulle's hero is not even vulgarly charismatic in that his immediately evident external traits are "haughtiness" and "roughness in method." Weber's commitment to "science" did not allow him to distinguish between the "charisma" of the charlatan and the prophet, or the tyrant and the statesman.[55] De Gaulle's man of character, like the charismatic leader, draws on largely mysterious and unanalyzable inner resources and gifts. But he is a political artist rather than a creator and source of human "values." He is part of an order of nature and justice which is incompatible with the domination of an unlimited, unmeasured human will.

The great-souled man of character, like the charismatic leader, sometimes shuns hierarchies, and is the source of new laws and new traditions. He is a potential "revolutionary" or founder. But he is not like those merely, or primarily subversive members of Lincoln's "tribe of the lion and the eagle" who deliberately tear down old laws and traditions because they "disdain a beaten path."[56] Like Lincoln, and Lincoln's model of statesmanship, de Gaulle and his leader are shepherds who protect the political community from wolves, from the fury of unmastered events and the threats posed by ideologues, demagogues, and tyrants. He performs the "difficult tasks" and "principal efforts"[57] largely by himself but not against the nation and community. In a broader sense, he exercises loyalty and fidelity. He is a servant of the nation, of the common good, and in de Gaulle's particular case, of France who is his "mother" (in Péguy's theological-political sense).

De Gaulle duly noted that the man of character "feels obliged by the humble justice that they (the people) render to him."[58] In *The Edge of the Sword*, de Gaulle spoke of the immediate, dramatic, and universal character of the hero's recognition by the people. As his *War Memoirs* makes clear, De Gaulle knew that not all or even most people would immediately or unqualifiedly render this justice. But unburdened of delusions, such as the misguided belief that Marshall Pétain could save the self-respect of the nation through accommodation with Hitler's Germany, and restored to the "better angels of their nature," to their good sense and goodwill, they would gradually recognize him for what he was, the savior and protector of the liberty and independence of France.

The man of character avoids the pitfalls of mediocrity, including the disfiguring passion for revenge. "Scarcely even does he taste the savor of revenge because action absorbs him completely."[59] He is absorbed in his tasks, in the requirements of the life of action. The confidence others give him helps to justify and strengthen his benevolence, for "he is a born protector."[60] He takes full responsibility for the consequences of his actions, generously sharing the advantages incumbent upon success but refusing to blame others for his failures. In contrast, Aristotle's magnanimous man does no harm, but not out of any generosity of soul or genuine solicitude for those under him but because doing harm is beneath him. Rather than taking full political responsibility, he acts rarely, that is, only on those exceptional occasions where actions are worthy of *his greatness*. His pride prevents him from being a shepherd or "a born protector." In Aristotle's description of magnanimity, one can find the philosophical analysis of Coriolanus's aristocratic disdain for the necessity of dealing with the hopelessly vulgar people.[61] The magnanimous man, like Coriolanus, refuses to accept the fact that he belongs to the same human and political "whole" as the people. Aristotle's magnanimous man is a political animal only in an extremely limited or qualified sense.

Here I think we find the originality and nobility inherent in Gaullist magnanimity. Aristotle's magnanimous man ironically expresses disdain for the vulgar. This Zeus-like man fails to appreciate the human possibilities inherent in the protective nourishment of the common good. Similarly, Weber's social scientific category of charismatic leadership severs the gifts of leadership from a recognition of the natural world or from "the rules of classical order" which give structure and direction to human choice. It thereby distorts the phenomena, making it impossible to make those distinctions that allow us to understand accurately and deeply the human and political world. In its turn, Nietzsche's beautifully seductive portrait of the human mastery and self-mastery of the Superman reflects its creator's rejection of that "sense of equilibrium, of the possible, of measure which alone renders durable and fecund the works of energy."[62] De Gaulle traces and follows a different path. Pierre Manent eloquently formulates the moral characteristic of de Gaulle's political model. It is located precisely in his

more than human blending of pride and humility. . . . In his political and moral being, de Gaulle owed nothing to democratic convention, legitimacy, or custom. In his political action, he never turned against democracy; indeed, he twice decisively helped to reinstate or consolidate it. Is not this weaving together of magnanimity and moderation distinctive of the truly great man?[63]

The restraint and moderation that accompanied de Gaulle's willful "assumption"[64] of France in June of 1940 is clearly foreshadowed in de Gaulle's account of the man of character. The man of character "abuses no one and shows himself to be a good Prince."[65] He is not Nietzsche's Caesar with the soul of Christ, an impossible contradiction formulated by Christianity's most eloquent enemy. But he is something like "Caesar reshaped by Christianity," as an associate of de Gaulle formulated it.[66] In his thought and action, magnanimity and a recognition of "common humanity" are combined in a remarkably unforced and "authentic" manner. He combines a sense of the distinction and hierarchy of human types, a recognition of the dynamic tension between the many and the great. But he does not distort that hierarchy or radicalize that tension to the point of precluding the existence of a common humanity or of a political world where the virtues of great-souledness and the natures and needs of the people sustain a network of mutual obligations.

Machiavelli's conditional recommendation that the Prince form an alliance with the many against the few was based on a cost-benefit analysis of the comparative harmlessness and malleability of the many and the few.[67] An alliance with the people can better sustain the longevity and solidity of the prince's rule. In Machiavelli's understanding, however, the prince's "humor" cannot unite with that of the people or the great in a common good because there is no justice or statesmanship that is capable of mediating the claims of the respective parts of the city. De Gaulle's man of character, in contrast, draws from himself in serving and uniting others. He "abuses no one" because of his generous nature and his recognition of the force of the claims of human justice. While quite capable of exercising "moderate Machiavellianism," de Gaulle and his hero reject what we might call the moral and political ecology of Machiavellianism.

De Gaulle's phenomenology of the man of character helps us recover the natural world obfuscated by a modern philosophy that flees from the articulations and demands of nature, a social science that aims to replace a political science of human nature with value-free causal analysis, and a democratic ideology that resists the distinctions and inequalities which nature contributes.[68] The virtues that democracy readily recognizes are social virtues: cooperation, sociability, even "good cheer." The man of character is benevolent and even in a certain manner humane, but he assuredly is not "nice." He is characterized by "asperity,"[69] by a rough and sharp hardness that cuts and hurts. He regularly is despised by mediocrities, legalists, and "bureaucrats" and by the intellectuals defined by their dogmatic egalitarianism. He will serve democracy, but he is not its product or natural fruit. He therefore exists in uneasy tension with the claims of egalitarian ideologies and rational-legalistic institutions and bureaucratic forms of modern society. But the analysis of *The Edge of the Sword* is more *extra*democratic than *anti*democratic in its lessons and import. De Gaulle aims to contribute to the civic education of democratic citizens and statesmen by showing the concrete limitations of the democratic dogma. He insists that asperity is only the surface of "powerful natures" and that such natures, however firm and inconvenient, offer profound supports for the regime of modern liberty. One can "only lean on something that offers resistance and . . . firm and inconvenient hearts are to be preferred to facile souls without a spring of life or action."[70]

Recall de Gaulle's famous remark at a press conference in Paris on May 19, 1958, in the midst of the unrest in Algiers which led to the collapse of the Fourth Republic. De Gaulle expressly (even angrily) denied any tyrannical or dictatorial intent.

Did I ever make any attempt on basic public liberties? On the contrary, I restored them. . . . Why should I, at 67, begin a career as a dictator? . . . [However] it is not possible to solve the national crises of the present time within the limits of everyday routine.[71]

The great French liberal Raymond Aron, always respectful of the General's greatness and historical importance but a frequent critic of his policies and style, asserted in 1960 that the man given absolute power in 1958 to reform the Constitution of France "has the soul of a paternal monarch or of a prince-president, not of a tyrant."[72] This remark succinctly captures and clarifies de Gaulle's self-understanding as presented in *The Edge of the Sword* and the political intentions of his work as Legislator of the Fifth Republic.

THE CRISIS OF AUTHORITY AND THE CULTIVATION OF PRESTIGE

"Of Character" is followed by "Of Prestige," a chapter that is probably a greater source of misunderstanding than "Of Character." If the discussion of character has given rise to the myth of de Gaulle's Nietzscheanism, the account of prestige has been a major source for the Machiavellian interpretations of de Gaulle's thought and action. De Gaulle certainly affirms the necessity for the statesman to carefully cultivate prestige through the subtle manipulation of the needs and sentiments, the "latent faith,"[73] of ordinary people. He also accepts, without anguish or moralistic scruples, the sometimes unsavory means that are inescapable requirements of the political vocation. In the decisive respects, however, he rejects the full-fledged Machiavellian philosophy of man and the political order.

The starting point that frames the contours of de Gaulle's purported Machiavellianism is usually ignored. The social realities that necessitate a radical rethinking of the problem of authority are precisely the contemporary crises of traditional institutions and sources of authority and the rise of new tyrannies within increasingly mechanized and collectivized modern societies. The "death of god" and totalitarianism are the twin threats to civilized order which provide the backdrop to the Gaullist evocation of prestige. "These are hard days for authority," de Gaulle notes. Both public authority and moral standards were in decay or decline. The old conventions, the traditional sources of moral and political authority, no longer held sway. He quotes without attribution the words of Sallust cited by Augustine in *The City of God* to illustrate the decay of the Roman Empire: "Nos dieux sont decrépits et la misére en tombe" ("Our gods are decrepit and misery ensues"). But in *The Edge of the Sword* de Gaulle rejected the view that this crisis of authority, of gods and "values," would last "indefinitely." Men are "political animals" who "feel the need for organization, that is to say for an established order and for leaders."[74]

The older European traditions, loyalties, conventions, and hierarchies would continue to be important sources of social cohesion. In every social order, there are more and less conventional sources of authority and social obedience; there must be recognized wellsprings of social reverence. Modernity weakens but cannot destroy that legitimacy which arises either from tradition or from established legal sources of authority. "Men do not change so quickly or so completely, nor does nature move by leaps. Authority exercised over other people still depends to a large extent upon the consecration of rank and services."[75] But the crisis of our time is coextensive with a crisis of institutions and traditions. "Conventions of obedience" have grown weak and are vulnerable to new theoretical and practical threats. Personal prestige will be the "mainspring of command" until a substitute is found for the moral legitimacy that Christianity once provided for the Western social order.[76]

De Gaulle locates "prestige" in an analysis of modern times while recognizing that there is a permanent tension, independent of the crisis of the modern social order, between the requirements of formal hierarchy, rank, and services and the character and prestige of leaders. De Gaulle does not side in a Machiavellian way with the self-assertive "Prince." Rather, he recognizes that perverse expressions of the natural human need for authority will fill the vacuum left by the exhaustion of liberal and Christian Europe. In 1932 de Gaulle saw new foundations of order emerging in modern societies. "What the masses once granted to birth or office, they now give to those who can impose themselves."[77] This recognition of personal prestige can take the relatively benign form of the acclamation of athletes or the power or influence of scientists and engineers. But it is most ominously seen in the phenomenon of the dictator "who owes his rise to nothing but his own audacity."[78] The "individualist" ethic of modern societies can lead to the triumph of a new despotism where the human will is unchallenged in its domination and manipulation of the human person. The cultivation of prestige is on one level, a necessary expression of the benevolent protection that the man of character provides for the legitimate political community.

If de Gaulle's moral and political intention is not Machiavellian, his political psychology is reminiscent of the Machiavellian tradition, as reformulated by his contemporaries such as Vilfredo Pareto and Roberto

Michels. The Machiavellians distinguish between the "humors" of the few and the many, between an ambitious elite that wishes to rule or dominate, and the mass of men who wish to be left alone but who are in fact controlled by others. De Gaulle's many, as we have seen, are "political animals" because "in their hearts [they] can no more do without being led than they can live without food, drink and sleep." But de Gaulle does not advocate tyrannical manipulations of the many by an ambitious and self-aggrandizing elite. Instead, in *The Edge of the Sword* de Gaulle tries to educate a new elite who are instilled with the "virtue of difficult times" which he calls "character." These self-reliant, passionate, and ambitious men will use their talents in the political and military service of a legitimate, constitutional state. De Gaulle encourages them to cultivate their own "personal prestige" through the development of resolute character and the mystery and reserve that are preconditions of effective leadership or command.[79]

De Gaulle provides a rich analysis of the austere bearing of those who pursue personal prestige. They deliberately cultivate a mysterious air, a personal manner that excites the interest of those around them. They combine a "reserve of soul" with a carefully crafted "economy of words and deeds."[80] De Gaulle is remarkably forthright about the sources of what we might call the Gaullist style. "In any event, a leader of this quality is inevitably distant, for there can be no authority without prestige, nor prestige unless he keeps his distance."[81]

Here we see a striking confirmation of that quality of austere reserve noted by many of de Gaulle's contemporaries. Writing in 1947, the resistance leader Emmanuel d'Astier somewhat disparagingly referred to de Gaulle as the "Symbol." D'Astier saw de Gaulle as a "great, cold prelate whose kingdom is France, a kingdom not perhaps of this world, and which he will share with no one." He complained that de Gaulle was incapable of friendship or any form of genuine human communion, and he noted his physical and spiritual remoteness, his economy of words and deeds, and his use of "three weapons: prestige, secrecy and cunning."[82]

D'Astier's presentation of de Gaulle is not intended to be flattering. But in no important respect does he disagree with de Gaulle's own account of the methods that the great political man must use, although he fails to sufficiently appreciate the personal sacrifices that he must make. De Gaulle's man of character who cultivates prestige is not simply engaged in theatrical self-presentation; he bears the almost superhuman weight of his responsibility. His pride is marked by a melancholy like the old and noble monument to which de Gaulle refers, whose sadness someone had commented on to Napoleon. "Yes," [Napoleon] replied, "as sad as greatness."[83]

De Gaulle notes in this chapter that men of character can sometimes unexpectedly reach the breaking point and suddenly withdraw from public life. Georges Pompidou, de Gaulle's successor as president of the Fifth Republic, remembered these words when de Gaulle resigned as president of France after losing the referendum on regionalization and the reform of the Senate in April 1969. The melancholy brought about by wounded pride and exhaustion from a lifelong crusade against the "forces of mediocrity" is also evident in de Gaulle's conversations with Malraux shortly before his death which were published as *Les Chênes qu'on abat* (*Felled Oaks*).

Let us return to the larger moral and political purposes that animate de Gaulle's discussion of prestige. Given the contemporary crisis, those with the "natural gift of authority" must acquire or develop the constant and necessary elements of the craft of leadership. De Gaulle wishes to encourage (in the military and political elite) those natural aristocrats, men with an inborn propensity to lead, to develop an art or craft of command that can be strengthened and exploited by the exercise of their "gift."[84] He believes that this cultivation of "character" and "prestige," by a self-selecting "elite" at the service of the greatness of the nation, would go a long way toward strengthening credible sources of public authority. There is a natural equilibrium to human and political life, and the proper balancing and interrelations of the elite and the masses are at the core of that equilibrium. The many desire a civic faith, authorities to look up to, greatness to admire and recognize. A decent liberal society must appeal to the "latent faith" of the many, a faith that survives the modern or democratic revolution. De Gaulle is responding to the erosion of traditional sources of authority, the weakening of the legitimate, constitutional state, and the rise of new ideological paganisms, totalitarian "Mollochs"[85] as he called them, in Germany and Russia. In *The Edge of the Sword*, de Gaulle presents a model of military and political prestige which appears to be a mirror of his own soul. Gaullist grandeur in this account resembles Weberian "charisma" but with this fundamental and vital difference: Gaullist "grandeur" is less a mysterious "demonic" charisma, a source of "values," than a partially crafted, partially natural mode of relating to the military and political community for the purpose of rekindling attachment to a legitimate, decent constitutional state. De Gaulle's efforts were animated by the desire to defend and reinvigorate moderate politics and the moderate state against forces of spiritual and political disintegration.

Prestige cannot be fully or adequately cultivated without the virtue of character. De Gaulle believes that ordinary human beings and citizens are willing to grant the man of character the "privilege of domination, the right to issue orders, the pride of seeing them obeyed, the thousand respects, homages and faculties which surround power."[86] They ask of the leader that he genuinely dominate events, that he possess and display "the qualities of daring, decision and initiative."[87]

The many are less democratic in this respect than the intellectuals, who cling more blindly to the egalitarianism of the democratic dogma. The people openly recognize their dependence on the energizing direction provided by leaders, as long as the leaders' projects "seek the perfection of the goal"[88] de Gaulle calls grandeur. Statesmen must touch this "spring" in men; they must nourish the sentiments and hopes of ordinary souls to contribute to an enterprise greater than themselves. De Gaulle, of course, recognizes that there are fraudulent prophets and statesmen who give the support of their energy and talents to destructive crusades, to revolutions and barbarities in the name of "some high-sounding justification." But he also recognizes the fact that even their deeds are marked by a kind of "somber magnificence,"[89] by a kind of distorted grandeur that is of a different order and quality than the protective magnanimity of the man of character.

This recognition does not establish de Gaulle's Machiavellianism, nor does it reveal a "value-free" understanding of power or an indiscriminate acceptance of all manifestations of "charismatic leadership." In his *War Memoirs* de Gaulle paints subtle portraits of the perverted grandeur of totalitarians such as Stalin and Molotov.[90] Elsewhere he speaks about the false grandeur of Mussolini, who failed to appreciate that true greatness must recognize measure and human liberty in order to do its work.[91] Burke speaks in similar tones about the tragic greatness of Cromwell. Sometimes our contemporaries, who are so quick to accept the legitimacy of a value-free science of man, respond in moralistic tones when great men recognize the complexity of human affairs, including the "greatness" inherent even in the actions of tyrannical souls who give a skewed witness to their humanity by their efforts to leave their mark on events. In such reactions, we witness the triumph of the egalitarianism of the democrat over his penchant for value-free social analysis.

THE PROBLEM OF MACHIAVELLIANISM

De Gaulle's "Machiavellianism" is ordinary political Machiavellianism, the kind of moderate Machiavellianism recognized by the classical political philosophers or by reasonable observers of political life as a constituent and permanent element of politics. Machiavelli himself already anticipates

Nietzsche's comprehensive transvaluation of values. His prince creates himself and is beyond good and evil even if his statecraft depends in a parasitic manner on the maintenance of the older moral framework, the world of "good and evil." The Machiavellian Prince must know how to use well both the beast and the man. His metaphorical teacher is Chiron the centaur, half-man and half-beast, the mythological teacher of ancient princes. In his resort to the beastly arts, he must combine the strength of the lion with the fox's capacity to pretend and dissemble. All of this is necessary because human beings are wicked and are incapable of observing faith. There is no recognizable common good or human fidelity that can be relied upon. Machiavelli's Prince must "appear merciful, faithful, humane, honest, and religious and to be so, but to remain with a spirit built so that, if you need not to be those things, you are able and know how to change to the contrary,"[92] as necessity and the times require.

De Gaulle's recognition of the "Machiavellian" dimension of political action does not entail Machiavelli's transvaluation of values. De Gaulle's emphasis is on the necessary priority of ends to means if the true "master" is to vivify the community with a vision of greatness, of those political summits otherwise unavailable to men. The Gaullist hero deals in the realm of "faith and dreams."[93] He is not, as Nora Beloff falsely claims, completely "free from the normal bonds of conscience."[94] But he does recognize that it is impossible to lead human beings to the summits without displaying "egotism, pride, hardness and cunning."[95] The man of character was described as rough in his method, as marked by asperity. He is not virtuous in the Christian sense, nor does he possess the Florentine's virtù. He does not transvalue values, but instead incorporates within himself certain dispositions and displays certain actions that reflect the complex and heterogeneous elements and requirements of a political world fit for man.

As we have already seen, de Gaulle notes that "evangelic perfection does not lead to empire."[96] This is undoubtedly true, but it raises perplexing questions about de Gaulle's relationship to Christianity and not just to Machiavellianism. De Gaulle does not insist with any relish or cynical glee that the statesman play the part of the beast. He does not reject ordinary or common morality. But he does admit that the man of character must be willing to use means that transgress the ordinary demands of Christian virtue. He recognizes a partial *autonomy* of political morality and the political art.

De Gaulle's statesman, unlike the Machiavellian Prince, is not self-serving. His "austerity" derives from his service to an ideal that transcends and guides his own quest for glory or ambition. But the cause of greatness, of service to the nation, demanded a self-conscious rejection of evangelic perfection. How does this rejection coexist with personal piety or faith or the requirements of individual virtue? With due recognition of the inscrutability of the human heart, the evidence suggests that de Gaulle was a serious, believing, and practicing Catholic.[97] There are impressive private testimonies to the reality and depths of his piety. Yet his political thought and action explicitly avoided openly Catholic or theological references or categories.

Malraux claimed that de Gaulle was singularly dedicated to two causes: to his idea of France and to his Catholic faith. About his faith de Gaulle spoke only with a kind of unparalleled discretion.[98] Certainly, his Catholic faith is evident in his critique of mass society and his support for new forms of "association."[99] It undergirds his partisanship for a "certain conception of man"[100] against the materialism and mechanization of the modern world. One discerns the influence of Péguy and Bernanos as well as that of the "personalist" tradition in politics and philosophy. Still, the question must be asked: did de Gaulle subordinate the well-being of his own soul to the categorical imperative of civic and national salvation? Did his "theological-political" partisanship on behalf of France confuse the temporal and spiritual realms in a manner that is somewhat idolatrous? And finally, did his acceptance of the necessity of *raison d'État* lead him to acquiesce in methods that are ultimately incompatible with both the demands of honor and considerations of common morality?

Consider, for example, his willingness to unconditionally abandon the *pieds noirs* and the pro-French Muslim harkis in Algeria, and his near complete capitulation to the National Liberation Front's (FLN) demands in Algeria in 1962 with seemingly little concern for the human consequences of such a capitulation and abandonment. Alain Peyrefitte, for example, records de Gaulle's disconcerting indifference to the fate of the French Algerian community or to France's Muslim allies.[101] De Gaulle was undoubtedly right that disembarkation from the Algerian War was the sine qua non for the modernization of France's polity and economy and the restoration of her place in the world. From 1958 to 1961 de Gaulle was willing to cover his Algerian policy in a cloud of ambiguity, misleading ultras and liberals alike.[102] After a long series of maneuvers, he negotiated what amounted to a French surrender to the FLN sealed by the Évian accords. One can understand his lack of empathy with the *pied noirs*. The community had largely been Vichyite in its sympathies during World War II, and significant elements of it had declared war on de Gaulle and the institutions of the Fifth Republic as his refusal to maintain Algérie Française became clearer.

But here we are not interested primarily in de Gaulle's policy so much as in the nature of his political morality. He manifested a striking and disturbing inattention to the principle of fidelity in carrying out his quite rational desire to free France from the Algerian quagmire. The consequences of this inattention were grave indeed: approximately one hundred thousand harkis and other opponents of the FLN were murdered after the precipitous French departure from Algeria in 1963.[103] De Gaulle, who had so nobly represented the cause of fidelity and national honor since 1940, allowed himself to be moved in the Algerian case only by the coldest requirements of state. This example reveals some of the moral limitations of a statesmanship of grandeur. It has an inherent tendency to separate the means from ends in the dialectic of means and ends which de Gaulle accepted in principle and which structures the morality of political action. Gaullist magnanimity is tarred by a somewhat unseemly acquiescence in the ideology of *raison d'État*.

None of these questions or reservations about de Gaulle's political morality in this case is intended to deny the moral seriousness of Gaullist magnanimity. De Gaulle, like his man of character, was a man of unswerving attachment to his principles. He believed that he had a mission: to remind a great European people of the continuing possibilities for national "greatness." He appreciated the necessarily Sisyphean character of such a mission in democratic societies dominated by commercial pursuits, the cult of individual pleasure, sundry ideological temptations, and the ethos of egalitarian mediocrity.[104]

It is sometimes necessary to employ the methods of "moderate Machiavellianism," such as intrigue, dissimulation, and secrecy, in pursuit of the seemingly inaccessible heights. But de Gaulle told Claude Mauriac in 1947 that the one unacceptable thing was to indulge in "politics" in the unprincipled sense classically analyzed by Péguy in *Notre jeunesse*.[105] The statesman must remain faithful to his core convictions both out of duty and wisdom "for the artful ones always end by being in the wrong."[106] The political artistry delineated and practiced by de Gaulle did not leave room for Machiavellian flexibility toward political principle itself or anything remotely resembling ordinary, merely self-promoting and self-interested political calculation. Above all, the statesman must recognize the ontological structure, characterized by fundamental natural limits as well as a margin of human liberty, within which political choice occurs. De Gaulle categorically rejected the big or ontological lie. He told Mauriac that the

communists could never ultimately succeed because "they lied systemati-
cally and that nothing durable had ever been seen based on lies."[107] As *The
Discord among the Enemy* makes clear, de Gaulle believed that the human
world is marked by broad, somewhat obscure, but naturally grounded
"Principles." The statesman must never forget this primordial ontological
fact if he wishes, in Péguy's words, to "produce works and men, nations and
races,"[108] if he truly wishes to leave his mark on events.

CONCLUSION

In the next chapter we must turn back to the founding moment of the
Gaullist enterprise in 1940. It is then that de Gaulle comes to sight as the
"good Prince" articulated in *The Edge of the Sword.*

As we will see, de Gaulle did not insist on the "legality" of his political
action in June of 1940 so much as its "legitimacy." Of course, the extralegal
but nontyrannical character of de Gaulle's political action is foreshadowed
by his portrait of the man of character. It is a conception of statesmanship
and political legitimacy which is unfamiliar to a positivistic, rationalistic,
and democratic social science. Such a science resorts to the familiar images
of the dictator or charismatic leader, hence the famous accusations of
Bonapartism, Nietzscheanism, or more generously, of anachronistic romanticism and the continuing difficulty of some otherwise very reasonable and
decent men to make sense of the Gaullist phenomenon.

Chapter 4

De Gaulle's "Mission" and the Legitimacy of Free France

Twenty-five years ago, when France was rolling toward the abyss, I believed it was my duty to assume the burden of governing until France was liberated, victorious and mistress of herself.

Seven years ago I believed it was my duty to return to her head in order to save her from civil war, to spare her from financial and monetary bankruptcy and to build with her institutions meeting the requirements of the times and the modern world.

> Address by Charles de Gaulle declaring his candidacy
> in the presidential election,
> November 4, 1965

In France, de Gaulle is often called the "man of June 18"—this, despite the fact that historians, ever anxious to dispel mythological readings of history, wish to minimize the epic importance of that date and the events associated with it. We are told *ad nauseum* that comparatively few heard de Gaulle's "Appeal," that de Gaulle did not even declare himself leader of the Free French movement on that occasion, and that the highlighting of that event owes more to retrospective Gaullist mythmaking and hagiography than to its objective importance in the scale of events at the time. But all these qualifications are beside the point. Undoubtedly, de Gaulle's appeal to resistance only successively and retrospectively took on the importance that it holds today in the narrative of French and world history. However, the elevation of this date owes less to the propaganda of some real or imagined Gaullist cult than to the fruits of de Gaulle's singular and initially largely unnoticed act: June 18 decidedly had weighty world-historical consequences. The "Appeal" of June 18, 1940 was the sine qua non of the Gaullist enterprise and of the moral recovery and political reconstitution of France. At the age of forty-nine, de Gaulle sharply broke with the established authorities and in effect declared that the French state had ceased to exist. The claimants to its fatally compromised authority no longer could demand his or any other patriot's services. From his near solitary acceptance of this fact, he drew the necessary conclusions. France was facing an abyss that could only be overcome by a "liberating act of moral will," one that realistically and fearlessly accepted all the facts about France's unprecedented situation. Someone must "assume" France, somebody must safeguard her sovereignty until the state could fully function in the normal circumstances that would follow France's participation in the anticipated victory in the world war.

Contrary to a certain legend, de Gaulle never insisted on the "legality" of his act or of the Gaullist enterprise that flowed from it. Rather, he asserted its "legitimacy" since his course of action—refusing to accept the moral and political legitimacy of the armistice and defending the liberty, honor, and independence of France within the order of nations—was the only one that lived up to the historical "mission" as well as the long-established "status" of France.

De Gaulle cultivated a unique theological-political language to explain his "mission" as savior-leader of France. He claimed that he embodied the "national legitimacy" since June 18, 1940 and that he continued to embody it even while not holding electoral office, even during his years in the political desert from January 1946 until June 1958 when the Fourth Republic embodied the sovereignty of France and represented it diplomatically before the world. This claim disturbed even basically sympathetic critics who feared that it entailed an excessively mystical (and partisan) conception of national and political life, reflected an unhealthy cult of personality, and showed a dangerous contempt for ordinary political processes (as well as the sovereignty and judgment of the French people). These reservations were expressed by liberals such as Raymond Aron (in a characteristically restrained and measured way) and Jean-François Revel (in a fiercely polemical manner) and in private by an otherwise devoted Gaullist, Olivier Wormser.[1] Without ignoring the dangers of an excessively "mystical" account of political life and legitimacy, especially in our "desacralized" liberal regimes, and without denying the more unsavory and "authoritarian" dimensions of the Gaullist cult of personality promoted by Gaullist partisans such as Malraux, it is nonetheless imperative to understand de Gaulle's claims to legitimacy *as he himself understood it*. It is impossible to deny that de Gaulle aimed to embody both a *mystique* and a *politique* of national resistance. However, his claimed embodiment of the national legitimacy was, in his own self-understanding, an act of moral will grounded in a realistic evaluation of the situation of and prospects for an independent France. De Gaulle's language about his "mission" and his "assumption" of the burden of France is quintessentially mystical but his enterprise itself is based on a level-headed and objective evaluation of the world crisis and France's situation and opportunities within it.

In his *C'était de Gaulle*, Alain Peyrefitte records a private conversation he had with de Gaulle on May 23, 1963 in the Elysée which perfectly encapsulates the moral and political understanding that animated the Gaullist enterprise and pervades de Gaulle's account of his action in the *Mémoires de Guerre*.[2] Peyrefitte asked de Gaulle what he understood by legitimacy and the difference between it and legality. De Gaulle, in his response, begins by differentiating normal from extraordinary times. In normal times "institutions and customs assure order." But de Gaulle insists that "real order" has certain essential moral and political preconditions: it must rest on "national independence, public liberties, the good functioning of justice, popular sovereignty." For de Gaulle, order normally presupposes the existence of a sovereign state that goes beyond maintaining order in the narrow sense of the term; authority in a more capacious sense must assure the functioning of justice and be broadly accountable to the populace. It must be embedded in a nontyrannical and independent state. De Gaulle contrasts this with other periods where order apparently continues to reign but where it "loses its sense" because beneath the surface real order is "exhausted." De Gaulle maintains that this is what happened with the armistice. It preserved an illusory order, one that sacrificed public liberties, the proper functioning of justice, and above all "the sovereignty of France" (the last-named process having begun with the Third Republic and its "regime of parties" which had allowed France's sovereignty to slip away). In his response to Peyrefitte, de Gaulle again asserts his Péguyan inspiration: "As Péguy said, 'Order and only order definitively makes liberty: disorder makes servitude. The order of liberty alone is legitimate.' "

In a Péguyist spirit, de Gaulle rejects the tenability of either a theoretical or practical compromise between ordered liberty and even limited despotism and between national sovereignty and a partial surrender of sovereignty to an imperialist and totalitarian enemy. He rejects the moral and practical validity of what Père Gaston Fessard insightfully called the regime of the "slave-Prince."[3] This regime is an incoherent compromise waiting to self-destruct, corrupting its adherents by blinding them to the dissolution of legitimate order and erosion of sovereignty that this compromise necessarily entails. In normal times, order is reflected in laws, institutions, and rules. But in extreme circumstances, when the legitimate state is absent, the deepest sources of order are temporarily separated from formal or legal order. In June 1940, de Gaulle was a revolutionary in the fundamental sense that he rejected the positivistic and traditionalist identifications of order with the established order, with whatever "order" that is. In a time of profound crisis, it is necessary to "relativize" our sense of order in order to avoid becoming "slaves." One must always place "the spirit before the letter."[4] For de Gaulle, it is the Vichy regime, rather than Free France, which rests on a fictive pseudoreality, and is an example of pompous and self-deluding posturing. It allowed the French to think that ordered liberty could somehow survive even in a regime whose founding act was a camouflaged surrender to and the institutionalization of collaboration with Hitler and National Socialism. De Gaulle rebelled in June 1940 in the name of reality—in the name of moral and political *clarity* about the nature of the disaster which confronted the French and the consequences of surrender for French dignity and morale.

In the *Mémoires de Guerre*, de Gaulle clearly and eloquently presents his self-understanding and the moral and political foundations of "Free France." We must follow his self-presentation with care if we are to comprehend the moral motives and political understanding that provide the Gaullist enterprise with its point of departure and its animating sense of purpose.

Near the conclusion of the long opening chapter, "The Slope," of Volume 1 of the *Mémoires de Guerre*, *L'Appel*, de Gaulle reflects on the political options still available to France at the end of May 1940. For all intents and purposes, the Battle of France had been lost. De Gaulle makes clear that at this point he "had no illusions." But, he adds, he "was determined not to abandon hope."[5] These words summarize that judicious mixture of realistic judgment and anxious but clear-minded hope for the future which characterized de Gaulle's political stance as the Battle of France came to a precipitous close. For de Gaulle, everything centered on maintaining the moral integrity and genuine independence of the state. Were statesmen available, men of insight and courage, patriotism, and the art of command, who could grasp the possibilities present even in France's forlorn position? It was de Gaulle's belief that France was not without options or sources of strength. De Gaulle presents his case for continuing the war from the Empire, establishing the French government and armed forces on a new basis in North Africa. Such a move would be based on a wholly reasonable recognition of the global character of the Second World War and the reversible character of the results of the Battle of France. De Gaulle writes:

If the situation could not, after all, be restored in the homeland, it must be re-established elsewhere. The Empire was there, offering its refuge. The fleet was there, to protect it. The people were there, doomed in any case to suffer invasion, but capable of being roused by the republic to resistance, that terrible occasion for unity. The world was there, able to give us fresh weapons, and later, powerful aid.[6]

But he recognized that it was essential that the state preserve its independence and thereby safeguard the future. It was necessary, above all, to avoid surrender "in the panic of collapse."

De Gaulle realized that much would depend on the attitude and determination of the High Command. In principle, it was capable of pursuing the honorable course, of exhausting all means of resistance, in a word, of adopting what de Gaulle called "the African solution" of continued resistance from the base of the Empire. In this case, it "could become the rescue buoy for the shipwrecked state."[7] If, on the contrary, it were to urge a weak, unsure, and vacillating state to surrender, it would contribute powerfully to "the degradation of France."[8]

De Gaulle writes that it was his meeting on June 1, 1940 with General Maxime Weygand, the commander-in-chief of the armed forces, which confirmed to him the defeatist attitude of and the inevitability of a choice for surrender by the High Command.[9] De Gaulle reflects at length on the revealing case of Weygand. He embodied the strengths and weaknesses of the regime. He had served Foch admirably and ably in World War I. He had devised the strategic plan by which Józef Pilsudski saved Poland from Bolshevism in 1920. He was a competent chief of the General Staff who "intelligently and courageously represented"[10] the vital interests of the army before the political authorities in the 1930s. What he decidedly was not, de Gaulle suggests, without explicitly using the phrase, was a man of character capable of initiating action, facing risks, and taking personal responsibility for people and events. He was a man who had all the virtues attendant to staff service but who lacked the moral qualities necessary for genuine and effective command. He was the wrong man to command the armies of France at the moment of her supreme crisis. He could only operate within a routinized or bureaucratized governmental and military structure to which he was habituated: "To take action on one's own responsibility, to want no mark upon it but one's own, to face destiny alone—the harsh, exclusive passion characteristic for a chief—for these Weygand had neither the inclination nor the preparation."[11] France needed the services of an authentic statesman, a man of character who would renew the state and actualize her continued possibilities for independence and action as the most severe crisis in her history tragically unfolded. But Weygand was not the man to do it.[12] He lacked strategic judgment, and he had woefully misjudged the revolutionary potential of mechanized forces in modern warfare. He then was immobilized in the face of the disastrous consequences of his comprehensive misjudgment. By age, turn of mind, and temperament, he lacked those dynamic qualities of energy, risk, and command necessary to rescue the state and to pursue global and ideological warfare. Weygand was carried along by, and contributed to, the currents of defeat.

Unlike de Gaulle's man of character, Weygand would not even attempt to "master" the abyss facing France. In the final weeks of the Battle of France, he fought for the only solution to which he was intellectually and temperamentally attuned: surrender. He found his "natural ally" in Marshall Pétain.[13] But the ultimate failure was systemic and political. A strong state and effective civilian leadership would never have maintained a weak and uninspired leader such as General Weygand in the post of commander-in-chief. It would have found a true commander, someone emboldened with the spirit of resistance and willing to take radical risks in recognition of the unprecedented situation facing France and the world. But the French state, the institutions of the Third Republic, had "neither—faith nor vitality." In the end, the regime "decided in favor of the worst surrender."[14] De Gaulle writes: "The price, for France, was thus to be not only a disastrous military armistice, but the enslavement of the state. So it is true that, face to face with the great perils, the only salvation lies in greatness."[15]

Chapter 2 of *L'Appel*, "The Fall," makes abundantly clear the absence of true statesmanship within what remained of the French state.[16] There was no one in a position of significant authority who was willing or able to act according to the requirements of greatness. The advocates of capitulation both abandoned honor and self-respect and misjudged the radically unprecedented character of the crisis afflicting France and the world. A decrepit Pétain chose ambition divorced from honor.[17] He accepted defeat because he saw the Battle of France as one more unpleasant episode in the game of nations and in the sempiternal rivalry between France and Germany. He had witnessed French defeat in 1870, helped win victory over Germany during the Great War from 1914 to 1918, and had now witnessed another unfortunate German victory. For him, the recent defeat was "cruel but normal."[18] Despite de Gaulle's own rhetorical tendency to minimize the importance of ideology in the life of nations, here he attributes Pétain's willingness to accept the leadership of France at the moment of national surrender to his fundamental inability to recognize the global and ideological character of the stakes involved in the conflict, as well as to "the shipwreck" of "old age." Pétain maintained only the outer shell of greatness, one worn by time, by embittered passions, and by sometimes misplaced ambitions. But at the *intellectual* center of Pétain's failing was a profound failure to recognize the nature of totalitarianism and hence the "ideological consequences of Hitler's victory."[19] One might generalize from de Gaulle's account of Pétain to the regime of Vichy more broadly: the Vichy episode was initially the result of the coming together of moral decrepitude and intellectual obtuseness. After November of 1942, with the German occupation of "unoccupied France" and the radicalization of Pétain's "National Revolution," Vichy becomes less an escape from ideological conflict than a symptom and an example of the ideological character of politics in the age of totalitarianism. Reality has a way of insinuating itself on those who try to evade it, leaving them with fewer and more difficult options than they might otherwise have had.

There are two favorable, or at least sympathetic, portraits of political leadership in "The Fall." One is of Premier Paul Reynaud, sometimes called the French Churchill for his astute and longtime recognition of the danger from National Socialist Germany. The other is of Churchill himself. The contrast with Churchill reveals the limits of Reynaud's stature. Reynaud was clearly a decent man, an unflinching patriot, a man of good intentions and eminent good sense, but he lacked the fortitude and courage of a true statesman or of a man of character. By the middle of June 1940, he had "reached the limits of hope."[20] He had long recognized the proper strategy and military policy for averting France's misfortunes and had been the public voice in Parliament and government for de Gaulle's ideas for military reform. But for all his courage and insight, Reynaud remained essentially a man of the established order. He could not master events outside the framework of a functioning state and normal circumstances. In a moving passage that reflects both de Gaulle's genuine feeling for Reynaud and his real appreciation for his limits, de Gaulle writes:

At bottom, the personality of M. Paul Reynaud was the right one for conditions where it would have been possible to conduct the war within a state in running order and on the basis of traditionally established data. But everything was swept away! The head of the government saw the system collapsing all around him, the people in flight, the Allies withdrawing, and the most illustrious leaders failing. From the day when the government left the capital, the very business of exercising power became merely a sort of agony, unrolling along the roads amid the dislocation of services, disciplines, and consciences. In such conditions M. Paul Reynaud's intelligence, his courage, and the authority of his office were, so to speak, running free. He had no longer any purchase upon the fury of events.[21]

Reynaud was not fit by nature or temperament to wrestle with "the fury of events." In principle, he recognized the necessity of the "African solution," but he was not willing to take those "extreme measures" (i.e., "changing the High Command, getting rid of the Marshall and half the Ministers, breaking with certain influences, resigning himself to the total occupation of France"[22]) that such a choice would have entailed. In de Gaulle's view, Reynaud, in his moment of weakness, was willing to investigate the terms of an armistice (although only with England's permission) mainly because he was not fully able or willing to do what was necessary to pursue the full and energetic continuation of war. He was too honorable to adopt the defeatist path of Pétain and Weygand, but he lacked the self-sufficiency and character to break with the past and to pursue a Gaullist option. He was one of a handful of politicians of the Third Republic who knew the nature of the enemy and genuinely appreciated what surrender would entail for France. But he lacked the courage to act consistently on his insights. De Gaulle speaks in a magnanimous, affectionate manner about the tragic dilemma facing this good man incapable of assuming the burden of France in her hour of need. De Gaulle's portrait is a concrete illustration of the incompleteness, even the ultimate powerlessness, of principled and intelligent leadership unsupported by the instinct and virtue of character. Reynaud, who might have saved France in 1936, was no Churchill (or de Gaulle) in 1940.

The only portrait of undisputed human and political greatness in the two opening chapters of *L'Appel* is de Gaulle's famous account of his first impressions on meeting Winston Churchill at Downing Street on June 9, 1940.[23] Churchill had the benefit of the support of an ancient and solidly established state, as well as a relatively unified people, supports that neither Reynaud nor, later, de Gaulle could rely on. But while they were powerful supports, they were not the sources of Churchill's own greatness of soul. He was a man of great culture and historical judgment who could grasp synoptically all the dimensions involved in global crisis and war. He was a "born protector," confident in his abilities and solicitous of his people. Like de Gaulle, he was a "man of character." De Gaulle writes in an elegant passage of lofty majesty:

Mr. Churchill received me at Downing Street. It was my first contact with him. The impression he gave me confirmed me in my conviction that Great Britain, led by such a fighter, would certainly not flinch. Mr. Churchill seemed to me to be equal to the rudest task, provided it had also grandeur. The assurance of his judgment, his great culture, the knowledge he had of most of the subjects, countries, and men involved, and finally his passion for the problems proper to war, found in war their full scope. On top of everything, he was fitted by his character to act, take risks, play the part out-and-out and without scruple. In short, I found him well in the saddle as guide and chief. Such were my first impressions.[24]

De Gaulle continues by praising Churchill's eloquence, which played such an indispensable role in clarifying the meaning of the world conflict and in elevating the spirits of the Allied peoples and forces. Churchill's rhetoric was an ennobling means of mastering events by channeling hope and connecting millions of human beings to the moral meaning of the unfolding drama. De Gaulle notes with admiration and respect:

Whatever his audience—crowd, assembly, council, even a single interlocutor— whether he was before a microphone, on the floor of the House, at table, or behind a desk, the original, poetic, stirring flow of his ideas, arguments, and feelings brought him an almost infallible ascendancy in the tragic atmosphere in which the poor world was gasping. Well tried in politics, he played upon that angelic and diabolical gift to rouse the heavy dough of the English as well as to impress the minds of foreigners. The humor, too, with which he seasoned his acts and words, and the way in which he made use now of graciousness, now of anger, contributed to make one feel what a mastery he had of the terrible game in which he was engaged.[25]

Writing in the mid-1950s, and with wartime grievances still fresh in mind, de Gaulle does not hesitate to write of the

harsh and painful incidents that often arose between us, because of the friction of our two characters, of the opposition of some of the interests of our two countries and of the unfair advantage taken by England of wounded France, which have influenced my attitude towards the Prime Minister, but not my judgment.[26]

Later in Volume III of the *War Memoirs*, when reflecting on Churchill's defeat at the polls in the election of July 1945, de Gaulle pays eloquent tribute to this statesman who "had always been convinced that France was necessary to the free world; and this exceptional artist (who) was certainly conscious of the dramatic character of my mission."[27] But he adds, somewhat unfairly, that Churchill "had quite naturally felt something of Pitt's spirit in his own soul."[28]

We shall return to the subject of the vexed relations between de Gaulle and Churchill, operating within broad contours marked by an overarching mutual admiration and support but marred by mutual suspicions and intense and ongoing frustrations. For now it is important to note what Stanley Hoffmann has observed: de Gaulle's opening portrait of Churchill also serves as a self-portrait.[29] Churchill is another man of character, another instance of political greatness or magnanimity. It is a tribute that de Gaulle pays to another shepherd or born protector, to a member of the tribe of the lion and the eagle. The final sentence of de Gaulle's introductory portrait of Churchill conveys de Gaulle's sense of the artistry of the man of character, an artistry shared by himself as well as Churchill. "Winston Churchill appeared to me, from one end of the drama to the other, as the great champion of a great enterprise and the great artist of a great history."[30]

Unfortunately, nothing resembling the indomitable Churchillian spirit was evident among the established leadership of the Third Republic. De Gaulle notes that there were many, even some at the upper echelons of the state, who looked with "horror" at the capitulation of France.[31] But no one seemed capable of *acting* to avoid or to respond to this capitulation. The president of the Republic, who personally opposed the armistice, did not even raise his voice within the Cabinet "to express the supreme interest of the country!"[32] (We should add that this had as much to do with the constitutional position of the presidency under the Third Republic as with the lack of initiative or judgment of the president.) This inability of the state to act decisively in defense of France's permanent interests and principles revealed the thoroughgoing corruption of the Third Republic. In a damning appraisal, de Gaulle writes at the end of "The Fall":

In reality this annihilation of the state was at the bottom of the national tragedy. By the light of the thunderbolt the regime was revealed, in its ghastly infirmity, as having no proportion and no relation to the defense, honor, and independence of France.[33]

This quotation helps us understand why the constitutional re-founding of France—the attaining of its "salvation" as well as its unity and victory—were constituent elements of the Gaullist enterprise from its inception.

The practical question facing de Gaulle and other responsible Frenchmen was what to do once the official or legal state had surrendered its very *raison d'être* and the enemy seemed at least temporarily to control France's destiny. At the beginning of Chapter 3 of *L'Appel*, "Free France," de Gaulle announces there was never any doubt in his mind about continuing the war.[34] This is what personal and national honor demanded. But he insists that this meant that in the continuing struggle Frenchmen could not fight simply as auxiliaries of the British empire. For de Gaulle, "what had to be served and saved was the nation and the state."[35]

What is so striking for a reader of de Gaulle's *War Memoirs* is the simultaneously instinctive and deeply reflective character of de Gaulle's decision to continue the struggle. Certainly, honor demanded France's continued efforts on the side of the Allies. But honor was not a merely emotional or romantic or traditional response to the nation's tragedy. An honorable course of resistance was nothing less than a requirement of reason and the sine qua non of the independence and self-respect of the nation. De Gaulle's decision to continue the war was heroic, but it was never merely romantic or quixotic in inspiration or character. Honor was paradoxically an end in itself and the most sober requirement of *raison d'État*.

What made de Gaulle's decision to continue the fight truly radical, susceptible to misunderstanding, and a source of future conflict with Great Britain and the United States was his insistence that not only specific Frenchmen but also France herself as a *sovereign political entity* must be brought back into the war. For de Gaulle this was the essential condition on which the "honor, unity and independence" of France would ultimately rest. If capitulation and armistice were the final word, even granting the possibility or likelihood of her eventual liberation by foreign arms, France's status and self-respect would be permanently undermined with tragic repercussions for the future. "Its self-disgust and the disgust it would inspire in others would poison its soul and its life for many generations."[36]

The way out of this potential tragedy could only lie with resurrecting a Free and Fighting France. As de Gaulle insisted, anticipating Free France's substantial if decidedly secondary contribution to the Allied war effort, "there is no France without a sword."[37] Some Frenchmen, such as Jean Monnet, offered their services to the British and the Allies, but opposed the creation of an official body to speak for France because they believed that it might appear to be under the sponsorship and control of the British.[38] Many preferred direct service to the Allied cause under the command of the British and American governments. They were content to be auxiliaries within the broader Allied and democratic cause. For de Gaulle, the decisive issue on which the future self-respect and independence of the nation rested was the maintenance or, more precisely, the revival of France's sovereignty, particularly as evidenced in a fighting force that would announce to the entire world that France had not been completely defeated by the enemy. The restoration of France

was bound to involve the reappearance of our armies on the battlefields, the return of our territories to belligerence, participation by the country itself in the effort of its fighting men, and recognition by the foreign powers of the fact that France, as such, had gone on with the struggle—in short, to bring our sovereignty out from disaster and from the policy of wait-and-see, over to the side of war and, one day, of victory.[39]

It was his principled and visceral opposition to the abandonment or compromise of sovereignty that was the source of de Gaulle's absolute rejection of the acceptability of an armistice with the Nazi regime. De Gaulle asserts in the third volume of his *War Memoirs* that the armistice was the "capital error of Pétain and his government."[40] He regretted that this capitulation to the enemy was not among those crimes with which Pétain had been charged by the High Court during his trial in July and August of 1945. For de Gaulle, some kind of "local" or field arrangements to bring the fighting to an end in metropolitan France were wholly appropriate.[41] These arrangements were necessary to protect civilians and to avoid unnecessary death and destruction. But, as we have seen, it was incumbent on the government to continue to uphold and manifest the *independence* and *sovereignty* of France from the base of the Empire. The abandonment, through its mutilation, of the sovereignty of France was the "poisoned spring" from which all the crimes, including service to the ideological and wartime designs of National Socialism, flowed. In a capital passage from *Salvation*, de Gaulle contrasts what ought to have been done with the poisonous path followed by the Vichy regime:

[The] government might have reached Algiers, taking with it the treasure of French sovereignty which for fourteen centuries had never been surrendered, continuing the battle, keeping its word to the Allies, and demanding their aid in return. But to have retired from the war with the Empire intact, the fleet untouched, the air force largely undamaged; to have withdrawn our African and Levantine troops without a single soldier lost; to have abandoned all those forces which, in France herself, could be transported elsewhere; to have broken our alliances; above all, to have submitted the state to the Reich's discretion—this is what had to be condemned in order to clear France of the stigma. All the faults Vichy had been led to commit subsequently . . . flowed inevitably from this poisoned spring.[42]

Pierre Manent has highlighted a most important feature of de Gaulle's political reflection.[43] De Gaulle's emphasis on the "treasure of French sovereignty which for fourteen centuries had never been surrendered" is a reminder and reaffirmation of the substantiality of the French nation, a spiritual, political, and cultural substantiality that makes it impossible for a great nation to be immediately and irrevocably defeated. Her sovereignty persists even if her previous, established means of action are temporarily limited or even eviscerated. The patriot, conscious of the nation's substantiality and greatness, must will her independence, and through this act of fidelity help to revivify and actualize her body and soul. De Gaulle knew that France, like all great nations, existed in a "whole," a "frame of space and time" that was infinitely broader than the limited period of the Battle of France or even of the "Thirty Years' War" beginning in 1914. Manent eloquently expresses the connection between the affirmation or recognition of the broader framework of space and time within which national sovereignty operates and the moral nobility of political life:

If the nation, the body politic, has lasted for fourteen centuries, and if the natural and noble desire is to see it last indefinitely, you could not properly consent to a defeat that means the forced obliteration of its independent life.

There is an auspicious disproportion between a great body politic and any defeat, however stunning: a disproportion of substance, a disproportion of weight. A tiny body politic—for instance, a small tribe—can be quite shaken out of legitimate existence by a stunning military defeat; not so a great body politic.[44]

De Gaulle, as we have emphasized repeatedly, was committed unwaveringly to the affirmation of the sovereign independence of France and to a course of action that would lead to France's participation in the victory over Nazi Germany. This commitment has led to sundry changes of romanticism, quixoticism, and sheer deluded, even megalomaniacal, posturing. But de Gaulle claims that from the beginning of his "mission" in June 1940 he had "no illusions about the obstacles to be surmounted."[45] De Gaulle realistically assessed the obstacles in the way of effective French resistance and of his own leadership. He knew, of course, that Free France would face the belligerent opposition of the enemy as well as the authorities in France who were committed to cooperation with them. He recognized the

moral and material difficulties which a long and all-out struggle would inevitably involve for those who would have to carry it on as pariahs and without means.

There would be the mountain of objections, insinuations, and calumnies raised against the fighters by the skeptics and the timorous to cover their passivity.[46]

But he also clearly appreciated the paradoxical liberation that this same pariah status would bring the Free French. Its adherents would serve, as he says in the Speech at Bayeux, as a kind of moral elite and noble conspiracy working for the resurrection of France. There would be something both ennobling and even exhilarating about their defiant struggle for the "rehabilitation of France."[47]

De Gaulle also was aware of the dangers that would flow from political and ideological divisions within the camp of resistance, a division that the Allies would try to exacerbate for their own aims and interests. (It is impossible to know with certainty if de Gaulle truly anticipated, as early as June 1940, something like the Allied and American efforts to foist General Henri Giraud onto the political and military leadership of "liberated" North Africa and the non-Vichy areas of the Empire.) The last two obstacles foreseen by de Gaulle were the obstruction by the communists with their "determination to side-track the national resistance in the direction of revolutionary chaos, to result in their dictatorship" and the Allies with their "tendency . . . to take advantage of our weakness in order to push their interests at the expense of France."[48]

De Gaulle clearly saw himself as the only available and morally reputable alternative to the future prospect of communist dictatorship in France. He appreciated the bankruptcy of the established order, fatally wounded by its complicity in the armistice and the transfer of power to Pétain. He knew that the Vichy regime would powerfully discredit the traditionalist as well as the fascist Right in France. He feared the communists' capacity to manipulate the resistance, despite their own slavish and disreputable adherence to the Hitler-Stalin Pact. The only "right" or nonrevolutionary, broadly liberal alternative that could claim full moral-political credit in a liberated France would be one that firmly rejected right-wing totalitarianism and authoritarianism in theory and practice (whether it be National Socialist ideology or Pétain's National Revolution) and that unequivocally resisted the armies of the Reich. In this judgment, de Gaulle was undoubtedly right. Moreover, Franklin Roosevelt's inclination to consider France finished as a serious European and global actor as a result of the weakness the French state showed in June 1940 could play into the hands of communist totalitarianism.

In a remarkably candid and intelligent "dialogue" between Harry Hopkins and de Gaulle in Paris on January 27, 1945, held on the eve of the

Yalta Conference, Hopkins told de Gaulle that it was the "stupefying disappointment" Americans suffered in watching the disaster of 1940 which overthrew America's "traditional conception of (France's) value and her energy." America could no longer "trust (France) to play one of the leading roles."[49] But the paradoxical course pursued by the United States as a result was at worst one of indulgence of, if not appeasement toward, the Vichy government, or at best the display of a broader and deeper sympathy for the Vichy regime than for de Gaulle and Free France. What the diplomatic Hopkins could not admit to de Gaulle on that occasion was the ultimate source of the friction between Free France and the United States, a source de Gaulle well recognized. Roosevelt had arrived at the firmest judgment that de Gaulle was at best a "prima donna" and an "egoist" and at worse a megalomaniacal posturer and aspiring despot.[50] This misguided judgment, more than Gaullist inflexibility or uncooperativeness, led to the darkest moments in U.S.-French relations: the American deal with the Vichyite Darlan in November of 1942 at the beginning of Operation Torch and the liberation of North Africa, the misguided efforts to impose the wholly unprepared and apolitical General Giraud on the French leadership in the first months of 1943, the rather pathetic and wholly unrealistic plans to place liberated France under American military government, and the final inexplicable delay of official American recognition of de Gaulle's provincial government until October 23, 1944, months after the liberation of Paris itself and the full functioning of a French state and administration.[51]

De Gaulle made one supremely reasoned and accommodating effort to explain himself and Free France to Roosevelt. In a remarkable letter dated October 26, 1942, only days before the establishment of the Eisenhower–Darlan agreement, de Gaulle explained the necessity for France to be a full partner in the Allied cause if disaster, including communist dictatorship, was to be avoided.[52] He reminded Roosevelt that France's defeat did not occur in a political vacuum. The United States and the other democracies owed much to France's supreme sacrifices as the main Allied force during World War I. Later, the democracies, including the United States, did not give France the support she counted on in dealing with the dangers of resurgent German power and imperialism. All the Allies had made radical mistakes, had pursued vacillating positions, and had shown inconsistent moral purpose in the face of totalitarian aggression. They had been and were in this effort together for the duration of the war. In other words, the larger context of the conflict (the "Thirty Years' War" beginning in 1914) and broader criteria of blame and praise must be taken into account if the

Allies were to see and act with necessary clarity and full moral integrity in their current, common situation. De Gaulle, without polemics, then reminds Roosevelt of exactly what is at stake in both the failure to see France's laceration in perspective and in the continuing American ambivalence, if not overt hostility, toward Free France:

France, then, feels deeply the humiliation inflicted on her and the injustice of the fate she has suffered. This is why France must again take up her place in the conflict, and while waiting, not be given the impression that she is entirely abandoned. She must feel that she is one of the countries whose effort has contributed to victory. This is important to the war and essential for the future.
  If France, liberated by the victory of the democracies, felt herself to be a conquered nation, it is to be feared that her bitterness, her humiliation and her divided loyalties, far from turning her towards the democracies, might lay her open to other influences. You know what these are. This is not an imaginary danger, for the social structure of the country is going to find itself more or less shattered by privations and spoliation. . . . In any case, whatever line France, thrown into a revolutionary situation, takes up, the reconstruction of Europe and even the re-organization of the peace of the world will find itself strained. Victory then must reconcile France to herself, as well as to her friends; and this will be impossible unless she participates actively in this victory.[53]

Roosevelt never responded to de Gaulle's letter.
  Let us return to the question of the motives or moral content that lay at the foundation of de Gaulle's decision for resistance. De Gaulle appreciated the apparent desperation and destitution of his own position. He recognized that he was starting from literally nothing with no established organization, force, following, or reputation behind him. But his "very destitution" showed him his "line of conduct."[54] The following passage from the chapter "Free France" explains de Gaulle's deliberately adopted "strategy" for the acquisition of political authority and the consent of the French through recovery of France's independence and pride:

It was by adopting without compromise the cause of national recovery that I could acquire authority. It was by acting as the inflexible champion of the nation and of the state that it would be possible for me to gather the consent, even the enthusiasm, of the French and to win from foreigners respect and consideration.[55]

We must stress the rational character of de Gaulle's acceptance of the need to be inflexible, of his considered refusal to "compromise" any of the reality or even the symbols of the independence or status of France throughout the war years. A recent biographer notes that de Gaulle's intransigence in defending France's right to determine the fate of her Empire and his heated opposition to British involvement in the Levant or to American political dictates may have been intensified by exaggerated suspiciousness. It is suggested that his ornery manner and his sometimes unfounded suspicions of Allied policies and intentions may even have been exacerbated by illness (malaria contracted in Africa) and fatigue.[56] It is difficult to know how much weight to give to these speculations. But we do know this: first and foremost Gaullist intransigence was *chosen* as an indispensable requirement of national moral and political recovery.

De Gaulle knew that he could not afford to depend finally on any foreign power for the defense of France's interests. This was true even of Britain and the great Churchill who, unlike Roosevelt and the Americans, "had always been convinced that France was necessary to the free world."[57] But de Gaulle judged that Britain naturally placed its own interests and, perhaps less naturally, the integrity of its alliance with the United States above its concern for the status of France. Free France, in fact, became a somewhat unpleasant obstacle in the path of unstrained Anglo-American relations. At various times, Churchill threatened more or less seriously to abandon de Gaulle and find other, more palatable, less prickly leadership for the French.[58] (Anthony Eden, in particular, wisely resisted this temptation.) It is fair to say that Churchill preferred a French option somewhere in-between a mere auxiliary of the British and the proud and capacious Gaullist affirmation of France.

Whatever the ultimate mixture of elements in de Gaulle's intransigence, it cannot be said that de Gaulle lacked self-knowledge or essentially mistook the judgments made about him by the main actors in the drama. In his manner and policy, he combined the asperity and roughness of the man of character with a principled "egoism" on behalf of France. De Gaulle openly recognized his inflexible manner but placed it in a properly political context:

Those who, all through the drama, were offended by this intransigence were unwilling to see that for me, intent as I was on beating back innumerable conflicting pressures, the slightest wavering would have brought collapse. In short, limited and alone though I was, and precisely because I was so, I had to climb to the heights and never then to come down.[59]

In a letter to Congressman Joseph Clark Baldwin, written eight days after de Gaulle's meeting with Roosevelt in Washington in July of 1945, a meeting intended to help reconcile the two camps, Roosevelt characteristically belittled de Gaulle. (He had done so already at the time of their first meeting at the Anfa conference in Morocco in January of 1943. In Washington, after the conference, Roosevelt transformed de Gaulle's perfectly reasonable references to Joan of Arc and Clemenceau as symbols of national resistance into indisputable evidence of his vanity and dictatorial ambitions.[60]) In his letter to Baldwin, Roosevelt noted that while de Gaulle is "very touchy in matters concerning the honor of France," he "suspect[ed] that he is essentially an egoist."[61] In his comments on the episode, de Gaulle suggests that Roosevelt failed to differentiate national egotism from personal self-seeking.[62] This failure of generosity and judgment explains why Roosevelt could not appreciate the chasm of political and moral motivation which separated the ambition of a statesman like de Gaulle from a mere usurper or tyrant *manqué*. In fact, for de Gaulle, dictatorship was destructive of the traditions and the "genius" of the French which demanded respect for the fundamental human liberties and the ongoing consent of the governed. Without respect for these moral foundations, the French would be decidedly and hopelessly ungovernable.

Let us turn now to a fuller discussion of de Gaulle's famous Appeal. As historians note, it was only later in June 1940 that de Gaulle formalized his position as leader of Free and Fighting France. For several days after the Appeal, he waited for other French officials, those with greater rank, reputation, and official sources of authority, perhaps the so-called Proconsuls in the various regions of the Empire, to come forward to lead the cause of resistance and liberation.[63] Yet, "no responsible man anywhere acted as if he still believed in her independence, pride, and greatness."[64] De Gaulle observed from the beginning of the debacle an "immense convergence of fear, interest, and despair which caused a universal surrender in regard to France."[65]

In one of the most important passages of his *War Memoirs*, one often interpreted to suggest de Gaulle's egotism and mysticism, de Gaulle announces in quasi-theological language the "mission" that was left to him because of the abdication and cowardice of others and because of his character and his capacity for command: "In face of the frightening voice of the general renunciation, my mission seemed to me, all of a sudden, clear and terrible. At this moment, the worst in her history, it was for me to assume the burden of France."[66]

De Gaulle's "mission" is first given voice in his Appeal. The Appeal is the first *public* rejection of the general renunciation of France by a public man, even if one without a widespread reputation or established authority. France needed such a public affirmation of hope and rekindling of the national spirit if the Vichyite spirit of renunciation of national pride and independence was to be resisted and reversed. Pierre Manent has clearly articulated the moral character of this act of will which is the Appeal:

The Appel du 18 juin was precisely this liberating act of will. It was liberating, first, because it was just that: an act of will. By it, a single man, without high title or command, who was soon to be outlawed and sentenced to death, said that political and moral man can rise above the circumstances, however dire. This act of pure moral will also convey more political understanding than could be found in the political and military establishment remaining in distraught France. . . . In this founding and pregnant proclamation, de Gaulle gave time and space, that is, faith and reason to the French cornered and blinded into despair.[67]

De Gaulle's Appeal was delivered over the BBC at 6:00 P.M. on June 18, 1940 after the French authorities had officially requested an armistice with Germany. It was delivered with Churchill's encouragement and support but strikingly on the same day as his monumental "Finest Hour" speech announcing the end of the Battle of France and prefiguring the Battle of Britain. The latter speech minimized the attention that the Appeal received, although it was highlighted in the world press and was heard by a sizable, if not immense, audience within Metropolitan France. Still, a week after de Gaulle's broadcast, the number of volunteers for the French Free army, drawn primarily from French forces trapped outside of France at the time of the defeat, totaled only a few hundred. But this proved to be the seeds of a force that, although never sizable in terms of the overall numbers involved in the Allied war effort, would come to play a serious role in the battle for North Africa and in the liberation of France, as well as the gradual rallying of a substantial part of the French Empire.

What precisely did de Gaulle say in his brief and pointed Appeal? He began by noting that the leaders of the French armed forces "have set up a government."[68] He highlights the connection between the army of France and the new political authorities, what would shortly (July 9–10, 1940) officially become the Vichy regime led by Marshall Pétain. De Gaulle proceeds to link their pursuit of an armistice with the military authorities' mistaken belief in the permanent "defeat of France's armies." De Gaulle then shows that the impulse for capitulation stems from a mistaken judgment about the meaning and the supposed finality of the Battle of France. But justice demands pointing out that the present lack of perspective and judgment of the French military authorities-cum-government derives from a previous misjudgment about the effects of mechanized force on the character of modern warfare and hence on policy and statecraft. De Gaulle enhances his moral authority by vindicating his position in the military and political battles of the 1930s over the impact of mechanization on strategy and warfare. De Gaulle states:

It is quite true that we were, and still are, overwhelmed by enemy mechanized forces both on the ground and in the air. It was the tanks, the planes, and the tactics of the Germans, far more than the fact that we were outnumbered, that forced our armies to retreat. It was the German tanks, planes, and tactics that provided the element of surprise which brought our leaders to their present plight.

But the success of Germany's offensive and the overwhelming power of its mechanized forces are not sufficient ground for despair. "But has the last word been said? Must we abandon all hope? Is our defeat final and irremediable? To those questions, I answer—No!"

De Gaulle's resounding, intransigent "No!" is an expression of hope grounded in an act of will, of primordial fidelity to the nation. But it is equally grounded in a "full knowledge of the facts." "The cause of France is not lost," de Gaulle claims, for the reason that "the very factors that brought about our defeat may one day lead us to victory."

The Battle of France, we have seen, belongs to a larger whole that de Gaulle would repeatedly call the Thirty Years' War. In this struggle, whose ultimate issue was German hegemony and, in the second phase of the conflict, the survival of liberal and Christian civilization itself, de Gaulle emphasized that "France does not stand alone." De Gaulle reminds the French and her allies in the common cause of the possibilities inherent even now in France's "vast Empire." He reminds his audience of the extent, the immense naval power and resources of the British empire, as well as its determination to continue the struggle. He anticipates the United States' future involvement in resolving the world crisis. One can surmise that de Gaulle thought that the survival of a free and independent Britain was so linked to America's historical heritage and political principles and so connected to its vital national interests that America would gradually be drawn into the conflict, despite its remarkable inertia and seeming indifference to the crisis. De Gaulle highlights the global character of the war: "This war is not limited to our unfortunate country. The outcome of the struggle has not been decided by the Battle of France. This is a world war."

The Appeal suggests de Gaulle's remarkable grasp of the nature of armed conflict among modern mass, industrial societies. In such conflicts, especially one marked by radical ideological cleavages and global territorial stakes, war takes on a "total" character, with the full mobilization of resources, industry, machines, fire power, as well as propaganda with its attendant "organization of enthusiasm" (in the famous phrase of French

historian Elie Halévy). The Second World War would be what Raymond
Aron astutely called an "industrial war, conducted by civilians in uniform,"
one carried out by "industrial societies capable of mobilizing all their men
and all their factories. Workers and soldiers, all citizens contributed to the
collective effort."[69]

De Gaulle clearly saw that in any competitive total mobilization of
industrial and social reserves the Allies were capable of winning what Aron
calls the "race for numerical superiority in men, armies, and munitions."[70]
De Gaulle dramatically limns these possibilities, which in turn require a
revivification of the spirit of the French and the Allies more broadly. He
stresses what is possible down the line if the Allies persist in their efforts:

Mistakes have been made, there have been delays and untold suffering, but the fact
remains that there still exists in the world everything we need to crush our enemies
some day. Today we are crushed by the sheer weight of mechanized force hurled
against us, but we can still look to a future in which even greater mechanized force
will bring us victory. The destiny of the world is at stake.[71]

De Gaulle ends his Appeal by directly evoking his personal authority
and by raising the standard of honor and hope. In his own name ("I,
General de Gaulle"), he calls upon French officers and men on British soil
now or in the future, as well as French engineers and skilled workers from
the armament factories now or in the future on British soil, "to get in touch"
with him. De Gaulle already spoke, if not for a functioning government or
state, then for the spirit of France attempting to incarnate itself in a body
through the reconstitution of an armed force dedicated to resistance and
liberation.

The dignified and stirring peroration of the Appeal speaks for itself:
"Whatever happens, the flame of French resistance must not and shall not
die."

We have spoken of de Gaulle's claim and use of personal authority, which
extended to the claim to speak for France herself. In recounting the
beginnings of Free France, de Gaulle speaks of his need to strike out of the
"frightening void of the general renunciation" and of his "mission" to
"assume France." This quasi-theological rhetoric baffles positivistically
minded historians, raises suspicions about de Gaulle's democratic creden-
tials, and leads to at times somewhat small-minded questions about the
"legality" of the whole Gaullist enterprise.

De Gaulle's sense of his mission has not generally been properly understood inside or outside of France. In a mistaken judgment, Alain Peyrefitte
recently stated that "De Gaulle did not have any need to be anointed by

universal suffrage because he had already been so by History."[72] But despite the misplaced enthusiasm of his partisans, de Gaulle makes no claims to the authority of history. His claim is more solid and substantial. Instead, he claims to have been prepared by his character, his grasp of the men, issues, and events characteristic of the unfolding drama, as well as his fidelity to the fourteen-centuries-old sovereignty of France, to act for France in the absence of "legal" public authorities committed to ordered liberty and independence. De Gaulle's claim is not to legality or to the Historical Process but rather to a personal legitimacy grounded in the order of natural justice or the common good as articulated in Chapter 2 of *The Edge of the Sword.*

There is no more convincing account of Gaullist legitimacy than that made in a series of wartime writings and books by the Jesuit philosopher and theologian, Gaston Fessard.[73] We have already referred to his striking formulation of the Vichy regime, the regime established by the armistice, as a "slave-Prince." The regime of the slave-Prince upheld an attenuated or compromised sovereignty, one shared with an intrinsically imperialist and totalitarian regime committed to the institutionalization of an Idolatry of Race. Yet this compromise-regime still claimed to embody the principles of order or the common good. In his writings, Fessard articulated three principles of the common good essential to the maintenance of political justice and national legitimacy. These are the protection of the basic security of citizens, the establishment of an order of right or law founded upon reasonable criteria of justice, and a fidelity to and realization of the "values" or "ideal" and the "mission" of the nation.[74] Fessard argued that Vichy could never have genuine legitimacy because its sovereignty was the product of an initial fraud or delusion: it had abandoned its duty and authority to arbitrate the nation's destiny while pretending that it remained, in the decisive respects, sovereign.

The Vichy regime was legitimate only as a "Prince"—only to the extent that it exercised independence. But it was essentially illegitimate as a "slave" authority beholden ultimately to Nazi direction and *diktat.*[75] It could never embody the second or third criteria of the common good, the establishment of justice and fidelity to the nation's "mission," because the Vichy regime's founding act was a grant of power from an essentially corrupt and intrinsically evil political order. The deportation of French workers to Germany to aid in the war effort and the handing over of tens of thousands of Jews to the Nazis, the adoption of anti-Semitic laws, and the increasing political oppression within so-called unoccupied France, all evidenced and were results of the corruption inherent in the original pact with the Nazi

Leviathan. Fessard suggested that Vichy was a "screen" between the French and reality.[76] It allowed the French to avoid the real and inevitable choice between absolute and naked surrender and an uncompromising affirmation of the mission and ideal of France. For Fessard, there was no moral and intellectual middle road between Vichy and Gaullism available. All other options involved an evasion of facts, a hope for a compromise that neither totalitarianism nor total war made possible.

During the war Fessard suggested that de Gaulle's and Free France's fidelity to the mission of France could and would, with its growing base and influence and the expanding support of the French people, grow into a regime, a sovereignty, that embodied the fundamental criteria of the common good. In contrast, Vichy could never embody the legitimacy that is grounded in fidelity to the "common good."

None of this is to suggest that Gaullism as a partisan political movement represented the only political course for decent Frenchmen after the Liberation. That would be to make a greater identification between de Gaulle and the cause of France than good sense requires or justifies. De Gaulle never felt comfortable with the very idea of political parties. He found it difficult to accept that in democratic politics, outside of periods of national crisis, there could be no nonpartisan party, no simple, universal and unmediated "rally" for the unity and interests of the nation as a whole. This effort at a nonpartisan rally behind the greatness of France is the second and more problematic Gaullism.

In 1940 de Gaulle genuinely embodied the only principled and fecund hope for France. His "partisanship" was for France, and only secondarily and instrumentally for himself. We have repeatedly emphasized the clairvoyant realism underlying de Gaulle's course of action. De Gaulle's romantic mystique was inextricably tied to a sober judgment of the prospects and possibilities for French recovery. Yet it was de Gaulle's *hope* and his *action* that helped restore the "reality" of sovereign France. De Gaulle's example suggests that hope is an indispensable element of political reality and one of the "metaphysical" and "religious" foundations of the statesman's political action and choice when his nation and civilization itself are imperiled. In a remarkable essay on "A Metaphysic of Hope" published in 1942 (in occupied France!) and with obvious allusions to de Gaulle, Gabriel Marcel explains the causal efficacy of hope and the political consequences of patriotic fidelity. In doing so he indirectly illumines the "religious" essence or underpinning of de Gaulle's "mission":

Here I take the example once more of the patriot who refuses to despair of the liberation of his native land which is provisionally conquered. In what, or in whom, does he place his hope? . . . Even if he recognises that there is no chance that he will himself witness the hoped-for liberation, he carries beyond his own existence the fulfillment of his desires, he refuses with all his being to admit that the darkness which has fallen upon his country can be enduring, he affirms that it is only an eclipse. Still more: it is not enough to say that he cannot believe in the death of his country, the truth is much more that he does not even consider he has the right to believe in it, and that it would seem to him that he was committing a real act of treason in admitting this possibility; and this is true whether he is a believer or not. In every case he has made a judgment, which lies outside all his power of reflection, that to despair would be disloyal, it would be to go over to the enemy. This judgment rests on a postulate which is actually very likely to remain implicit but which we must examine. It consists in the affirmation that in hoping for liberation I really help to prepare the way for it, and that, inversely, in raising a doubt about its possibility I reduce the chance of it to some degree. It is not that strictly speaking I impute a causal efficacy to the fact of hoping or not hoping. The truth is much rather that I am conscious that when I hope I strengthen, and when I despair, or simply doubt, I weaken or let go of, a certain bond which unites me to the matter in question. This bond shows every evidence of being religious in essence.[77]

The Péguyist de Gaulle appreciated that there could be no realistic political course of action without an underlying mystique to claim men's loyalties and energize their wills. If the Marxists genuflected before the determinisms of History, de Gaulle appealed to the soul's capacity for fidelity to a common world, the world of the nation and civilized order. The Gaullist mystique transcends while informing the present historical moment by linking one's action to the broad inheritance of the past as well as to future humane possibilities shaped by the action of men. Such fidelity is the political reflection of the "theological virtue" of Hope.

Chapter 5

Democracy, Greatness, and Civilization: De Gaulle and a "Certain Conception of Man"

Democracy is the unchallenged and only legitimate social and political regime and "ideal" of the modern world. To question it in any significant way is to place oneself outside the spectrum of respectable political action and discourse; it is to risk consigning oneself to the category of the reactionary or retrograde. Yet Charles de Gaulle, arguably the greatest statesman of the twentieth century, was an ambivalent democrat, one without any illusions about the strengths and weaknesses of the democratic order. We must ask, was he then a reactionary, a noble anachronism briefly interrupting the approaching end of history? Does he speak to the political condition of modern democratic man?

De Gaulle cannot be called an ambivalent democrat because he, in any way, rejected the principles of popular sovereignty or the institutions and practices of constitutional government. He most emphatically did not. De Gaulle exercised what he himself called a "monarchy"[1] as the leader of the Free French movement during World War II, and he again exercised near total executive prerogative during the months after his return to power in June of 1958. But after the Liberation, de Gaulle restored the political parties (whose rampant and irresponsible partisanship he had only contempt for), scrupulously respected the civic and public liberties, and willingly stepped down from office in January of 1946 when it became clear that his constitutional design for a presidential Republic was at fundamental odds with the parliamentary regime supported by the full range of parties in the Constitutional Assembly. De Gaulle began his practice of appealing to the good sense of the "people" through referendum in 1945, a practice he would utilize throughout his eleven-year tenure as president of the French Fifth Republic. De Gaulle did not believe that *vox populi, vox dei*, but he did appeal to the people to rally to the national interest or common good as articulated by a statesman-president who transcended ideological and partisan sectarianism. De Gaulle's reputed "Bonapartism," his use of plebiscitarian techniques, was not evidence of a propensity for dictatorial rule. Instead, it was part of a considered design to make heard or manifest a "general will" that speaks for the long-term and deepest interests of a united France. De Gaulle was not only a respecter (and sometimes manipulator or educator) of the popular sovereignty, but he was also a liberal who respected those liberties, from freedom of the press to religious liberty, which are at the center of the liberal conception of human freedom.

De Gaulle, as we shall argue, fully understood the problems that modern democracy posed for the sustenance of human dignity and liberty. As a Catholic and conservative military officer, as a partisan of the greatness of France, it might have been expected that de Gaulle would be tempted by the allure of a national and military dictatorship that would put to an end the moral and political decadence and institutional weakness of a dispirited democracy. Of course, in 1940 the Vichy regime carried out its National Revolution after fatally compromising France's sovereignty by accommodating itself to the Nazi occupation and domination of France. De Gaulle could not accept such a fatal abandonment of sovereignty even if he shared some of the principles of the National Revolution and much of its critique of the Third Republic. But while recognizing the thorough corruption of the Third Republic, and refusing his assent to the "regime of the parties" that characterized the Fourth Republic, de Gaulle refused to abandon democratic principles and institutions or his loyalty to the republican character of contemporary France.

De Gaulle was undoubtedly a convinced constitutionalist and a (somewhat reluctant) democrat, but he dreamed of a strong, unified republic that would restore the greatness of France. At some point, we must ask whether there is something utopian about de Gaulle's partisanship for greatness. Democracy, understood as the modern regime of liberty, the regime of equal rights and universal citizenship, is above all a "middling" or mediocre regime. This is not meant in any necessarily pejorative sense. The philosophic architects and political analysts of modern democracy are in universal agreement about the antiaristocratic character of democracy and the democratic regime. Democracy, characterized sociologically by the growing equality of conditions, is a regime that self-consciously rejects the aristocratic or gentlemanly spirit. One need only look at the most important texts of the modern political philosophy to establish the point.

Modern liberty as formulated by such diverse thinkers as Machiavelli, Hobbes, Montesquieu, and Constant is above all prosaic and bourgeois, rejecting the conceits of the vainglorious, firmly identifying democracy with the security of the individual, suspicious of all claims by priests and gentlemen to rule in the name of some good (some "greatness") higher than that of the comfortable preservation of the rights-bearing individual.

TOCQUEVILLE ON DEMOCRACY AND GREATNESS

The greatest philosopher of democracy, Alexis de Tocqueville, helps us to see the problems or tensions inherent in the Gaullist effort to link modern liberty and the demands of greatness. And he shares, to a remarkable extent, de Gaulle's identification of these two seemingly opposed goods.

Modern democracy is explicitly identified by Tocqueville with mediocrity and not greatness. In the concluding chapter of Volume II of *Democracy in America*, Tocqueville describes what can be discerned about the new democratic society that was emerging throughout the European-Christian world and that had come to fullest fruition in America. Its most striking characteristic is its mild, humane, and utterly *mediocre* character. Tocqueville writes in a striking passage:

[G]ood things and evil in the world are fairly evenly distributed. . . . Everyone feels some ambition, but few have ambitions on a vast scale. . . .

There is little energy of soul, but mores are gentle and laws humane. Though heroic devotion and any other very exalted, brilliant, and pure virtues may be rare, habits are orderly, violence rare, and cruelty almost unknown. . . . Life is not very glamorous, but extremely comfortable and peaceful. Seeking for the most general and striking of all these various characteristics, I notice that what has been said about personal fortunes applies to other things in a thousand different ways. Almost all salient characteristics are obliterated to make room for something average, less high and less low, less brilliant and less dim, than what the world had before.[2]

Tocqueville is saddened by the relative absence of great men and great exertions in this new democratic world. He recognizes that a profound justice is embodied in this new democratic social state and regime, a justice that is grounded in the "idea of humanity," in the recognition of the human dignity and the right to liberty of *all* and not just some accidentally or historically privileged class of human beings. And yet this "just" democracy threatens some of the highest human excellences and risks confining human beings to a new herdlike "mass" or democratic despotism charac-terized by a loss of genuine human individuality and even the notion of personal independence and responsibility. As Pierre Manent has observed, in democracy, nature (the rightful recognition of the justice of democracy) threatens nature (human excellence or greatness as well as human choice and responsibility).[3] This is the ultimate problem of democracy, so pro-found and seemingly tragic, for Tocqueville. At points, Tocqueville seems to fear that the virtues and vices of democracy and aristocracy belong to "two distinct kinds of humanity . . . each of which has its peculiar advan-tages and disadvantages, its own good points and its bad."[4] Tocqueville comes close to suggesting that human "justice" and human "excellence" belong to two dramatically opposed and unsynthesizable social conditions and political orders. And yet, while warning that friends of human liberty and dignity in modern times must firmly reject aristocratic privilege, while establishing that equality is the necessary foundation of any libertarian order in our time, Tocqueville remains in some very real sense a partisan of human greatness. His "holy enterprise" is to protect the independence and dignity of man in an age prone toward equalitarian or democratic despotism.[5] Tocqueville rejected any effort to sustain or resurrect aristo-cratic *society*, but he attempted to support those "aristocratic" dimensions of the human soul which are natural to human beings and which are necessary for the survival of human liberty. One can turn to Tocqueville's own political activity in order to hear what Raymond Aron has called his Gaullist tone or voice.[6] Like de Gaulle, Tocqueville believed that a politics of greatness was necessary to prevent the dehumanization, the thorough-going "enervation" of men. In a letter dated March 8, 1841, Tocqueville explained to a befuddled John Stuart Mill why he, Tocqueville, did not side with the "peace party" advocating easy accommodation between France and Britain during the Anglo-French crisis of 1840. Tocqueville believed that it was imperative for France to maintain her national self-respect. He criticized the great liberal Guizot for humiliating the nation's honor by trying too hard to avoid war with Great Britain. He writes:

I could not approve the revolutionary and propagandistic language of the greater part of the partisans of war, but to chime in with those who were loudly asking for peace, at any price, was even more dangerous. I do not have to tell you, my dear Mill, that the greatest malady that threatens a people organized as we are is the gradual softening of mores, the abasement of the mind, the mediocrity of tastes; that is where the great dangers of the future lie. One cannot let a nation that is democratically constituted like ours and in which the natural vices of the race unfortunately coincide with the natural vices of the social state, one cannot let this nation take up easily the habit of sacrificing what it believes to be its grandeur to its repose, great matters to petty ones; it is not healthy to allow such a nation to believe that its place in the world is smaller, that it is fallen from the level on which its ancestors had put it, but that it must console itself by making railroads and by making prosper in the bosom of this peace, under whatever condition this peace is obtained, the well-being of each private individual. It is necessary that those who march at the head of such a nation should always keep a proud attitude, if they do not wish to allow the level of national mores to fall very low.[7]

Tocqueville supported a proud and semi-imperial foreign policy in order to correct the soft, humanitarian, materialistic, and antipolitical impulses of democratic peoples. It is for this reason that the same Tocqueville who actively worked in the French Assembly for the elimination of the slave trade enthusiastically supported the colonization of Algeria in the 1830s and 1840s. It is for the same reason that Tocqueville, who was so profoundly critical of the failure of the French Revolution to live up to what he saw as the promise of 1789, the great effort to keep together liberty and equality, could praise in *The Old Regime and the Revolution* the almost transhuman heroism, the great exertions and sacrifices of the armies of the Revolution and Empire![8] Tocqueville believed that all manifestations of greatness in modern times which did not undermine democratic equality and liberties must be highlighted or *talked up.* De Gaulle's "politics of grandeur" entails a similar correction or mitigation of the spirit and mores of democracy, without rejecting the justice or necessity of democracy. De Gaulle, like Tocqueville, recognized that modern citizenship and statesmanship must operate within the fated or predestined circle of modern democracy.[9]

De Gaulle's politics of grandeur, therefore, is not a reactionary, anachronistic, or nostalgic effort to revitalize a lost or half-forgotten aristocratic treasure. It is, instead, a self-conscious effort to deal with the problem of democracy, particularly as that problem comes to light in modern France, still torn in his lifetime by the great struggles between Left and Right engendered by the cataclysm that was the French Revolution.

DE GAULLE ON MODERN CIVILIZATION

De Gaulle believed that "France cannot be France without greatness." Elsewhere in this book, we analyze the two principal speeches of de Gaulle, the Appeal of June 18, 1940 and the Discourse at Bayeux of June 16, 1946, which are inspired by de Gaulle's service to the greatness of France. In them we see the two defining moments of de Gaulle's statesmanship: the effort to save the independence and honor of France, to sustain and rekindle the never-before-abandoned sovereignty of France against an unprecedented tyranny, and his efforts to re-found France's republican institutions by establishing the competency and impartiality of the state. Both of de Gaulle's principal actions, those of resistance and re-founding, were motivated by one imperative: national and personal honor. But his statesmanship occurred not only within the context of France, her history and tragedies, but also within the larger horizon of a modern and democratic world. Therefore, it is necessary to turn to an analysis of an important wartime speech that helps clarify de Gaulle's analysis and evaluation of modern democracy. The imperative of "greatness" is only fully comprehensible in light of both the distinctive character and history of the French nation *and* the nature of modern democracy itself.

It is undoubtedly the case that Charles de Gaulle was not a philosopher but rather a soldier, a statesman and, in time, the founder of a new political order. His warnings in *The Edge of the Sword* against a priorism in military and political affairs, his recognition that ever-changing circumstances are at the core of the life of political action, and his belief that action is largely intuitive and in some existential sense prior to reflection, all reflect de Gaulle's belief that political action can never simply be ruled or dictated to by thought.[10] But it is also the case that de Gaulle was a man who constantly reflected on what he called the "philosophy of action"[11] and more generally, on the preconditions and possibilities for human liberty and greatness in modern, democratic times. The discourse that best expresses de Gaulle's larger or more comprehensive reflection about the character of the modern age is one that he delivered to the "Cercle Français" at Oxford University on November 25, 1941. The speech is increasingly recognized in France today as de Gaulle's most incisive analysis of totalitarianism and as one of the most revealing expressions of his "political philosophy."[12] The speech deals most immediately with the subject of Franco-British relations and how collaboration between these two great and ancient nations can "ensure that victory [in World War II] will bear fruit."[13] But its larger theme is that of the "crisis of civilization," a crisis whose depths and severity can only be addressed by a partnership between the two great homes of Western liberty and by a statesmanship fully cognizant of the crisis of our times.

De Gaulle begins his discourse by citing the French nationalist writer, Barrès, highlighting the special importance of those "places where breathes *l'esprit*" (spirit, mind).[14] De Gaulle pays tribute to Oxford University as a preeminent example of such a place. The "atmosphere" of the University is the product of a long tradition of disinterested thought and therefore the appropriate location for a relatively disinterested discussion of the deepest issues of modern politics and thought.[15] It appears that spirit, mind, and reflection are absolutely necessary for both the diagnosis and the successful resolution of the modern crisis. Action, after all, needs thought to understand the circumstances that it faces and to overcome the tyranny of the merely material, of the merely given. For this reader of Henri Bergson, if human beings are to remain fully human, it is imperative that mind continue to "triumph over matter," that the human spirit not become a prisoner or plaything of impersonal social and historical forces and processes. For de Gaulle, this liberation is the great precondition and in a certain sense, the very definition of our humanity. And it is also what is most profoundly threatened by the generalized standardization and collectivization of life, thought, and society in the contemporary age. This theme will be developed further in this chapter.

The first half of the speech, dealing with the past and present of Franco-British relations, is a kind of prolegomenon to the fundamental theme of the piece, the aforementioned crisis of civilization.

De Gaulle knows that the alliance between Britain and France is of comparatively recent origin. England was arguably, by any ample historical criteria, the hereditary enemy of France. But de Gaulle is not a simplistic realist who asserts the mere geostrategic determination of Franco-British relations. It is no longer sufficient to say, with the nineteenth-century French statesman and historian Adolphe Thiers, that British and French relations are determined by the fact that "Britain is an island."[16] Of course, the fact that Britain is an island requires it to control the sea routes leading to it in order to ensure the freedom of its commerce and its political independence. Thiers's formula adequately describes the position and motivation of Britain *before* the rise of German power and imperialism at the end of the nineteenth century and before the rise of totalitarianism and collectivist movements in the twentieth century, which pose a threat to *all* of Europe, and even to the principle of civilization itself. De Gaulle presents a lucid account of the sources of traditional French and British enmity and the initial reasons for the Franco-British entente at the beginning of the twentieth century. It is an account that Churchill, for example, would not quarrel with. De Gaulle writes:

[Britain] could not permit any form of hegemony to be established on the European continent, for the State exercising such supremacy would immediately become a pretender to the empire of the sea. Hence the frequent periods of political tension between London and Paris throughout the seventeenth, eighteenth and nineteenth centuries. Hence their repeated conflicts. Hence, too, at the beginning of the present century, the complete reversal of their mutual relations brought about by the influence of your King Edward VII. The *Entente Cordiale* came into being almost overnight when Germany, led by the Prussians, raised the standard of Pan-Germanism, threatening the balance of power by mounting victories, and crying from the lips of Kaiser Wilhelm II: "Our future is on the seas!"[17]

De Gaulle then proceeds to show that some of the responsibility for this Thirty Years' War (the great conflict between Germany and Europe beginning in 1914 and, of course, ending in 1945) lies with and was facilitated by the "political divergence" between Paris and London.[18] What the Free World needed was the closest political, military, diplomatic, and, one must add, spiritual coordination and connection between France and Britain. Instead, French and British policy involved no coherent and unified strategy for dealing with Germany. Whatever prudence one can allow to the acceptance of the recovery of a liberal Germany, the lackadaisical acceptance of the Nazi regime after 1933, first by London and then rather clumsily by Paris, made no sense whatsoever. The failure to appreciate the character of the Nazi threat, the following of a misplaced appeasement policy toward an insatiably imperial and hostile regime, the failure to coordinate an effective and firm response to German rearmament or the militarization of the Rhineland, the acquiescence by France to the abandonment of her ally Czechoslovakia, an abandonment orchestrated by London in the misconceived and futile effort for peace, were emblematic of a profound spiritual and political incapacity on the part of the democracies.[19]

De Gaulle warns, in November of 1941, that Nazi Germany has an obvious interest in exacerbating the separation of Britain and France. Germany hopes to prevent any Anglo-French rapprochement after the disastrous events of May and June 1940. Berlin understandably "seeks to open wounds and then constantly rub in salt to irritate and inflame"[20] them. The Germans also seek to revive old memories of British and French animosity, an animosity associated with the great names of Joan of Arc, Marlborough, Nelson, Wellington, and l'Aiglon among others.[21] These are quarrels, memories, and names that de Gaulle, the French patriot, steeped as he is in the political and military history of France, is deeply conscious of. De Gaulle's magnanimity and statesmanlike prudence consist in large part in his clairvoyant ability to recognize Britain both as the hereditary enemy and as a very real friend and partner in a common struggle for the maintenance of European liberty and civilization. On one hand, present-day proponents of a unitary, homogeneous Europe too readily forget history, that is, the longstanding and to some extent still living quarrels and memories that divide European peoples. On the other hand, the partisans of Vichy were oblivious to the fact that the fate of Britain and France was (and is) inextricably tied together. Some misguided French patriots could not forget that Britain favored a German recovery after 1918, that Britain failed to prepare for war in the 1930s, and that it was in no serious position in 1940 "to give substantial help to France in her hour of danger."[22] De Gaulle has not forgotten these wounds, and he is careful to remind his audience of Britain's role in the disaster culminating in the June 1940 armistice in France. But de Gaulle knows that blame for the debacle of 1940 is not the exclusive property of the British. He, more than anyone, is cognizant of the corruption of the political and military elites of the French Third Republic: embodied in their failure to accept de Gaulle's proposals for the establishment of a dynamic professional army with offensive capacities made possible by the mechanized tanks and air corps. De Gaulle knew that the French authorities too willfully ignored reality and developed a "static" strategy appropriate to the "static" and decadent character of their regime.

Yet, de Gaulle is convinced that the French people have not fallen victim to German propaganda or to shortsighted Vichy-inspired resentment of a supposedly untrustworthy and duplicitous Albion. De Gaulle is convinced that the peoples of France and Britain can see beyond the "abyss" of 1940, that they realize the absolute indispensability of a friendly union between France and Britain, and by implication that they recognize "Free France" as the symbol and embodiment of that union. De Gaulle is sufficiently distant from a cold and calculating, geopolitical, or power-political realism, to speak of Britain and France as "friends." He makes this point by quoting the great British national poet Shakespeare, from whose font of human wisdom de Gaulle repeatedly drank. He states:

There can be no doubt that the French people, in the depths of the abyss into which they have temporarily fallen, have never better realized the true worth of the British, never more clearly seen that "liberation" is synonymous with "British victory," never felt more certain that their future independence cannot be achieved unless there is a friendly union between our two countries. I am convinced that, for their part, the British people recognize as never before the vital necessity for such collaboration. This springs, in the first place, from the same generous instinct that inspires a man to go to the rescue of his friend. Shakespeare has well expressed the British attitude:

> I am not of that feather, to shake off
> My friend when he most needs me . . .[23]

The development of modern technology, particularly the advent of mechanized warfare, of airplanes and tanks, has made such a dogmatic geostrategic realism obsolete (one can add today the development of nuclear weapons).[24] Britain and France have a visible interest in maintaining friendly relations. In the modern, technologically driven and mechanized world, no island is any longer an island unto itself. The very hardheaded and nonutopian de Gaulle recognizes without lament, or enthusiasm either, the realities of Anglo-French and European "interdependence."

Accordingly, de Gaulle recommends an enhanced, "stronger and more sincere Anglo-French collaboration than has as ever yet existed."[25] Such collaboration is "rendered imperative by excellent reasons of practical policy and the most valid arguments of sentiment, but it is above all made necessary by a duty common to both our great and ancient nations—the need to preserve our civilization."[26]

As we have already seen, it is a mistake to think that de Gaulle's deliberations about foreign affairs were based solely on geostrategic concerns or calculations of the balance of power. Domestic considerations, for example, the maintenance of the unity and honor of France, were prime considerations and motivations for de Gaulle. Of course, de Gaulle was no romantic in either aspect of his statesmanship, thought and action, in foreign affairs. He recognized that calculating the balance of power was the beginning of wisdom in international relations. But it was only the beginning. Great and ancient nations had margins of liberty of action in world affairs that were unavailable to small nations or nations whose survival was threatened by imperial or hegemonic powers. Great nations must concern themselves not only with protecting their interests and maintaining their independence, and not only with sustaining their national honor and self-respect, but also with serving the cause of civilization and humankind. De Gaulle called this most elevated and rare dimension of statesmanship the "querelle de l'homme."[27] He truly believed, and in a most realistic way, that nations like Britain and France could provide important and at times indispensable service to the common cause of humanity. The "querelle de l'homme" is an essential element of a politics of grandeur. Greatness is not then simply at the service of the "power" of the nation but of the principles of civilized human order. And "great and ancient nations" are the building blocks, the constituent elements of a truly cosmopolitan or civilized world order. As we shall see, de Gaulle believed that the most sublime task for modern statesmanship was the protection of a "certain conception of man"[28] threatened by the general evolution of modern society.

It was de Gaulle's considered and longstanding view that modern life was characterized by a crisis of civilization. In the midst of world war, de Gaulle locates that conflict within the larger "whole" that is the crisis of European civilization. De Gaulle rejects the view that the "revolution" through which the modern world is passing during World War II is due solely or even primarily to the "ambition" of Hitler.[29] De Gaulle rejects this as a "summary verdict," one that ignores the deeper sources and causes of the European crisis. He also rejects the claims that the "catastrophe must be attributed to the German people's eternal appetite for domination."[30] This rejection comes from a man who had noted, in his first book (*La Discorde Chez L'Ennemi*), the corrupting attraction of the German elite to Nietzschean ideas about the Superman and power politics and who firmly believed that modern (post–1870) Germany regarded war as its "prime industry!" De Gaulle was firmly opposed to the Allies' toleration of German economic recovery and military rearmament in the 1920s (before Hitler's advent to power) and opposed the reconstitution of a centralized German Reich, as he called it, after 1945. This man of the Right, this proponent of a politics of grandeur, absolutely rejected a philosophy of Machtpolitik which recognized no higher principle than the power and power-prestige of the nation. He rejected what one might call the anti-European imperialism that infected German political and military elites from the 1880s onward and made them forget that Germany was one face or manifestation of a "common European home." In brief, de Gaulle was fully cognizant of the intellectual and deeply spiritual pathology of the German mind and soul. Yet he rejected an explanation of the Thirty Years' War that separated the rise of National Socialist totalitarianism from the more general evolution of modern times:

But it remains to be seen whether the combination of the Nazi system and German dynamism was due to mere chance, or whether this fusion was not itself the upshot of a more particular evil. To put the matter bluntly, it may have been the result of a crisis in civilization.[31]

It is important to understand what de Gaulle means by civilization. Surprisingly, de Gaulle makes no distinction between the Old Regime and a modern world beginning in the sixteenth, seventeenth, or eighteenth centuries. For two thousand years, since at least Roman times and the beginning of the Christian religion, the West has been one unitary civilization. During this period, various "conceptions, customs, and laws have spread throughout the world, altering the spirit of the peoples and even the very face of the globe."[32]

There, of course, have been important political, national, religious, and social differences among the peoples of this civilization "born in Western Europe." But despite these differences, "despite the clash of armies,

a sort of common ideal, a like recognition of what the collectivity owes to the individual and of what the individual owes to the community, together with respect for freedom and justice, asserted themselves among the nations according to their stage of evolution. The fundamental principle on which our civilization is based is that each man should be free to think and believe as he chooses; that he have liberty to determine his opinions, his form of work and his use of leisure.[33]

A reader is forced to confront the accuracy of de Gaulle's account of the common ideal that characterizes this two-thousand-year-old civilization. Why, for example, does de Gaulle exclude classical Greece from his otherwise capacious category of Western civilization? Is it because Greek politics, philosophy, and culture predate Christianity and therefore did not sufficiently recognize the dignity and liberty of the individual? Has de Gaulle adequately described the fundamental principles of Western civilization through its long history and transmogrifications? A skeptical student of political theory or a partisan of the Enlightenment might argue that some of the liberties described by de Gaulle such as freedom of opinions, belief, and enterprise are preeminently modern liberties. The very notion of the individual with individual rights is a product of modern political philosophy's break with an older classical-Christian (scholastic or Christian Aristotelian) conception of man's duties as well as the sources of his dignity and liberties. De Gaulle seems to treat the Reformation, the French Revolution, the modern capitalist and industrial revolutions, and the rise of a new democracy in America as mere secondary events or even epiphenomena of a largely continuous civilization that is dedicated to the same lofty and humanizing ideal of civilized order:

This civilization, born in Western Europe, has weathered many storms. It has been seriously threatened by barbarian invasions, partitions brought about by the feudal system, discord inside Christendom, the upheaval of the French Revolution, the rise of the nationalist spirit, social strife, and the advent of great industrial undertakings. But, so far, it has always managed to retain sufficient internal vitality, sufficient power of attraction, to enable it finally to carry the day. More than that, it has moved like a conqueror through the world, gaining vast regions, much to their advantage. So saturated has America become with this civilization of ours that it may truthfully be said to have reached its fullest expression beyond the Atlantic. It has penetrated Asia, Africa, and Oceania. As a result, first of colonization and then of the gradual emancipation of innumerable peoples, the moment was fast approaching when all the inhabitants of the earth would have recognized the same high principles and been clothed in the same dignity.[34]

De Gaulle's position is not as idiosyncratic, farfetched, and ahistorical as it might appear on first impression. De Gaulle, I suggest, believes that the heart of Western civilization is Christian and medieval and that this civilization is essentially a liberal or libertarian one in that it recognized the basic dignity of the individual and tolerably well protected basic human liberties. De Gaulle shares the view of many important and diverse nineteenth-century liberals such as Tocqueville, Chateaubriand, and Michelet that European-Christian civilization "tends essentially towards the freedom and development of the individual."[35] Western civilization then begins not with classical antiquity, with its discovery of politics and philosophy, but with the Gospel's recognition of the spiritual dignity and "equality" of all men before God. From this perspective, modern democracy is the "final conquest of the Gospel," the political embodiment of the recognition of the sacred value of each created and ensouled human being. In this view, it does not matter in the final analysis that "democracy" was merely latent in the feudal institutions and way of life of the Old Regime. This civilization, by its origins and principles, inexorably tended toward the realization of democratic and libertarian principles. De Gaulle also shares, as we shall see, the view of such thoughtful conservative liberals as Tocqueville (in *The Old Regime*) and de Jouvenel (in *On Power*) on the subsidiary but connected point that the "liberties" of men were often better respected under the Old Regime than under the dispensation of the modern democratic state.[36] The erosion of traditional social and corporate bodies and institutions (the various *corps*) goes hand in hand with the rise of individual "rights" and the augmentation of state power. The dialectic of individualism and collectivism within modernity has been traced by serious students of modern politics such as Robert Nisbet and Pierre Manent.[37] It was recognized by the astute de Gaulle.

De Gaulle's analysis of the "classical" period of the ancien regime in *France and Her Army* suggests that he favored the strengthening of the modern state for the sake of the unity and greatness of the nation while opposing any fundamental efforts to abolish or seriously erode the historic liberties of the French people. Undoubtedly, some tension exists between de Gaulle's sympathy for a unitary and aggrandizing French state and his defense of the individual against the collectivizing tendencies of modern politics. Contrary to Tocqueville's analysis in *The Old Regime and the Revolution*, de Gaulle seems to believe that the Old Regime at its peak established an exemplary, non-"ideological" compromise between these two divergent requirements and goals.[38]

In *The Edge of the Sword*, de Gaulle notes the weakening of traditional sources of authority and the enhanced "recognition given to the value of individual in modern times."[39] He also recognizes that "individualism is out of favor, and everywhere the claims of collectivism are being pushed to the forefront."[40] This is not evidence of a contradiction on de Gaulle's part. There is an essential connection between the weakening of traditional institutions and "corporate" liberties, and between the rise of individual skepticism and "authority" and the widespread collectivization of modern life. If de Gaulle is right, the individual *needs* a social context of authoritative traditions and institutions for the development and exercise of genuine individuality. Modern individualism, as opposed to Christian or medieval liberty, divorces the individual from the "natural equilibrium" of authority and liberty, and of the few and the many within which the dignity of the "humble masses" can be promoted and protected.

De Gaulle proceeds to describe the Second World War as a struggle between two dimensions or aspects of modernity: that "Western" civilization which remains dedicated to the freedom and development of the individual and a

diametrically opposite movement, a movement which admits no rights save those of the racial or national collectivity; a movement which denies the individual the right to think, judge, or act as he sees fit, depriving him of the possibility of so doing and giving the dictators inordinate power to define good and evil, to decree what is true and what is false, to kill or let live as best suits the interests of the group they represent.[41]

De Gaulle understands that the National Socialist and fascist collectivisms have provided new opportunities for the "eternal ambitions" of the Germans and the "spasmodic pretensions" of the Italians. Most deeply and disturbingly, such collectivism "is part of the general evolution" of modern times.[42] One should add, of course, that de Gaulle did not exclude the class-based collectivism of communism from his general condemnation of totalitarianism. Writing after the German invasion of the Soviet Union, de Gaulle realized that the Soviet Union was likely to be a crucial ally in the struggle against Nazi Germany. Whereas de Gaulle never underestimated the "totalitarian" character of Soviet communism, it is probably the case that he saw nationalist and racialist collectivism as posing a graver threat to the survival of Western civilization than the class-based and supposedly international or cosmopolitan collectivism of communism. As de Gaulle wrote in his *War Memoirs*, "in the long run there is no regime that can hold out against the will of nations."[43] There was something profoundly *unnatural* about communism, while the "fascist" regime perverted national and political impulses that de Gaulle believed were intrinsic to men and strengthened by the "democratic" or mass character of modern society.

De Gaulle understands that modern collectivism, racism, and nationalism are precisely *modern* movements unintelligible without the phenomenon of the mass society and its "citizen," the mass man, whom Michael Oakeshott has tellingly called the "individual manqué," the anti-individual.[44] De Gaulle is a "good European" and French patriot and has nothing but contempt for the illiberal, unmeasured, and "pagan" character of the "fascist" Right.

It is absolutely necessary to differentiate de Gaulle's emphasis on the unity and greatness of the nation from the imperialism and nationalism of the fascist Right. De Gaulle wished to rally or unite (*rassemblé*) the French people in order that they could overcome the debilitating partisan and ideological strife that has been a source of immense political conflict and national grief. He wished to unite the French in the name of a standard, France and her greatness, which transcended mere partisanship. He recognized the existence of a "common good" that could transcend individual and partisan "interests" and rights while recognizing their legitimate place in the realm of "civil society." In de Gaulle's understanding, France itself was part of a larger entity, Europe, which itself was the living embodiment of the "common ideal" of civilization. De Gaulle's emphasis on political and national unity is not then antiliberal. Respect for liberty, for the human person, is necessary for human self-respect and honor. De Gaulle's liberalism consists in his belief that the individual has "the right to think, judge or act as he sees fit." But de Gaulle is not endorsing the merely idiosyncratic exercise of human freedom. Human beings are responsible beings, and true individuality consists in the responsible exercise of human freedom. Such liberty is liberty under "God and the laws"[45] as Tocqueville put it, a liberty guided by the conscience and by an articulated sense of self-limitation. But the totalitarians claim the very power to define what is good and evil and what is true and false. De Gaulle's "Christianity" is evident in his refusal to accept the ideological claim that the will of the party or state can define the nature and contours of what is or is not humanly permissible. De Gaulle is liberal *and* Christian in his recognition of inherent limits on the exercise of human will and in his political refusal to deify the state even as he recognizes the "natural" character of the political and the moral authority of a properly constituted "state." De Gaulle is also premodern and Christian in his refusal of the modern "lie," the belief that political actions and human will are solely responsible for the human world, that they make everything and are the highest things. De Gaulle rejects the "paganism" of the Right as he recognizes a truth that is perverted almost beyond recognition by them; there is a sacredness proper to the city, to the political world, which is not sufficiently or properly recognized by liberal or bourgeois politics.

What precisely are the characteristics of the mass society which provide such powerful support for the establishment of mass or "democratic" tyrannies in the twentieth century? De Gaulle gives a dramatic description of a world transformed by the presence of machinery or technology, one in which human beings are increasingly aggregated and in which every kind of uniformity has become the order of the day. De Gaulle describes a world in which human individuality, the human soul or "essential I" ("*le quant de soi*"),[46] is becoming a prisoner and plaything of material forces, of a general mechanization of the human order itself. He describes a standardized world of chilling uniformity:

A world where human beings are herded together for work and pleasure, and where even their thoughts and interests are determined for them; in a world where housing conditions, clothing, and food are gradually standardized; where everyone reads the same things in the same papers at the same time; where, from one end of the earth to the other, they see the same films, and hear the same news, ideas, and music broadcast; in a world where, at the same hours, similar means of transport take people to the same workshops and offices, restaurants and canteens, sportsgrounds and theatres, to the same buildings, blocks or courts for work, food, recreation, and rest; where men and women are similarly educated and informed, and all lead the same busy life and share the same worries.[47]

De Gaulle observes a world in which human beings have become increasingly indistinguishable. In such a situation, "only a tremendous effort can preserve the individual as such."[48] De Gaulle implicitly evokes the "querelle de l'homme" and calls for nothing less than a statesmanship that works for the preservation of the elementary conditions of both genuine individuality and its correlate, the *civitas*.

But the difficulty of this task is exacerbated and complemented by the fact that the masses "far from reacting against such standardization, are actually developing a taste for it and encouraging the process."[49] The mass man finds strength and emotional solace in the conformity of an utterly communal existence. He cannot accept the burden of freedom, and he prefers the support and identity of the crowd. "And it is precisely in the modern tendency that the dictators have sought and found success for their doctrines and ritual."[50] The totalitarians offer mass men a false *ersatz* grandeur, one that offers the "hope of dominating others" but in return demands the comprehensive abandonment of political and individual liberty and the "enthusiastic" adaptation of "the organization of termites."[51]

De Gaulle's rhetoric may seem somewhat exaggerated and excessively anguished, but its character is understandable given the fact that he is writing at a time, in the middle of the twentieth century, when the destruction of Western liberty was more than a distinct possibility. But he is not idiosyncratic in his language, concerns, or insights. The most penetrating and perspicacious of nineteenth- and twentieth-century political and social thinkers, from Tocqueville and Burkhardt to Nietzsche, Spengler, Ortega y Gasset, and Bernanos, were in agreement about the dangers of creeping conformism and its enervation of the human spirit accompanying the development of a mass democratic society. Winston Churchill himself expressed this view in his 1925 essay "Mass Effects in Modern Life," an essay remarkably complementary to de Gaulle's speech in its analysis of threats to genuine human individuality in the modern age.[52]

In retrospect, the various analyses of "mass society" undoubtedly have the virtue of pointing out the threats to genuine human individuality within modern, egalitarian societies. However, they tend to identify that threat, in a somewhat one-sided and exaggerated way, with the mechanization and standardization of human beings. These analyses tend to collapse or homogenize the experience of liberal and totalitarian modernity. The threat to human individuality within our liberal societies stems as much from the very mildness and "individualism" of such societies and from the attendant decline of civic virtues (which often accompany the augmentation of state power) as from excessive regimentation of social life. But on the fundamental point de Gaulle and his predecessors are undoubtedly right: modernity poses powerful new threats to the integrity and liberties of the individual, and totalitarianism is diametrically opposed to "modern liberty" while remaining its bastard child and its "frère-ennemi."

De Gaulle's purpose in the Oxford speech is emphatically not to denounce democratic principles and institutions or to call for the creation of a civilization or world order where a new aristocracy can somehow gain social mastery. That is the path of Nietzsche and his remarkably vulgar and "democratic" epigones. Instead, de Gaulle calls for the "party of freedom" to transform the vitally important if limited victory in the world war into a more widespread campaign against the general tendency of our age. De Gaulle calls for a sustained effort at "spiritual regeneration" in the social, moral, and political spheres.[53] Such regeneration must be led by Britain and France, two great "homes" of freedom and the "liberties of man," on behalf of the "cause of civilization."[54] In this perspective, the quarrel between Burke and Paine, between historic British liberties and the French "rights of man," are antiquated—republican France and monarchical Britain are both recognized as homes and champions of the "liberties" of men.

De Gaulle calls for the creation of a political and social order in the West "in which the liberty, security and dignity of the individual can be safeguarded and elevated to such a degree as to seem more desirable than any possible advantages to be obtained by their abolition."[55]

De Gaulle's recognition of the pathological dimensions of mass society did not lead him to turn against the democratic desire for adequate social provision. De Gaulle's support for a welfare or social security state and his repeated call for the "association" of capital and labor and for worker participation in business enterprises are evidence of his "Christian" and "democratic" concern to provide for the security and dignity of the ordinary individual. Without adequate provisions for all citizens, the masses might be attracted to the false promises and the destructive class hatreds promoted by communist totalitarianism.

These were among de Gaulle's major themes during the years of the RPF's political engagement (1947–1952), and he would renew and reemphasize them during and after the crisis of May 1968. His critics are right that his ideas about participation and association have often lacked any real specificity and concreteness. De Gaulle never went much further than evoking the need for a political alternative to both totalitarian communism and a social order dominated by the profit motive. Echoing a theme in the modern tradition of Catholic social thought, de Gaulle wished to humanize the industrial order by making "Man a responsible being instead of a mere tool."[56] He wished to introduce greater consultation with and decision making by workers within business enterprises. The majority within the Gaullist movement, favoring social stability and the promotion of economic growth, believed that "participation" could be socially disruptive and would discourage investment in France. A small group of "Left Gaullists" believed that it was the necessary foundation for a social revolution within liberty. In any case, de Gaulle had only limited hopes from participation despite his sometimes hyperbolic talk about the availability of a third way of social and political development. As he wrote in the *Memoirs of Hope*, the "spiritual sickness resulting from a civilization dominated by materialism could not be cured by any form of government."[57]

De Gaulle concludes his speech by reminding his audience, "the *elite* of our modern youth," that "ideas lead the world."[58] De Gaulle quotes a poet who says that it is impossible to understand the plains without ascending to the "heights."[59] In his Oxford address, de Gaulle has ascended to the theoretical heights in order to address the crisis of civilization. De Gaulle was the rarest of statesmen because he was one of the most reflective. He knew that "ideas rule the world," that they have real causal efficacy. In his November 25, 1941 address, he calls for nothing less than the renewal or modernization of the common ideal of responsible individuality which, in his view, has been the key to the vitality of Western civilization.

In November of 1941 de Gaulle still hoped that a British and French alliance could forge a new European bloc, one allied to but genuinely independent of the Americans, and one maintaining cordial but tough-minded relations with the Soviet Union. He hoped that this new Europe, as he told Churchill, could give "primacy in world politics to a certain conception of man despite the progressive mechanization of society."[60] His sometimes violent disputes with Churchill whom he admired profoundly ("the great champion of a great enterprise and the great artist of a great history")[61] stemmed from his fear that Churchill was undermining the possibility of building an independent Europe, a genuinely powerful bloc of free European peoples which would shape the character of post–World War II international relations. He could not understand why Churchill, who had substantial national resources, an uncontested legitimacy and authority, as well as immense spiritual authority as leader of the Free World, did not more intransigently defend the interests of Britain and Europe, particularly near the end of the war. In his *War Memoirs*, de Gaulle criticized Churchill's failure to be more prickly, more intransigent, one might say more "Gaullist," in his relations with Roosevelt and the Americans.[62]

The November 25, 1941 speech at Oxford reveals important dimensions of de Gaulle's political and moral vision. That vision underwent no essential change between 1940 and 1970, although de Gaulle's attitude toward Britain was permanently affected by Churchill's choice for the primacy of the relationship with America and his distance from the project of building Europe. (He encouraged that project but kept Britain to the side as a friendly outsider and not an active participant. His eyes were always principally directed toward the United States and the Common-wealth and Empire). But as de Gaulle's speeches during a triumphant visit to Great Britain in April of 1960 reveal, he remained a profound admirer of British liberty and civilization, with its fusion of tradition, monarchy, and parliamentary government into a stable and coherent "framework of liberty."[63] In 1958, on returning to power, one of de Gaulle's first acts was to honor Churchill for his support of Free France and for his great deeds as a leader of the Free World during the final episodes of the Thirty Years' War. In 1960 de Gaulle, despite their previous disagreements, praised the "immortal glory" of Winston Churchill who was an inspiration not only for the British peoples but also for "many others,"[64] most notably de Gaulle himself. However, the important point to recognize is that from de Gaulle's point of view England's choice for subordination to America's leadership and unqualified hegemony necessarily meant a spiritual and political distancing, although not a break or schism, with de Gaulle's understanding of Europe and France.

To appreciate de Gaulle's thought and action more fully, we must understand the ways in which both heated conflict and genuine admiration characterized de Gaulle's action toward and evaluation of a great nation such as Great Britain. For de Gaulle, Britain and France belonged to Europe, a unitary civilization sharing high ideals and yet characterized by a national diversity that includes the "proud sizing up and rough interplay between bodies politic."[65] The Oxford speech shows that the proud and profoundly patriotic de Gaulle realized that one could not be a true patriot apart from being a partisan of civilization and "a certain conception of man."

Chapter 6

De Gaulle's Constitutional Correction: Executive Power and the Theory and Practice of Modern Republicanism

Our whole history is the alternation of the immense sorrows of a divided people, and the fruitful grandeur of a free nation grouped under the aegis of a strong state.
— Conclusion of the Speech at Bayeux

De Gaulle is not only the man of June 18, the trustee of the honor of France, but also the man of June 1958, the founder or legislator of a reconstituted republican regime or political order. His is, in fact, the most illustrative and successful example of a political founding within our time, perhaps of any time since the American Founding two centuries ago. His political founding or re-founding is the completion of his work begun in 1940. As the *War Memoirs* attest, de Gaulle always understood the establishment of a new, reformed republican regime and revitalized state to be the aim and crowning act of liberation and victory, the necessary condition for the "Salvation of France." This chapter examines de Gaulle's understanding of constitutionalism, particularly as delineated in his speech at Bayeux and secondarily as reflected in the Constitution of 1958. We will attempt to uncover the moral foundations of Gaullist constitutionalism and to relate de Gaulle's constitutional doctrine to various other liberal and republican reflections on constitutionalism and the requirements of free, energetic, and effective government.

In the final volume of his *War Memoirs*, de Gaulle displays his acute awareness of the various obstacles to the effective re-founding or reconstitution of France at the end of World War II, in the period immediately after the Liberation. The country had been materially and economically devastated, exhausted, and impoverished by the occupation and war. But accompanying the "physical devastation" was the even greater obstacle to her ultimate recovery which lay in the "moral depression" that seems to have gripped the French spirit.[1] De Gaulle discreetly but clearly suggests that this moral depression has its roots in that fundamental division that has crippled France since 1789—one opened up by her great but destructive Revolution. France's national unity had been torn apart by a great division within her national spirit; because of this continuing division no regime had been able to establish a true political and constitutional equilibrium after 1789. As François Furet well observed, with the Revolution, France found herself a new society but not a commonly accepted regime.[2] (De Gaulle also suggests that Napoleon Bonaparte's excessive or unmeasured efforts at European hegemony had fatally compromised France's borders and left her open to foreign attack and further humiliation.[3]) In sum, the weakness of the French state was a partial result of the enduring division between the Old Regime and the Revolution in the French psyche and political order and the legacy of revolutionary and imperial overreach.

The great moral-political task underlying the Gaullist constitutional project is to heal, through personal example, through a new political mystique or spirit, and through new institutions and a new Constitution, the spiritual and political divisions that perpetuated French weakness and doubts and that were the obstacles to the unity and grandeur of the nation. For a further clarification of this task, let us turn to an examination of the speech at Bayeux. We have already highlighted the central importance of this speech delivered about six months after de Gaulle's resignation as provisional president of the French Republic, ten months before his founding of the *Rally of the French People*, and twelve years before his return as Legislator of a new French Republic.

De Gaulle's choice of Bayeux as the location for a speech on the need for constitutional re-founding was no accident. He spoke on the second anniversary of his historic appearance in that city, the first in Normandy to be liberated by the Allies after D-Day and the first French city to acclaim de Gaulle and thereby to seal the legitimacy of his enterprise. According to de Gaulle, the events at Bayeux were the beginning not only of the victory and liberation of continental France but also of the rebirth of the legitimate and sovereign state. In the first part of the speech, de Gaulle reiterates the classic Gaullist themes on the character of an independent and self-respecting state. In the process he exaggerates, in a salutary manner, the independence of action then available to the French state:

It is here, also, on the soil of our ancestors, that the state was reborn! A legitimate state, since it was founded on the interests and the feelings of the nation; a state whose true sovereignty was born of war, liberty and victory, whilst servitude only had the appearance of it; a state upheld in its rights, its dignity and its authority in the midst of its vicissitudes of destitution and intrigues; a state saved from the interference of foreign powers; a state which was able to gather round itself again a united nation and a united Empire, to re-assemble all the forces of the country and of the French Union and to carry itself to final victory together with its allies, to treat as an equal with the other great nations of the world, to maintain public order, to mete out justice and finally to begin the reconstruction of the country.[4]

The choice of the Bayeux setting then links resistance with liberation and victory and true victory with the reconstitution of the state. De Gaulle notes that the work of liberation and victory had been "carried on outside the earlier pattern of government" since the old order had "ceased to be operative in the general turmoil."[5]

"Salvation" had to "come from another direction," from that moral elite which was the "conspiracy" of Free France.[6] This small vanguard, rallying above narrow feelings of party or class, dedicated to the recovery of France, eventually returned the entire French people, initially stunned and disoriented by defeat, to their better motives or selves. In de Gaulle's salutary account of events, the French had never really accepted defeat in their hearts and souls. The Vichy regime was illegitimate and came to be widely recognized as such because it had forsaken "the highest interests of the country."[7] At Bayeux, de Gaulle speaks in order to help shape a new constitutional order for a Fourth Republic. When the Constituent Assembly eventually put forward a Constitution in September of 1946 which repeated the fundamental errors of the Constitution of the Third Republic, de Gaulle spoke thunderously against it at Épinal on September 29, 1946.[8] From there it is only a short time until the creation of the anti-Fourth Republic, RPF.

In the first part of his speech, de Gaulle outlines the obstacles to the re-founding or revitalization of the state. De Gaulle highlights France's historic inability to find a universally recognized regime, the foreign threats that have plagued her for over a century, her immense partisan and ideological divisions and hatreds, and the rise in the post–world war of a new ideological and political division in Europe and the world, what Raymond Aron aptly named "the age of empires."[9] All of these helped make the revitalization of the state both a pressing necessity and an elementary requirement of civic morality.

In Chapter 1, we have already quoted de Gaulle's eloquent passage from the speech at Bayeux rejecting the "adventure" of dictatorship on both moral and practical grounds. A key discussion in the second to last chapter of the War Memoirs further illuminates de Gaulle's rejection of dictatorship. In the Memoirs de Gaulle freely admits that he exercised a "monarchy" or even a temporary "dictatorship" (in the sense of extralegal or extraconstitutional rule) after June of 1940.[10] De Gaulle then explains why he did not attempt to perpetuate his monarchy–dictatorship in the differing but nonetheless problem-ridden circumstances of post–Liberation France.

He knew that circumstances had changed and that a refusal to recognize this would condemn France to further upheavals and continuing divisions. During the war, he had repeatedly promised to restore full political choice through elections to the French people once the national emergency was over.

To what upheavals would I condemn France by claiming to impose my absolute authority officially and for an unlimited period, once the danger which had put it into my hands had vanished? During the conflict, my declarations had deliberately left no doubt as to my resolution to restore its power to the French people once events would permit elections. If my power had been increasingly recognized, it was to a large degree because of this commitment.[11]

This passage reveals the moral principle that undergirded de Gaulle's sense of his political "mission." He understood the untenability of a Machiavellian manipulation of the popular will. He recognized the moral foundation of any deeply rooted political legitimacy. His authority depended in large part on the reliability of his words and promises, on the integrity of his character, and on the sense that he represented a genuine common good. De Gaulle was fully aware that people would not recognize the legitimate reasons that would lie behind his continued despotism. Moreover, this choice would only redound to the advantage of the communists, the only cohesive and disciplined political force in post–Liberation France.

De Gaulle, as we have seen, fully appreciated the liberal and democratic character of modern political legitimacy. In a capital passage, de Gaulle explains why he, as a "champion of France," and not the spokesman for a class or party, could not rally the French people through dictatorship. Such a rally must occur in accord with and not in opposition to liberty.

Opposition would be all the more certain since, save in periods of public danger, there can be no such thing as a lasting dictatorship, unless a single faction, resolved to overpower the rest, supports it against all comers. As the champion of France rather than of any class or party, I incited hatred against no one and had no clientele who favored me in order to be favored in return.[12]

De Gaulle goes on to state that only a great "national ambition" for empire or genuine danger from abroad could justify dictatorship in the modern context. De Gaulle cites the example of the two Bonapartist empires. But damningly he asks, "Yet how had each of these Caesarian regimes ended?"[13] De Gaulle's choice is not that of Bonapartism. De Gaulle sees no principle of restraint operating within Bonapartist Caesarianism; it is prone, by definition, to go too far, to surpass reasonable and salutary political and moral limits.

De Gaulle's choice is for grandeur *within* liberty, for a revitalized republican order at home, and self-respect and grandeur accompanied by rejection of hegemonic pursuits abroad. In order to avoid the triple danger of either the self-destructive adventure of dictatorship, or Caesarian reaction to disorder or communist totalitarianism, de Gaulle proposed a comprehensive republican re-founding for France.

Despite abundant denunciations of the Bayeux address at the time of its delivery as antirepublican and Bonapartist, de Gaulle's constitutional doctrine is best viewed as a continuation but modification and correction of the Montesquieuan tradition of *liberal* constitutionalism. De Gaulle's speech is also a constitutionalist and political correction and redefinition of the French *republican* tradition with its overwhelming bias toward forms of legislative or parliamentary supremacy. The distinctive character of de Gaulle's constitutional doctrine is revealed in a central sentence from the address which links the doctrine of the separation of powers to the establishment of a fortified national executive. The executive both operates within the separation of powers and transcends it by guaranteeing the effective operations of the constitutional order and by representing and maintaining national sovereignty and independence. De Gaulle writes:

But all the principles and all experience show that legislative, executive and judicial power should be sharply divided and soundly balanced, and that above political contingencies there should be a national arbiter to give continuity to the different combinations.[14]

Let us try to unpack the meaning of this pregnant affirmation. One might begin by comparing this remark with the famous account of liberty made by Montesquieu in Book 11 of *The Spirit of the Laws*:

So that one cannot abuse power, power must check power by the arrangement of things. . . . Political liberty in a citizen is that tranquility of spirit which comes from the opinion each one has of his security, and in order for him to have this liberty the government must be such that one citizen cannot fear another citizen.

When legislative power is united with executive power in a single person or in a single body of the magistracy, there is no liberty, because one can fear that the same monarch or senate that makes tyrannical laws will execute them tyrannically.

Nor is there liberty if the power of judging is not separate from legislative power and from executive power.[15]

De Gaulle reaffirms an aspect of the Montesquieuan argument about political liberty and the separation of powers. He forthrightly affirms that "principles" (which in de Gaulle's writings usually suggests an articulation of the permanent or natural order of things) and experience (especially the experience of despotism) demand the sharp division and sound balancing of legislative, executive, and judicial power. On one important level, de Gaulle reaffirms liberal constitutionalism against the republic of the deputies or the sovereignty of the popular assembly so dear to the dominant currents of French republicanism. He does so both in the name of political liberty and, more importantly, in the name of effective government. De Gaulle knows that the reaffirmation of the liberal doctrine of the separation of powers necessarily entails the strengthening of executive power, both in its powers of autonomous or independent action and in its capacity to block or limit legislative initiative that "is not necessarily gifted with clairvoyance and complete serenity"[16] and that cannot represent the unity, cohesion, and capacity for collective action of the body politic. On one level, de Gaulle attempts to renew liberal constitutionalism within the French context by restoring executive energy and limiting the dangers of legislative tyranny and shortsightedness. But de Gaulle is not simply rearticulating or reformulating the Lockean notion of executive prerogative and the independent federative power in the realm of foreign affairs. Nor does he accept the Montesquieuan doctrine of an order of separated powers in which no unitary source of political command operates. In such a system, "necessity" forces the executive and legislative arms of government "to move, but still in concert."[17] In Montesquieu's constitutional doctrine, necessity replaces human deliberation as the ultimate mover and ruler of men. Decisions are finally driven by necessity because they *must* be made. Despite the reality of political contestation, decisions are finally made independently of the wills of the legislative and executive powers and their respective partisans. Montesquieu's constitutional doctrine neutralizes politics for the sake of individual liberty, for that "tranquility of minds" which is the modest end of his liberal politics.

Montesquieu also rejects legislative primacy. He sees the legislature's potential for political aggrandizement within a representative regime and acts to fortify the blocking or vetoing power of the executive. But as Book 19, Chapter 27 of *The Spirit of the Laws* attests, the executive as envisioned or described by Montesquieu is precisely a *partisan* executive supported by a sizable *party* within civil society and by no means a national "arbiter" who simultaneously operates within and guarantees the continuity of the constitutional order.[18]

Some ambiguity remains in de Gaulle's presentation of the relative weight of the "dignified" (ceremonial) and "efficient" (governing) dimensions of the executive in the operations of government. That ambiguity is reflected in both the Constitution of the Fifth Republic and its constitutional practice. The original Gaullist doctrine as revealed in the Bayeux address and reiterated in de Gaulle's testimony to the Constitutional Advisory Committee in August of 1958 suggests an executive with a more restrained involvement in the execution of day-to-day government than de Gaulle's own practice suggests.[19] The president as arbiter is supposed to represent the indivisible sovereignty and unity of France even as the politically and morally necessary separation of powers suggests the functional division of political powers and institutions. In a qualified sense, de Gaulle shares the first premise of representative liberalism (the liberalism of Thomas Hobbes and John Locke) which establishes both the indivisibility and popular origins of political sovereignty. The president, the protector or upholder of sovereignty, must be elected directly or indirectly by the people; he must be the nation's *representative*. It is hard to know if de Gaulle does so because of a profound commitment to democratic principles or because a viable constitution must be adapted to the requirements of modern times as he puts it in the concluding paragraph of the Bayeux address.[20] The Bayeux address, like the unamended original Constitution of the Fifth Republic, proposes the indirect election of the president of the Republic though "elected by a college which embodies Parliament, but with a wider scope and composed in such a way as to make of him President of the French Union as well as of the French Republic."[21] A controversial referendum amended Article 6 of the Fifth Republic's Constitution in 1962 in order to establish the direct election of the president.[22] In the *Memoirs of Hope*, de Gaulle explains that such a change was necessary in order to establish the full legitimacy and capacity for independent action of his successors who would not share his historical mission or "contract" with the French people.[23] De Gaulle wished to strengthen the legitimacy of the executive by establishing its undisputed republican and representative character. However, the president also transcends what one might call the circle of competing representations that characterizes a liberal representative regime. The president as arbiter represents the primordial and irreducible capacity for political action which liberal theory tends to ignore or replace and which liberal practice usually or typically reintroduces through the back door as an extraconstitutional exception, such as the prerogative power that Locke gave to his theoretically subordinated but often practically liberated or dominant executive. This is one aspect of the ambivalence of the modern executive brilliantly analyzed by Harvey C. Mansfield.[24] De Gaulle's notion of executive arbitration explicitly aims to correct the ambivalence of liberal constitutionalist theory and practice. The executive as arbiter is the locus of the possibility for political action characterized by the effective joining of deliberation and action. We will return to this theme later in the chapter.

In a famous discourse on the French Constitution at his ninth press conference as president of the Fifth Republic on January 31, 1964, de Gaulle discusses the two levels of presidential authority as conceived by Gaullist doctrine and as embodied in the Constitution. De Gaulle rejects any notion of executive diarchy but affirms the practical divergence between the premier as head of government, caretaker of political, parliamentary, economic, and administrative concerns and circumstances, and the president as arbiter of the national and political order. But he clearly states that

the indivisible authority of the State is entrusted completely to the President by the people who elected him, that there is no authority—either ministerial, civilian, military or judicial—which is not entrusted and maintained by him, finally that it is his duty to adjust the high office which is his own with those whose management he entrusts to others.[25]

For de Gaulle, the president is the only "man of the nation"[26]—the only political representative of the nation fully and unequivocally *responsible* for its destiny. This understanding is already implicit if presented in a less aggressive manner, one less likely to offend republican sensibilities, in the Bayeux address.

We have spoken at length about the place of the executive or the executive as arbiter in de Gaulle's constitutional doctrine. The independent legislature as representative of opinions, interests, "local" needs, and concerns—in a word of modern civil society—also plays an important role in de Gaulle's constitutional doctrine. But it by no means plays the central role that it plays in classical liberalism as the sole authoritative *representative* of civil society (Locke) or in the French republican tradition with its identification of republicanism with parliamentarianism, and with a single dominant assembly at that. In a manner reminiscent of Hegel's political philosophy, de Gaulle identifies the executive with the moral and political *universality* of the state, with the political community as a unity or whole, while the legislature entails the legitimate but necessarily fractured and partisan representation of particular or partial wills. One might say that according to de Gaulle legislative representation is necessary for the free and healthy functioning of civil society but that legislative representation barely touches upon, in fact it risks becoming a serious obstacle to, the effective organization and constitution of the state. De Gaulle's deemphasis of parliamentary authority led many critics to denounce the Constitution of the Fifth Republic as antirepublican. However, Gaullists such as Michel Debré vigorously and effectively countered that the end of an assembly regime would lead to more effective and more truly popular government.[27] Despite his downplaying of the dignity of legislative representation, de Gaulle recognized, however grudgingly, that democracy demanded the ability of civil society to attempt "to orientate public action and legislation"[28] according to its interests and needs. But that representation is but one element, limited and partial, within a political order and dynamic that must be subject to the president's political and constitutional arbitration.

The Bayeux address calls for the establishment of a bicameral legislature. The second chamber embodies a higher level of both representation and responsibility. It is elected and composed differently (by general and municipal councils) than the first and has the authority to publicly examine and amend the proposals of the first and more popular assembly as well as the right to put forward its own proposals. De Gaulle envisioned it representing local and regional interests (which have "inclinations and rights" too[29]) and the overseas territories attached to France through the French Union. (This need was fundamentally altered by the process of decolonization that had been effectively begun after de Gaulle's return to power in 1958.) De Gaulle, in accord with his cherished notions of participation and association as a means of correcting the regimentation and anomie of mass society, proposed the representation of corporate interests (social, economic, cultural, organizational) in the second chamber. Article 69 of the 1958 Constitution places such corporate representation not in the Senate but in an Economic and Social Council, established to give its opinion on bills, ordinances, and decrees at the government's request.

It is universally recognized that the Bayeux Constitution of 1958, as de Gaulle called it,[30] limited the power, influence, centrality, and role in governance of the legislative authority. The government, that is, the executive, was given a share in legislative power (the right to issue decrees) and the power to call for popular referenda, the president was given the authority to appoint the premier, the number of legislative committees was radically reduced, the legislature's role in determining the budget and economic policy was curtailed, and its members were barred from holding Cabinet positions in the government (so-called Parliament–Cabinet incompatibility).[31] The legislature still remained an important lawmaking body and a check on executive capriciousness or extremism. It was given the power (although circumscribed from that of previous French republican constitutions) to censure the premier and his government. In principle, the premier was to be responsible to Parliament, although appointed by the president of the Republic. In one reflection of the gap or tension between the theory and practice of the Constitution, de Gaulle began the practice of removing the premier from office. De Gaulle did all he could to limit both the practical and moral authority of the legislature. There were three underlying reasons behind the persistent distrust of the legislature in de Gaulle's thought and practice.

The first is the most obvious and has already been mentioned. De Gaulle and his collaborators in the formation of the Fifth Republic (Debré et al.) believed that the failure of French republicanism—reflected in France's ongoing search for a stable, recognized, and legitimate regime capable of governing—was essentially linked to the reality of parliamentary dominance. In this sense, de Gaulle's re-founding as outlined in the Bayeux address entails a liberal correction of republicanism, in the name of the separation of powers properly understood. Second, de Gaulle associated legislative dominance with party government and party governance with partisanship. He linked the collapse of the Third Republic to its excessive partisan and ideological sectarianism. He lamented the reconstitution of the party spirit after the Liberation and devotes some time in his *Memoirs* to a criticism of established political authorities (e.g., Blum, Herriot, and the leaders of the Christian Democratic MRP) who had faithfully rallied to the national cause during the great crisis but who returned with a vengeance to specifically partisan causes during peacetime.[32] De Gaulle saw party government as corrupting of civic spirit, as incompatible with effective governance, and as leading to a self-absorbed and oligarchic political process, one that can be only fraudulently representative. One can agree with most or all of de Gaulle's criticisms of the assembly regime and excessive partisanship while maintaining that his critique of partisanship goes too far in downplaying the necessary role of interests and parties in articulating and representing the will of civil society. De Gaulle sometimes spoke and acted as if the "national interest" was wholly distinct from the free play of sectional, individual, and partisan interests, as if the common good in a modern individualist society was a kind of platonic "Idea" that transcends the particularity of partisan wills.

De Gaulle, of course, had to accommodate himself to partisanship. He established something resembling a party in 1947, the so-called RPF, but he characteristically refused to recognize its partial (even if public-spirited) character. He stubbornly insisted on its character as a "rally" of *all* the French people (with the exception of the "separatists," i.e., the communists). In 1944 he legalized the old parties in part because he needed their support, but also because he genuinely, if halfheartedly, recognized that modern liberty was impossible without partisan contestation. This second reason leads us to the third.

For de Gaulle, legislative bodies are not and cannot be governing bodies. They lack the twin prerequisites of energetic, effective, and good government: a capacity *to act* (in the name of the unity and cohesion of the nation) and the capacity *to administer* a stable structure of state organization which helps provide a "little comfort, security and happiness" for the people while increasing the power and fraternity of the French nation.[33] While recognizing the *necessity* of a separation of powers, de Gaulle located governance in the dual foundation of executive energy and administrative competence and stability (hence, de Gaulle's pride in establishing a national school of administration, the *ENA*, the École Nationale d'Administration, which would become the backbone of the French administrative apparatus during both the Fourth and Fifth Republics and the source of a new French meritocracy-oligarchy). De Gaulle rightly discerned that the political unity of the nation needed to be institutionalized through executive authority if the continuity of a people and its capacity to act in the world were to be sustained. But he never sufficiently appreciated the partisan dimension of politics proper and the fact that the rally of the people or nation will only occur *in extremis*, during a national crisis. Citizens of modern democracies are necessarily as divided as they are united. And they are more properly individuals and consumers than citizens. De Gaulle never felt wholly comfortable with the "mediocrity" attendant to modern liberty, even as he recognized that the prudent framer of a constitutional order must "take the times as they are."

What of the judicial power which de Gaulle mentioned in his statement about the indispensability of the separation of powers? De Gaulle says nothing more about it, discussing neither the rationale behind it nor its institutional features. He shared Montesquieu's view that "power of judging" must be separated from executive or legislative control and made as "invisible and null"[34] as possible; that is, the law must not be an instrument of intimidation, a terrifying power used arbitrarily against citizens. But de Gaulle's concern in the Bayeux address clearly lies elsewhere: he wished to fortify the executive and reform or re-found French republicanism by definitively severing it from the parliamentary spirit. The Fifth Republic's Constitution established a Constitutional Council with the authority to judge the constitutionality of laws and to protect the basic rights of citizens. In 1971 the council extended its jurisdiction to the Preamble of the Constitution, with its obligatory references to the Declaration of the Rights of Man and Citizen of 1789 as well as the quite expansive list of rights reaffirmed in the Preamble of the Constitution of 1946.[35] France's turn toward judicial liberalism may very well represent an advance in the check on arbitrary power, but it also reflects the full modernization of French politics—a turn not so much toward Madisonian-style judicial review but rather toward judicial activism and much more exclusively rights-centered political discourse and practice. De Gaulle's concerns with an independent judiciary were less flamboyant and far less characterized by doctrinaire concerns with the ever-expanding rights of the individual.

Let us return to the presidency—de Gaulle's central and animating concern in this speech. De Gaulle treats the presidency in two central paragraphs of his address. He begins by reasserting the independence of the executive as a central requirement of the separation of powers properly understood.

It is obvious that the executive power cannot be dependent on a Parliament composed of two Chambers exercising legislative power unless we are prepared for a confusion of authority that would turn the Government into nothing more than an assembly of delegations.[36]

De Gaulle insists on the independent election of the president since a president dependent on legislative election would quickly lose authority and be unable to rule. He would be a mere delegate and instrument, an errand boy, of the truly sovereign body. This sovereign body is paradoxically incapable, because of its plurality, its representative features, and its partisan character, of embodying and acting for the nation as a whole.

How, then, can this unity, this cohesion and this discipline be maintained in the long run, if the executive power emanates from another authority with which it must balance, and if each member of the Government, which is collectively responsible to the entire nation, is only the representative of a single party.[37]

For this reason, de Gaulle insists that executive power must flow from "the head of state, placed above party feeling." The president will appoint the premier "who is to direct the policy and work of the government."[38] (See Article 20 of the 1958 Constitution: "The Government shall determine and direct the policy of the nation.")

Like the president under the 1958 Constitution, he is to share in broad, but partial, legislative and administrative powers to promulgate laws and decrees. He must preside over the Councils of the government. (See Article 9 of the 1958 Constitution.)[39] De Gaulle identifies the president's tasks with the maintenance of national "continuity," and he reiterates his central role as constitutional and political "arbiter." De Gaulle writes:

He must also act as arbiter over the heads of the Council in any political contingency, normally through the council or in moments of grave confusion by calling on the country to make its sovereign wishes known by means of elections.[40]

What precisely is the significance of de Gaulle's introduction of the theme of presidential arbitration? We have already presented some thoughts on this subject, but it is necessary to further delineate the central Gaullist idea that gained constitutional status in Article 5 of the 1958 Constitution. Whatever de Gaulle's final thoughts about the precise relation of power between the president and the premier and government, or whether his constitutional doctrine presupposes the possibility of so-called cohabitation (his public doctrine as opposed to his private thoughts and wishes seem to be compatible with the practice of cohabitation), de Gaulle never deviated from his repeated claim that the president stands largely outside of the quotidian political processes, that he transcends political contingencies in their narrow and specific sense. He represents the indivisible sovereignty, the primordial unity of the body politic, and he embodies that political element that acts to maintain transpartisan unity at home and to promote independence and grandeur in the larger world. He must guide and direct the nation, and he must have the power to free the nation from a potentially crippling political impasse through the power to dissolve the legislature.

Many see in de Gaulle's executive doctrine a residue of monarchism or an effort to synthesize French monarchical-Bonapartist and republican traditions. There is some truth to this insight: at an institutional and spiritual level, de Gaulle did hope to heal the inauspicious divide in the nation's consciousness opened up by the Revolution. But more fundamentally de Gaulle's correction of the French republican tradition's reduction of constitutional governance to a regime of the assembly represents a recognition and reflection of "the dialectic between the idea of representation and man's political condition."[41] De Gaulle brought out into the open what previous liberal and republican theoreticians and practitioners had left deliberately dangling in the dark, namely, the inability of a representative legislative power "to incarnate . . . the political unity" and "the greatness of the nation."[42] Majority consensus within a legislative body can certainly represent the well-being and the legitimate interests of civil society. But modern legislative bodies are representative without being genuinely deliberative; they cannot unite thought and action through a deliberation constitutionally designed to culminate in action. They are empowered to pass laws of varying degrees of generality, but they cannot carry out national "arbitration" or conduct foreign policy. Such tasks demand the most profound conjoining of deliberation with a capacity for quick and decisive action. Pierre Manent has best captured the distinctive qualities that forbid legislative governance and make possible and necessary a quasi-independent executive in our liberal regimes:

The immediate link between deliberation and action is a necessary condition for political action, and more generally for all human action. And since the unity of deliberation and action cannot reside in the legislative body, it will come forth in the executive power. One can truly deliberate only on what must be decided by oneself; one can decide wisely only on what one has oneself deliberated.[43]

De Gaulle also was attuned to the demands of political and national emergencies. Liberal regimes may be threatened by internal disorder and conflict, by tyrannical and totalitarian parties or movements (as in Weimar Germany in 1933 or potentially by the Communist party in France in de Gaulle's time), and by foreign threats (as happened to France in 1940). De Gaulle believed that liberal regimes must anticipate such contingencies by "constitutionalizing necessities," to use Harvey Mansfield's apt formulation.[44] De Gaulle affirms this central responsibility of the president: "On him devolves the duty, if the nation is in danger, of safeguarding national independence and the treaties concluded by France."[45]

Article 16 of the 1958 Constitution, which allows the president of the Republic to take whatever emergency measures are necessary to protect "the institutions of the Republic, the independence of the Nation, the integrity of its territory or the fulfillment of its international commitments," clearly incorporates de Gaulle's understanding. It would later provide an important means for de Gaulle to constitutionally respond to the putsch by renegade military elements in Algeria in April of 1961. (The state of emergency proclaimed by de Gaulle under Article 16 would last until September 29, 1961.) De Gaulle believed that the failure to anticipate potential crises and the absence of an embodiment of the political condition of France was a fundamental reason for the collapse of both the Third and Fourth Republics in 1940 and 1958.

Let us turn briefly to an excursus on the relationship between the constitutional doctrines of Charles de Gaulle and the great German political sociologist Max Weber. A parallel between their political thought, or at least their constitutional doctrines, has been suggested by such diverse authorities as Wolfgang Mommsen, Julien Freund, Raymond Aron, and Allan Bloom among others.[46] These two great political men were singularly concerned with the greatness of their nations and their capacity to act in the world. For this reason, both were intent on the establishment of rationalized political institutions that could preside over the "modernization" of their countries. Both were "national liberals" who disliked the disruptive role of local notables in a national legislature, who were concerned about maintaining the possibilities for independent selection of great leaders within a democratic process, and who believed that one must counter local and parliamentary particularism by establishing and constitutionally fortifying, in Max Weber's phrase, "a bearer of the principle of the unity of the Reich."[47] Bloom and Mommsen are right to suggest that the correction of German liberal parliamentarianism that Weber envisioned after 1918 ran broadly along the same lines as de Gaulle's constitutional re-founding in 1958. Weber, of course, did not desire anything remotely resembling the "correction" that 1933 afforded. But if we read Weber's specifically political writings, we see an inordinate emphasis on the dual themes of charismatic leadership (the Fuerher principle) and the power and culture-prestige of the German Reich. Charismatic leadership is a needed correction to the "iron cage" of soulless, bureaucratic domination. Weber's express concern for charismatic leadership and for the free display of the greatness of the nation on the world scene reflect his efforts, paradoxically, to moderate and constitutionalize some of Nietzsche's political and philosophical themes. However, there is nothing reminiscent of the Gaullist reflection on the ontological and political connections between liberty, grandeur, and measure. Weber's political moderation is philosophically ungrounded, and his philosophy of human action provides the most problematic moral foundation for a self-limiting, constitutional order.

Let us return to an examination of the text of the Bayeux address. De Gaulle begins the final paragraph of the speech by referring to Solon, the founder or legislator of democratic Athens. De Gaulle notes that Solon once had been asked, "What is the best form of constitution?" to which he replied, "First, tell me, for what people in what epoch."[48] De Gaulle proceeds to point out that his own proposed re-founding is for the French as *they are*, faced by difficult and dangerous times. De Gaulle does not have a choice of his times. His is necessarily a political founding within modernity, within democracy. He is not founding an abstract "best regime" according to the "nature" of man simply or a closed and cohesive classical city according to the requirements of ancient liberty.

De Gaulle, however, echoed classical foundings in evoking the sacred character of the unity of the *patrie*. In this sense, his is a "theological-political" founding, an at least partially "ancient" founding within modernity as Will Morrisey has suggested.[49] But de Gaulle knew that the effort to move too far beyond a primarily constitutional correction of modern politics supplemented by a statesmanship and hortatory rhetoric evoking the greatness of the nation would only lead to new national divisions, arouse the resistance of modern peoples, and force the choice for the destructive "adventure" of dictatorship. For this reason, de Gaulle's re-founding, despite its quasi-heroic rhetoric, is necessarily limited in scope and ambition. De Gaulle knew, for example, that he could do very little to transform the character or to reorient the souls of modern French democrats. He could elaborate a rhetoric of grandeur, which would call the French toward the heights; he could establish an executive that would be an institutional source for *rassemblement*; he could leave a rich literary record of his deeds and his own service to France. But he could not shape the young or reorient society toward a different model of social and economic organization. He must settle for democratic mediocrity and, like Sisyphus, fight the endless battle, in order to make some limited difference.

It is now widely recognized and accepted that, beginning in 1958, de Gaulle established the first truly legitimate political and constitutional order in postrevolutionary French history. His Constitution has adjusted relatively well to such political innovations as cohabitation between a president and premier of differing political affiliations. The Fifth Republic has seen the deideologization or banalization of French politics, with the increasing obsolescence of the communists and the collapse of any hard or neo-fascist Right. (Even Le Pen and the National Front, though reactionaries and ruffians, to be sure, do not advocate the jettisoning of France's democratic institutions. They have no alternative to de Gaulle's regime.) De Gaulle established what François Furet has called a "republic of the center" by reforming France's institutions and by creating a national mystique that transcended the fratricidal ideological division of Left and Right opened by the conflict between the Old Regime and the Revolution. This achievement was no historical accident. It was a self-conscious, deliberate act of statesmanship, as we have tried to establish throughout this book. We have finally seen the end of that French exceptionalism that made French politics the most interesting in Europe for over a century and a half.

Yet, for all of de Gaulle's success, it is arguably the case that the French are suffering from a profound malaise today. The nation is preoccupied with its economic difficulties, including record-level unemployment. While society gladly rejects the heroic burdens and demands of Gaullist grandeur, the nation cries out for a rearticulation of fundamental national purposes, that is, for statesmanship. The political class responds with the evocation of the inexorable "European" destiny of France but leaves that destiny vague and its relationship to distinctively national purposes largely undefined. The drift continues. Some have suggested that de Gaulle is largely and paradoxically responsible for the malaise of contemporary French society. It is said that his largely necessary institutional correction of French parliamentarianism went too far in consolidating a presidential monarchy and establishing an oligarchic, largely unresponsive, unrepresentative, and impenetrable executive-administrative state. This is the criticism of Jean-François Revel, for example.[50] He sees the French presidential state as the equally pathological antithesis of the old Italian system of parliamentary ungovernability, corruption, and irresponsibility. Clearly, this criticism is overdrawn. Whatever one thinks of the quasi-imperial styles of a Giscard or Mitterrand (somehow they were not "men of character" in the Gaullist sense), or however much one regrets the absence of an authentic tradition of local self-government in France, this system established by de Gaulle respects modern liberty in the context of a centuries-old administered state and society.

As our treatment in Chapter 2 of de Gaulle's analysis of the Old Regime made clear, de Gaulle believed that for the French liberty meant less an active participation in ruling themselves than being ruled by a regime that respected basic human liberties and where real checks originating from institutions and public opinion existed on governmental arbitrariness. Not all of the limitations of present-day French society or the failure of the present political class to exercise statesmanship can be blamed on faulty Gaullist foundations. De Gaulle himself recognized that a constitution is more than institutions. It needs a spirit or mystique. It needs virtue or character which constitutions cannot guarantee but can only allow by not inhibiting, as the Third or Fourth Republics clearly had. De Gaulle is a founder within modernity who knew that there could be no unproblematic solution to the problems of modern liberty or modern democracy: how does one make citizens out of self-seeking individuals and a self-absorbed civil society? How does one represent the whole in a regime that denies a common good? How does one represent the political condition of man in a time and in a regime that denies the palpable truth that men are political animals?

Chapter 7

The Unity of Europe and the Greatness of France: De Gaulle's Vision of a Europe of Nations

This chapter compares and contrasts the Gaullist vision of a "Europe des patries" with that of transnational European integration which has been the dominant understanding guiding the construction of a "united Europe" since the end of the Second World War. We examine the ways in which de Gaulle has been both a partisan of European unity and a critic of the dominant spirit informing the process of European integration. We argue that de Gaulle shows the need for Europe again to become the subject of philosophical speculation, moral vision, and a political action and statesmanship informed by such speculation, vision, and action. Moreover, he saw the project of constructing Europe as an opportunity for greatness in our time. He understood that a Europe that would live in continuity with its traditions and institutions and would maintain its soul, would have to be built by and through a *mystique*, the dedication to a great and transcendent goal, and not through *politique*, or a petty and purposeless politics of interest.

CONSTRUCTING EUROPE

We begin by sketching a brief outline of the European project and the philosophical underpinnings of that project. The making or building of a united Europe has been at the center of European political life since the end of the Second World War. The project of a united Europe was, no doubt, delayed by the exigencies of the Cold War, specifically, by the domination of Central and Eastern Europe by an imperial and totalitarian

enterprise after 1945. Nevertheless, the movement toward a more fundamental unity among independent, democratic European states coincided
with the maintenance of an Atlantic defense community, tying the United
States to the defense of the territorial integrity and political independence
of noncommunist Europe. The European "project" can probably be dated
from Sir Winston Churchill's famous Zurich speech of September 19, 1946,
where he called for the establishment of a United States of Europe,
centered around and cemented by Franco-German reconciliation, which
would become one of the main pillars of international political life along
with Russia, the United States, and Britain and its commonwealth.[1] A
series of decent and farseeing statesmen, associated mainly with Christian
democratic and "Atlanticist" political currents, such as Robert Schumann
in France, Alcide de Gasperi in Italy, and Konrad Adenauer in Germany,
propelled Europe forward by helping to create the infrastructure by which
a unified Europe and a more developed European political consciousness
might develop. They strove to build Europe "step by step," hoping to
weaken archaic nationalisms along the way.[2]

The European Coal and Steel Community (ECSC) was established in
1951, and after a failed effort to create a supranational European defense
force (the European Defense Community, or EDC) in 1953–1954, a customs union or Common Market was established by the Treaty of Rome in
1957. A European community dealing with the production and management of atomic energy was also formed (Eurotam). The original six continental West European democracies (Italy, the Benelux countries, France,
and the Federal Republic of Germany) that established the EEC in 1957
proceeded to build a supranational Europe. (De Gaulle we shall see, tried,
largely unsuccessfully, to reorient its character.) This community would
expand in the 1970s and 1980s, adding Denmark, Ireland, Britain, Norway,
Spain, and Greece as members. (In the 1990s the former communist
nations of East Central Europe would also begin knocking at the European
Community's door, wanting to share the identity of and join the process
called "Europe.")[3]

The Community would enter a second major phase toward European
integration or unity in the 1980s under the leadership of Jacques Delors,
the then president of the Brussels-based European Commission. In 1985
the European Community committed itself to the elimination of all trade
barriers remaining within the states comprising the EC. With the signing
of the Maastricht Treaty in February 1992, the states of the European
Community committed themselves to economic and monetary union to
be followed by the end of the decade by a more thoroughgoing political

integration characterized by the development of a common European policy on such fundamental questions as foreign affairs, defense, social policy, immigration, and justice. With Maastricht, the project of transnational European integration proceeds apace. Of course, it has run into all sorts of practical difficulties and obstacles, including conflicts of national interests, problems associated with economic and monetary integration, and disputes about the role of federalism and subsidiarity within the Community. But the vision of an integrated transnational Europe that slowly erodes and qualifies the sovereignty of the component states of the Community remains the guiding vision of European integration, at least in the eyes of Delors and his colleagues and successors in Brussels.

MONNET VERSUS DE GAULLE

The true "inspirer" of that union, as Charles de Gaulle called him, was the French businessman, diplomat, and administrator, Jean Monnet, who had played an outstanding role coordinating Allied trade and commercial policy during the two world wars.[4] The leading critic of the vision of an integrated, transnational European entity was de Gaulle himself. De Gaulle respected Monnet's intelligence, moral integrity, and political skills, but he believed that the architect of transnational Europe was an antipolitical utopian who wished to weaken the unity-in-diversity which was the source of the European genius itself. The inspirer of Europe, the visionary behind the ECSC, the EDC, and the EEC, responded, in turn, by denouncing de Gaulle's political ideas and vision of Europe as being thoroughly "obsolete." He believed that de Gaulle's emphasis on the centrality of the nation-state ignored the dangers inherent in the perpetuation of national sovereignties and indirectly contributed to the risk of the outbreak of new wars and another round of self-immolation in Europe.[5] Both de Gaulle and Monnet recognized the realities of cultural, commercial, and political interdependence in Europe, but they wished to shape that interdependence in fundamentally different and incompatible ways. De Gaulle was a critic of Monnet's vision of Europe, but he was a friend of the enterprise of building a "united" European community. De Gaulle was a good Frenchman and a "good European" as Nietzsche put it. He was a patriot and not a nationalist or an imperialist. While he most certainly believed in the continuing efficacy of the concept of the balance of power, one of the eternal and inalienable truths of the political universe, he was never attracted to German-inspired notions of "power politics." He was never afflicted by "atavistic attacks of fatherlandishness and soil addiction"[6] as Nietzsche so strikingly put it. His attachment to France and to Europe was both reasoned and passionate, avoiding the Scylla of utilitarian calculation and the Charybdis of mere rootedness, of racialist soil worship or nationalist xenophobia.

Some critics have not sufficiently appreciated de Gaulle as a "good European" because they mistake his rhetoric about, and statesmanship at the service of building Europe, as a mere cover for his partisanship for France. There is real truth in Harold Macmillan's remark in 1961 after his conference with de Gaulle at Birch Grove: He talks of Europe and means France.[7] But this view is not ample or generous enough. As we shall see, in de Gaulle's self-understanding, he was a partisan of Europe precisely because he was a partisan of France and her greatness.

For de Gaulle, the enduring realities of political life were the nation and the state. He believed that any realistic European confederation would have to be built on the firm realities of the nation-states. During his third press conference at the Elysée, dated September 5, 1960, de Gaulle clearly articulated his understanding of the centrality and solidity of the states as the building blocks of a more comprehensive European community:

The states are, in truth, certainly very different from one another, each of which has its own spirit, its own history, its own language, its own misfortunes, glories and ambitions; but these states are the only entities that have the right to order and the authority to act. To imagine that something can be built that would be effective for action and that would be approved by the peoples outside and above the states—this is a dream.[8]

De Gaulle had an understanding of Europe as a civilization composed of distinctive but complementary peoples, each with its own "spirit." These distinctive spirits could not be ignored without effacing the heterogeneity that enriched and gave vitality to the European spirit. For de Gaulle, Europe was a heterogeneous whole, a unity-in-diversity, and the various *patries* were the corporate expression of that diversity. But as with Montesquieu, the "spirit" of a people is the product not only of destiny and circumstances, of accident and geography, but, most importantly, also of politics and statesmanship. The spirit of a people, if it is to become a force in the world, that is, if it is to be truly efficacious, must be "exploited by politics."[9] The state is that entity which provides moral unity to a people and organically unites its past, present, and future into an enduring and dynamic whole. The state alone allows the sentimental attachments of the fatherland to be deepened and transformed into a national entity pursuing substantial political purposes. De Gaulle did not deny, as some have suggested, the growing reality of a supranational European "civil society," but he believed that that society, by itself, has neither the authority nor the capacity to act politically. It must be molded and exploited by politics even while one recognized that the irresistible movement toward interdependence and transnational civil society does not negate or eliminate the unavoidable reality, necessity, and moral dignity of the states.

During his press conference of May 15, 1962, following the Belgian and Dutch vetoes of the Fouchet Plan, a de Gaulle-inspired project for political as opposed to supranational integration of Europe, de Gaulle discussed his understanding of the necessarily political character of the effort to build Europe. He began by denying that he had ever spoken of a "Europe des patries," although he willingly identified himself with the spirit behind that notion. De Gaulle eloquently attested to his vision of a plural Europe:

I would like incidentally, since the opportunity has arisen, to point out to you, gentlemen of the press—and you are perhaps going to be very surprised by this—that I have never personally, in any of my statements, spoken of a Europe des patries, although it is always being claimed that I have done so. It is not, of course, that I am repudiating my own; quite the contrary, I am more attached to France than ever, and I do not believe that Europe can have any living reality if it does not include France and her Frenchmen, Germany and its Germans, Italy and its Italians, and so forth. Dante, Goethe, Chateaubriand belong to all Europe to the very extent that they were respectively and eminently Italian, German and French. They would not have served Europe very well if they had been stateless, or if they had thought and written in some kind of integrated Esperanto or Volapük.[10]

De Gaulle opposed an artificial, supranational process of European integration which he considered as lifeless, bloodless, and untenable as those languages such as Esperanto invented by well-intentioned but naive and stateless cosmopolitans. De Gaulle sees these three great European intelligences as indicative of the very meaning of what it means to be a good European. By being eminently Italian, German, and French, they embodied and enriched the spiritual and cultural heritage of Europe. They were precious manifestations of the same Western civilization, but they would not or could not have been themselves without the "determinative milieu"[11] from which they sprang. But by being genuine cosmopolitans and good Europeans, they shaped that determinative milieu by being spiritual "legislators" of their respective peoples. One must note that the references to Dante, Goethe, and Chateaubriand suggest a notion of the Europe that is historical, spiritual, cultural, and "poetic" as well as political and, secondarily, economic. De Gaulle eschewed what he perceived to be a narrow, soulless, technocratic understanding of common European inheritance.

De Gaulle continues in his May 15, 1962 press conference to reassert the primacy of the states as the "active, authoritative and responsible elements" that can build an enduring and substantial new Europe. The *patrie* is a "human and sentimental element," which must be guided by politics, by the architechtonic institutions, activities, principles, and mores associated with the state. De Gaulle asserts that

It is only the states that are valid, legitimate and capable of achievement. I have already said, and I repeat, that at the present time there cannot be any other Europe than a Europe of states, apart, of course, from myths, stories and parades. What is happening with regard to the Economic Community proves this every day, for it is the states, and only the states, that created this Economic Community, that furnished it with funds, that provided it with staff members; and it is the states that give it reality and efficiency, all the more so as it is impossible to take any far-reaching economic measure without committing a political action.[12]

Transnational Europe, the Europe inspired by Jean Monnet and other supranationalists, is a "myth, story and parade" for de Gaulle. De Gaulle did not oppose extranational technical "organisms" to deal with the common "technical" problem confronting the nations of the European Community. The various administrative boards and commissions dealing with trade and economic policy, coal and steel, atomic energy, and industrial and agricultural issues and policies could serve important common purposes. De Gaulle did not hesitate to affirm the Treaty of Rome and the institutions of the European Community after his return to power in 1958. But de Gaulle incessantly repeated that everything of importance, including important "technical questions" themselves, needs to be settled by the coordinated political action of states.

Monnet did not deny that European integration is not and cannot be a simply technical process, but he ultimately believed that the political action necessary to create a supranational Europe would lead to the obsolescence of national sovereignties and of politics itself in the specific and most ample sense of that term. Monnet was a partisan of a liberal, supranational European *administrative state*. The Fouchet Plan, with its outline of a "Union of States" and with its plan to have such a union directed by a council of the heads of states or government of the member nations of the Community, was an effort to derail the Monnet-inspired supranational integration in the direction of a Europe of states where national sovereignties coexisted with, and balanced, the emerging sovereignty of the European entity then in the process of creation.[13]

De Gaulle then firmly believed that European unity would come about as the result of *political integration*. But for European "unity" to be established there must be, in de Gaulle's word, a "federator" to establish a durable federation. The only candidates for the job of "federator" available in the post–World War II world were the totalitarian Soviet Union and the liberal but imperial and hegemonic United States. There had, of course, been federators available in the past such as Napoleon and Hitler,[14] both of whom illustrate the fact that not every federator wished to create a federation compatible with national and political liberties. Recognizing the absence of an external federator and the danger of a centralized and homogenized confederation, Europeans must gradually and deliberatively create their own federation with each state delegating a part of its sovereignty to a common confederal state. This was, de Gaulle said in December 1951, especially necessary in matters of economics, defense, and culture.[15] (Europe, we can see, must be built comprehensively from the bottom to the top, from the subpolitical to the transpolitical.) The European Federation de Gaulle envisioned would be much more than an invigorated League of Nations characterized by an effective system of collective security such as the "Covenant and Arms," a League of Nations with political will and armed might as envisioned by Churchill in the 1930s. It would be a genuine political community with the capacity and willingness to act as a unity and "personality" in the world. However, de Gaulle did not wish to efface or eliminate the essential characteristics of national sovereignty.

There is a tension in de Gaulle's espousal of both national and confederal sovereignty. Monnet's vision of an eventual undiluted supranational European sovereignty was undoubtedly more consistent than de Gaulle's support for a mixed system of conjoining national and confederal sovereignties. However, there is something disturbingly inhuman about the simplicity of Monnet's European vision. Monnet undoubtedly recognized the inexorable movement toward technological and commercial interdependence in the economically advanced parts of the world. He wished to encourage the functional and economic integration of free Europe in order that political sovereignties would be slowly but surely defanged and made effectually obsolete. Yet he misunderstood the complexity of human affairs: that technical interdependence of civil societies can coexist with the persistence of national passions and loyalties. De Gaulle, in contrast, recognized the complexity of European loyalties and reality, and the concomitant need to develop a genuine balance of power between emerg-

ing European institutions and consciousness and national sovereignties
and attachments. In the best and most humane sense of that term, de
Gaulle's European vision was conservative. He wished to conserve amidst
change and to adjust older institutions that had served the peoples of
Europe well to unfolding and inexorable social and historical forces and
realities.

EUROPE: THE NEED FOR POLITICAL INDEPENDENCE

For de Gaulle, the establishment of a united Europe was possible only if
Europe constituted "a political unity distinct from other entities."[16] In a
private note on the subject of Europe, dated July 17, 1961, de Gaulle
observes that Europe can become a genuine, corporate whole acting in
history, a "political personality" only if it has a "personality from the point
of view of defense. Defense is always at the base of politics."[17] He goes on
to argue that Europe cannot be a distinct political personality if it allows
itself to be either conquered *or* semipermanently protected by other political communities. The allusion to the dangers of both Soviet imperialism
and dependence on the power of the United States to deter that imperialism is quite apparent. De Gaulle continues by arguing that a continuation
of the then present state of things, namely the relative powerlessness of
Europe in relationship to the two superpowers, in regard to its own defense,
is incompatible with the "making" of Europe. "On the contrary, we are
blocking the making of ourselves."

De Gaulle continues by explicating what it would mean for Europe to
have "its personality in its own defense." To begin with, it is necessary for
Europeans to develop "plans" and "means" that are their own (this, as
France was developing her own nuclear deterrent, the "force de frappe").
The armed forces and the overall strategic direction of European defense
should not be under the control of non-Europeans (or of an American
"generalissimo" as de Gaulle rather snidely expressed it in the first chapter
of the *Memoirs of Hope*).[18] Despite his bitter disparagement of Atlanticism
from 1949 onward (and his accompanying and paradoxical support of the
Atlantic Charter, which he renewed on January 14, 1969 after the crushing
of the Prague Spring in Czechoslovakia), and despite his drive to construct
a Europe independent of American hegemony, in this private note de
Gaulle expresses his recognition that an independent, self-reliant Europe
would need allies. The natural ally, given its common civilizational roots

and the existence of a hostile, "totalitarian" Soviet Union, would be Europe's "cousin,"[19] the United States:

Certainly, it is natural and, in the world conjuncture, it is necessary that [Europe] has also some allies, that is, that it unites its defense to that of other countries who wish also to defend themselves against the same adversary, but who, to accomplish this, have their own direction, plan and means, also.[20]

But de Gaulle, who recognized the powerful place of egoism and will to power in the life of nations, knew that Europe could not rely on the United States to defend its independence and liberty. Even if this were possible, it would not be desirable since it would be incompatible with the maintenance of the political integrity and self-respect, the "personality" of Europe. Most importantly, if war were to break out in Europe, America would be able "to have the battle of Europe without disappearing. Europe cannot." Both self-respect and necessity demand that Europe take control of its political destiny by exercising control over its own defense which, as we have seen, is the base of political life and the effectual manifestation of the reality of sovereignty. For de Gaulle, a united, politically vigorous Europe would be an ally of, but not subservient to or dependent on, the United States.

Jean Lacouture and Raymond Aron, among others, are correct to argue that de Gaulle's project was in no essential sense anti-American, that he remained a friend and partisan of the "world of freedom" (he refused to use the term common in American parlance, *the free world*), and that he loyally carried out France's responsibilities to the Western world during the various Berlin crises of 1958, 1959, and 1961 and again during the Cuban missile crisis of 1962.[21] Undoubtedly, however, his withdrawal of France from the integrated NATO military command in stages between 1958 and 1966, his quasi-neutralist public rhetoric, and his opening to the East after 1965, with an accompanying rhetoric that at times suggested that the communist states had ceased in any meaningful sense to be communist at all, helped to undermine the solidarity of the Western alliance and served Moscow's stated goal of freeing Western Europe from American "influence." In his *Memoirs*, published in 1983, Raymond Aron, a committed Atlanticist and a measured critic of aspects of de Gaulle's foreign policy, has formulated an ambiguous and equitable judgment about de Gaulle's "great design" after 1958. On the one hand, he believed that, despite everything, de Gaulle understood the necessity of the Atlantic Alliance and of a continuing American commitment to Europe. He believed that de Gaulle had too great a sense of the Soviet Union's imperial ambitions and of the importance of sustaining a balance of power in Europe "to break with the United States and to push the Americans out of Europe."[22]

On the other hand, Aron delivers a harsh but accurate judgment about the consequences of de Gaulle's heated rhetoric and often immoderate efforts to distance Europe from reliance on American influence and power. Interestingly, the polemical rhetoric and anti-Americanism perceived in some of de Gaulle's speeches and symbolic actions are completely absent from his extremely measured private reflection of July 17, 1961. Here is Aron's second and harsher judgment about the public consequences of vulgarized Gaullism:

It was General de Gaulle who legitimated anti-Americanism. In moments of crisis, he demonstrated his solidarity with the West, but more often than not he represented France to be threatened equally by the two Great Powers. He attributed responsibility for the Six-Day War to American involvement in Vietnam. He gave the French the habit of seeing the wrong enemy, of taking the Soviet Union as an ally and the American Republic as a Great Power threatening French independence. Today, twelve years after the General's death, French diplomacy remains partially paralyzed by this inversion of roles, by a vision of the world that I consider contrary to reality.[23]

EUROPE: CIVILIZATION IN CRISIS

Let us return more precisely to the subject of Europe. De Gaulle believed that European unity was possible and natural because the European peoples formed a common "civilizational" whole. He writes in the chapter on "Europe" in the *Memoirs of Hope*:

I myself had always felt, and now more than ever, how much the nations which peopled it had in common. Being all of the same white race, with the same Christian origins and the same way of life, linked to one another since time immemorial by countless ties of thought, art, science, politics and trade, it was natural that they should come to form a whole, with its own character and organization in relation to the rest of the world.[24]

For de Gaulle, Europe is a culture and civilization as well as an increasingly interdependent economic and social community. De Gaulle's understanding of Europe differs from newer, more sociological and economistic definitions of Europe which emphasize common economic ties (a common market) and the interdependence of its civil society. De Gaulle integrates the old and the new, tradition and modernity, into his account of the meaning of Europe. But at its core, Europe is a common civilization, inseparable from its Christian origins. It is, in a certain sense, civilization itself, the civilization that allows "all the inhabitants of the earth" to recognize the "same high principles and [to be] clothed in the same dignity."[25] But for de Gaulle, as we have discussed in Chapter 5, this civilization and its Christian heritage are witnessing and experiencing a crisis of grave severity. According to de Gaulle, Europe, and more generally the West and the modern world, are plagued by the death of God and by a concomitant crisis of authority, the weakening of belief in all gods and values, which has paved the way for ersatz religions and totalitarian neo-pagan collectivisms. But the free world, too, is plagued by the weakening of genuine human individuality and institutions of moral and political authority. In his prewar *The Edge of the Sword*, de Gaulle writes about the collectivization and standardization of modern life, which is both symptom and cause of the present civilizational crisis:

Individualism is out of favor, and everywhere the claims of collectivism are being pushed to the forefront. . . . From Sydney to San Francisco, taking in Paris on the way, clothes are being cut to the same pattern. Even faces are beginning to have an uncanny resemblance to one another. Without, perhaps going so far as to agree with M. Maeterlinck that humanity is reverting to the conditions of the ant heap, we cannot help but realize that it is up in arms against individualism and independence.[26]

THE POLITICS OF GRANDEUR

One way in which the sterilizing homogeneity of modern mass society can be overcome is by reasserting the distinctive characters, milieus, traditions, and spirits of the particular peoples of Europe, the peoples who predate the democratic movement and the homogenization of individual and national faces and souls. Europe cannot be great unless it is a plural Europe, a unity-in-diversity, and Europe, as with individuals and nations, can be nothing without greatness. The modern movement, the movement for democratic liberties and individual social security, but also of a dehumanizing mass, technological society, that is, the movement of mediocrity, of leveling, must be countered by a politics and statesmanship of grandeur. This statesmanship will not negate or actively oppose the democratic movement of modern times, but it will attempt to moderate, humanize, and elevate it. It will accept the pediment of democratic justice and legitimacy, but it will enlarge and vitalize the modern and democratic emphasis of "liberty, equality and fraternity" with a reinvigorated traditional and aristocratic understanding of the importance of "honneur et patrie." (De Gaulle's Free French movement used both mottoes as rallying cries.)[27] As de Gaulle wrote about the circumstances surrounding his ascension to power in June of 1958, "(I)t was in a time which on all sides was drawn towards mediocrity that I must bid for grandeur."[28]

As is clear from our previous discussions, grandeur (greatness) is an ambiguous and elusive term that de Gaulle never precisely defined. But its connotations and characteristics are not all that difficult to comprehend. As Ghita Ionesco has written:

Its analogous, if not synonymous meanings are legion: greatness, height, power, rank, prestige, nobility, dignity, esteem, respect, authority, reliance, honor, magnanimity, generosity, charisma, perhaps even uniqueness. However different they may sound separately, most of them can be jumbled together into the patchwork of *grandeur*.[29]

For de Gaulle the greatness of Europe must be built on the actions of great and free and ancient peoples. De Gaulle, following Péguy, believed that there were "elected" peoples and nations (it is not so clear if that election comes from Providence, nature, destiny, or some process of self-selection of a combination of some or all of these factors) who are mysteriously destined to play a special role in the political life of nations.[30] France was such an elected people and nation, according to de Gaulle. In Volume II of his *War Memoirs*, in the section discussing and criticizing the Yalta Agreement, de Gaulle links the absence of France to the laceration of Central Europe, to the enforced communization of states such as Poland with the shameful complicity of Roosevelt and a weak and unprotesting Churchill.[31] The weakness of France meant the weakness of all the ancient, dignified, and "great" peoples of Europe. De Gaulle would often assert, "There is a pact twenty centuries old between the grandeur of France and the liberty of others."[32] Service to France and her greatness was a form of service to the liberty and greatness of Europe and the human race. To be French, and more importantly to be a servant of this greatness, to be de Gaulle, was for him to be a participant in a drama of world historical importance and significance.

With these observations in mind, it can be seen that, in de Gaulle's eyes, his "Appeal" of June 18, 1940, asserting that "Whatever happens, the flame of French Resistance must not and shall not die,"[33] was an act of European as well as French affirmation and patriotism. De Gaulle's intransigent defense of the honor, integrity, and indivisibility of the French nation and its sovereignty was not the act of an embittered nationalist or xenophobe but the moral affirmation by a good European of a free Europe and a free France. Throughout the war, de Gaulle appealed to the patriotic examples and inspirations of Joan of Arc, Danton, and Clemenceau. What these three remarkably different statesmen-heroes, Catholic saint, Jacobin revolutionary, and bourgeois and anticlerical writer, statesman, and war leader, had in common was their refusal to surrender the principles or ideals that they associated with their beloved *patrie*. Like de Gaulle, their very "*raison d'être* [was] honor, without compromise, in the service"[34] of France. The very democratic patrician, Franklin Roosevelt, could only see in de Gaulle's appeal to such intransigent French patriots the marks of an intolerable megalomaniac. Churchill, in contrast, for all his differences with de Gaulle, saw in him the indomitable representative of everything that the word "France" represents. The more heroic and aristocratic Churchill saw in de Gaulle's intransigent defense of French sovereignty the defining characteristics of a "good European." Roosevelt saw only an anachronism and an incipient despot.[35]

THE PROBLEM OF COMMUNISM AND DE GAULLE'S "PLAN" FOR EUROPE

De Gaulle's defense of a Europe of nations and states and his understanding of the special place for the greatness of France within Europe does not date only from the period of his presidency. In the third volume of his *War Memoirs*, de Gaulle writes of his "plan" for a reinvigorated Europe, which "could find equilibrium and peace only by an association among Slavs, Germans, Gauls, and Latins."[36]

De Gaulle's "image of Europe" was an image of an association of great, free, and ancient peoples and nations. De Gaulle had understood the fact that the "momentarily tyrannical and aggrandizing"[37] character of the Soviet Union would delay the construction of such a European association. In the long run, however, de Gaulle believed that communism was bound to collapse because it violated the deepest wellsprings of human nature and because it could not resist the national aspirations of those peoples who were victims of its aggrandizements. Communism was "antinatural" in that it contradicted two inalienable impulses rooted in human nature itself: the desire to be free and the wish to improve one's lot.[38] De Gaulle believes that the communists could continue "to impose on their peoples a system which is contrary to human nature, or to make those corrections in that system which are, little by little, being demanded by the rise of new elites and by the silent pressure of the masses."[39]

The second course of action was by far the more likely, de Gaulle believed, because of the "natural" character of both national ambitions and of the impulses that were stifled by communist totalitarianism. De Gaulle sometimes succumbed to a reductionist vision of revolutionary ideology. "The banner of ideology in reality covers only ambitions. And I believe that it has been thus since the world was born." [40] De Gaulle did recognize the ideological character of the Soviet Union, and he never ceased calling that regime "totalitarian." He never shared the anti-anticommunism of a large part of the European intellectual Left. But he finally did not take ideology seriously as a source of human inspiration or as an explanation of political and diplomatic conduct. De Gaulle was and is, no doubt, correct that national sentiments and impulses are far more resilient than the utopian elements of revolutionary ideologies. But his tendency to reduce ideological claims to some underlying and determinative national sentiments and ambitions led to serious misjudgments about the intentions and character of the Soviet leadership and regime. He misunderstood the partially ideological inspiration of Stalin's cruel tyranny and believed him to be a cruel and pitiless tsar who shared the imperialist dreams of Mother Russia. De Gaulle never underestimated the totalitarian character of Stalin's regime, but he saw him finally as a perverse embodiment of the dreams of a half-civilized imperial people.[41] Similarly, he failed to appreciate the extent to which East European communist leaders such as Wladyslaw Gomulka and Nicolae Ceausescu remained communist ideologues with no sympathy for de Gaulle's dream for an independent Europe of free nations from "the Atlantic to the Urals." During de Gaulle's visit to Poland in September 1967, President Gomulka of Poland flatly responded to de Gaulle's presentation of his European vision by stating that he was quite happy with Poland's alliance with the Soviet Union.[42] In the case of Romania, de Gaulle failed to appreciate the tactical and temporary character of Ceausescu's "liberalism" and his "opening" to the West as well as the totalitarian character of his nationalism. He also vastly underestimated the sheer viciousness and criminality of the man and his regime. De Gaulle was right to anticipate the ultimate failure of the totalitarian project, but he was wrong to identify a future outcome with present realities and even to partially confuse an oppressive party-state with a reemerging civil society or with underlying national sentiments. He misjudged the nature of the "whole" within which he was operating. De Gaulle's pursuit of détente entailed cozying up to communist tyrants, and it arguably helped delay the self-emancipation of civil society in the East of Europe. Those, such as Regis Débray, who argue that the collapse of communism has vindicated de

Gaulle's relative abstraction from ideology in the 1960s, and who mock the "obsession" of principled anticommunists with a Soviet "threat," are morally obtuse and are deaf to the self-understanding of the communist episode on the part of those who experienced it.[43]

Emblematic of de Gaulle's misjudgment about realities in the East was his oft-stated identification of "Russia" and the "Soviet Union." De Gaulle seemed to ignore the ways, emphasized with great clarity by figures as diverse as Alexander Solzhenitsyn and Boris Yeltsin, in which communism mutilated the national spirit and traditions of Russia and pursued policies inimical to its "national interests." True Russian patriots were never beguiled by the artificial and crudely propagandistic "Great Soviet Patriotism" put forward to satisfy the masses by a corrupt party oligarchy.[44] De Gaulle fully appreciated the ways in which communist totalitarianism stifled national ambitions in Eastern and Central Europe, but he failed to apply this logic to the case of Russia itself. He failed to carefully differentiate Russia and the Soviet Union and to understand the ways in which the authentic Russian spirit and national ambitions were undermined by the ambitions of a Leninist party and ideology. Regardless of de Gaulle's inability to understand the relations between ideology and national interest in the Soviet Union, it is nonetheless true that de Gaulle recognized that an association of European peoples from the "Atlantic to the Urals" could not arise without the eventual and effectual decommunization of the Soviet Union and the "lowering of the Iron Curtain." He insisted that his call for an association of European peoples, including the Slavs, was not a description of the possibilities of a *full* accommodation or détente with the communist regimes of the East but an "anticipation of the future resurrection" of the vitality and the political energies of a Europe lacerated and nearly mutilated by the Thirty Years' War of 1914–1945 and by the subsequent hegemony of the two peripheral continent-states after 1945. However, his hope for an accommodation with "Russia" in the 1960s sometimes belies this understanding and reveals a "contradiction" at the heart of de Gaulle's "grand design."

A full examination of de Gaulle's European "plan" would necessarily involve a study of his changing views on the German question, his early efforts to prevent the reconstitution of a unitary German "Reich," and his later acceptance and reconciliation with the Federal Republic of Germany, culminating in the Franco-German Treaty of 1963 and the great requiem mass attended by de Gaulle and Adenauer on the occasion of the signing of that treaty.[45] De Gaulle's reconciliation with a free, Western-oriented, and European Germany may have been his greatest and most enduring act of statesmanship. The territorial, political, economic, and ideological conflicts between France and Germany had been at the center of Europe's travails for nearly two centuries. De Gaulle did what Churchill had recommended in his Zurich speech: he established a firm and full partnership with the Federal Republic of Germany and allowed France to "recover the moral leadership of Europe."[46] One would also need to chronicle the complex relationship with Britain, and things British, de Gaulle's admiration for British liberties, his quarrels with, but underlying gratitude and immense admiration for, Churchill, his fears that Britain's friendship with the United States would result in an "Anglo-Saxon hegemony" in Europe, and his subsequent vetoes of British application for membership in the European Community.[47] Let us make this provisional observation: all of de Gaulle's actions, from his qualified support for détente with the East, to his reconciliation with Germany and his opposition to British membership in the European Economic Community in the 1960s, were guided by to his efforts to construct a new Europe of nations. In this new Europe, France and other free peoples would restore the self-respect and independent status of Europe as a spiritual, cultural, political, and economic force in the world.

His "plan" was already formulated at the time of the "Appeal," and it guided his statecraft from 1940 until his resignation as president of France in April of 1969.

DE GAULLE AND EUROPEAN "REALITIES"

It is often said that this concern for the greatness and rank of France was an anachronism that ignored the objective situation of a middle-range power such as France in a diplomatic system that was both bipolar and global. It is claimed that de Gaulle obtusely ignored the growing interdependence and depoliticization of European and even global society. This is precisely the position adopted by Ghita Ionesco in his fascinating, erudite, and opinionated book, *Leadership in an Interdependent World*. Let us examine Ionesco's book, which is the most thoughtful and sympathetic argument for the "anachronistic" character of de Gaulle's European vision and policy. Ionesco believes that contemporary global interdependence is the meeting point of several processes: the microelectronic and communication revolutions of the twentieth century, the debilitation of the Marxist-Leninist ideologies and regimes, and the principal political, social, cultural, and economic activities of our time, which are informed by the global information revolution.[48] Ionesco follows Jean Monnet, the architect of the European Community and the theoretician of European supranationalism, in asserting the relative obsolescence of national sovereignty in a Europe that has become an increasingly homogeneous, economically interdependent entity and is part of a larger global process of interdependence and modernization. Ionesco believes that the processes of global interdependence cannot be stopped by any human will, least of all by a traditional or historically minded statesmanship. Prudently managing the inevitable relativization of such "proud concepts as state, sovereignty and, yes, power itself" becomes the task of statesmanship in our time.[49] The fall of communism, the last fundamental obstacle to a world of liberal interdependence, according to Ionesco, is the great opportunity for and vindication of the Monnet-European project. Ionesco expresses profound admiration but also frustration and a fair degree of condescension toward the two European statesmen of our time who have been the most articulate and thoughtful partisans of national sovereignty and critics of the project for supranational European unity, Charles de Gaulle and Margaret Thatcher.[50] Ionesco faults de Gaulle for rarely referring to society at all in his writings and discourses. A critic of the student movement and of the extremism of the thought and practice of 1968, Ionesco nonetheless sees a large element of truth in the claims of Michel Crozier and Alain Touraine that the events of May 1968 were largely the consequences of a blocked or stalled society that resulted from the modernization of France.[51] De Gaulle had encouraged and understood this modernization in strictly political terms, as alleviating the class struggle and political divisions and increasing the relative international standing of France. Ionesco renews a Comtean or Saint-Simonian vision of modernity as a social order where the knowledge of scientists and producers has replaced the proud leadership of statesmen and generals. In Ionesco's historicist framework, de Gaulle is a noble and anachronistic embodiment of a political world that predates advanced, interdependent modernity.

According to Ionesco, contemporary French society prefers the enjoyments of consumer society, the accoutrements of American modernity such as Coca Cola and rock and roll, to the burdens of a politics of grandeur. About this matter, Ionesco is undoubtedly right. The French reject de Gaulle's obsession with the independence and rank of France. His intransigent defense of French sovereignty in 1940 undoubtedly saved France from generations of self-doubt and self-disgust and helped to restore France to her place in the family of free nations. It surely served the cause of Western liberty against totalitarianism during the Berlin crises and the Cuban missile crisis of 1962. But his deeply political perspective finally has no contemporary or enduring relevance. "His memory seems to haunt now more frequently the otherwise contented French people."[52]

Ionesco, like Georges Pompidou, de Gaulle's prime minister and his successor as president, compares de Gaulle to Philepomenon of Megapolis.[53] Philepomenon was an ambitious Greek military leader and statesman who led the Achean League, "the last bastion of Greek civilization before it was swamped by the inevitable advance of the legions of the Roman Republic."[54] Despite his efforts, the League succumbed to the Roman assaults, and Philepomenon was finally defeated in battle and lost his life. Fully aware of the wholly different circumstances facing these two heroic statesmen, Ionesco nonetheless applies Polybius's critique of Philepomenon to de Gaulle. Polybius believed that Philepomenon had exaggerated the irreversibility of Greek civilization because it had reached such unparalleled heights. Ionesco, though admiring de Gaulle's very real moral and political accomplishments, also laments his failure to appreciate and accept the inevitable globalization of human customs and the full implications of the modernization of French domestic life, which his statesmanship was ultimately powerless to resist. In a word, Ionesco believes that the transformation of France from a nation into a society, "into a human association which is simply useful, without any proper character, purpose, or end,"[55] is both inevitable and, on balance, morally estimable. De Gaulle differs from Ionesco not in his failure to appreciate the globalization of human customs but rather in his conviction that such a process of standardization ought to be moderated by a statesmanship that resists those forces of dispersal, as he called them, those forces of individualism and purposeless association that would not only prevent France from being herself but also ultimately undermine the preconditions of any vigorous civil society.

De Gaulle also believed that the supranational European project defended by Ionesco lacked any adequate political reference point. Transnationalism assumes that politics can arise semi-spontaneously out of the dynamic interactions of an interdependent global and European society. But the nation could not be replaced without some of its most valuable and distinctive attributes and functions being lost.

Ionesco intelligently discusses de Gaulle's profound indebtedness to the Catholic poet and philosopher Charles Péguy.[56] Péguy was convinced that the nation embodied the sacredness distinctive to political life, which the modern world ignored precisely by replacing the pagan and Christian "cities" and their dedication to higher spiritual goods with a merely bourgeois society grounded in the free play of interests and individual self-assertion. Like de Gaulle, Péguy was a patriot of eternal France, that France which transcended what he regarded as the relatively superficial distinction among regimes. He identified France neither with the Old Regime nor with the work of 1789. Péguy criticized those who believed either that all was darkness before January 1, 1789, and then electricity appeared, or that satanic destruction unfolded as in the Right's counter-revolutionary but equally partisan historical vision. He believed that the nation embodied that communion which made a free people a genuinely corporate entity. The nation, its form, its history, its culture, and its struggles, gave, to quote Pierre Manent,

a concrete content—a "carnal" one, to borrow a term used with much effect by a poet and thinker greatly admired by de Gaulle, Charles Péguy—to the democratic abstraction of the sovereignty of the people and the general will: it is *this* people which wants to govern itself, to be represented by a parliament elected by all the citizens, etc.[57]

Péguy feared the simultaneous "de-republicanization" and "de-Christiani-zation" of France. He feared the loss of the mystique of Christian France, of monarchical France, of even revolutionary France, with its heroic defense of the French nation and its doctrine of the rights of man, into the politique of a nation transformed into a civil society or an association. Péguy helped provide the poetic and spiritual inspiration for de Gaulle's identification of the mystique of the nation with the transpartisan politics of *rassemblement*, of the rally or unity of the people through dedication to the greatness and rank of eternal France. Modern bourgeois liberalism, the political and ideological divisions stemming from the French Revolution, and the standardization and collectivization of modern customs and prac-tices—all suggested to de Gaulle the need for a statesmanship that, as he told Malraux, cries out to herself and the world that France exists. This statesmanship is not simply reactionary, quixotic, or eccentric. It is a mystique based on the deepest reflections about the nature of modernity, France and her history, and the theological or mystical or "carnal" precon-ditions of political life itself. In the words of the famous first paragraph of his *Mémoires de Guerre*, de Gaulle writes that his "certain idea of France" is inspired by both sentiment and reason. It is a mystique grounded on historical sentiments and memories, but supported and buttressed by ra-tional reflection.

Unlike Ionesco, de Gaulle does not believe that there can be a united Europe that is more than a common market unless it is a confederal Europe built on the great historical nations and states of Europe. Europe itself must be a political and not just a social and economic project. Supranationalism is an untenable halfway house between a unitary European political community and a confederal union of European states. Supranational unity evades the decisive and ultimately unavoidable question of where sovereignty lies, even as it contributes to the depoliticization and homogenization of European peoples.

The political question remains: where does this ultimate authority to decide the most important questions that affect the destiny of the nation reside? Who decides the very criteria of citizenship? Who has the power to make peace and war? What are the precise boundaries of the community? If these defining marks of sovereignty do not lie with the state or nation-state, then they must in principle lie with some other body of authority. Without reaffirming Carl Schmitt's dialectic of friend and enemy as the defining feature of political life, de Gaulle recognizes the indispensable centrality of the question of territoriality and boundaries to political life itself.[58] To evade this question is to abandon one's responsibility as a member of a civic community that exists in a framework of both time and space and is larger, and one might say deeper, than any mere association of individuals.

De Gaulle was a partisan, then, of a confederal Europe, of a *Europe des patries*. Yet he did not have full confidence that his plan to help remake Europe according to his image of nations would succeed. At the end of his life, weary because the French had broken their contract with him, de Gaulle expressed to Malraux the pessimistic sentiment that he was witnessing the end of Europe, the end of an independent, political, Christian Europe of great nations. He feared the death through exhaustion and enervation of Europe as a civilization. In *Felled Oaks*, Malraux reproduces de Gaulle's beautiful and pathetic lament:

France was the soul of Christianity—today, let us say, the soul of European civilization. I did all I could to restore her. . . . Good luck to this federation without a federator! . . . You know as well as I do that Europe will be a compact among the States, or nothing. Therefore, nothing. We are the last Europeans in Europe, which was Christianity. A tattered Europe, but it did exist. The Europe whose nations hated one another had more reality than the Europe of today. It is no longer a matter of wondering whether France will make Europe, it is a matter of understanding that she is threatened with death through the death of Europe.[59]

De Gaulle had real forebodings about the health and political vitality of the European peoples. The death of God hangs like an ominous shadow over the materialistic and hedonistic pursuits of our commercial societies.

The crisis of our civilization, the crisis of gods and values, of credible authority, persists unabated. De Gaulle acutely felt the depoliticization of Europeans, evidenced by the decline of European statesmanship and by the inattention of the European political class to the political preconditions, the constitutional dimensions, and the military "base," as he called it, of European unity. For de Gaulle, Europe was a worthy and humanizing project only if Europeans recognized that it was not the ultimate project, only if they affirmed its political character and the continuing need to maintain, and if need be, to exercise the sword.

It is striking how relatively absent de Gaulle's voice is from the present European conversation. Of course, partisans of national integrity and sovereignty still appeal to de Gaulle. He is an important and penetrating critic of the economistic European project. But his partisanship for the greatness of Europe and a Europe of nations does not seriously inspire our contemporaries. Despite his protestations, perhaps it should be seen as a partially reactionary or premodern vision substantially in tension with the anticivic, commercial, and utilitarian character of modern times. The very great de Gaulle was undoubtedly right to believe that Europeans do not aspire to greatness, that they do not have substantial *national ambitions*. In the end, he told Malraux, "I entertained them with flags."[60] Nonetheless, de Gaulle himself, and his vision of a Europe of nations, stand as permanent reminders of the political and even spiritual qualities without which any future Europe could only call itself impoverished.

Notes

CHAPTER 1

1. Andrew Shennan, *De Gaulle* (New York: Longman, 1993), p. viii.

2. Ibid.

3. This work originally appeared in French in three volumes between 1984 and 1986. It was released as two volumes in English, the second and third volumes *The Politician* and *The Sovereign* being abridged into a single volume entitled *The Ruler*. The English-language editions appeared as Jean Lacouture, *De Gaulle: The Rebel 1890–1944* (New York: W. W. Norton, 1990) and *De Gaulle: The Ruler 1945–1970* (New York: W. W. Norton, 1991).

4. See note 1.

5. Daniel Chirot, *Modern Tyrants* (New York: Free Press, 1994), p. 418.

6. Charles de Gaulle, Press Conference of May 19, 1958 in *L'ésprit de la Ve République: Mémoires d'espoir suivi d'un choix d'Allocutions et messages 1946–1969* (Paris: Plon, 1994). See p. 610. For an English-language text, see *Major Addresses, Statements and Press Conferences of General Charles de Gaulle: May 19, 1958–January 31, 1964* (New York: French Embassy, Press and Information Division), p. 6.

7. Quoted in Lacouture, *The Ruler*, p. 482.

8. Quoted in Nora Beloff, "Enigma" in F. Roy Willis, ed., *De Gaulle: Anachronism, Realist or Prophet?* (New York: Holt, Rinehart and Winston, 1967), p. 110.

9. John Weightman, "Fatal Attraction," *The New York Review of Books*, February 11, 1993, p. 12.

10. Charles de Gaulle, *The Edge of the Sword* (New York: Criterion, 1960). The French edition can be found in a convenient one-volume edition of de

Gaulle's prewar writings entitled *Le Fil de l'épée et autres écrits* (Paris: Plon, 1990), pp. 141–225.

11. Charles de Gaulle, *Vers l'armée de métier* can also be found in *Le Fil de l'épée et autres écrits*, pp. 227–326. The English-language edition is entitled *The Army of the Future* (Philadelphia: Lippincott, 1941).

12. De Gaulle's most open and emphatic rejection of a Nietzschean philosophy of the will is *La Discorde chez l'ennemi* in *Le Fil de l'épée et autres écrits*, pp. 7–140. Remarkably, this work has never been translated into English. De Gaulle's *La France et son armée* can also be found in *Le Fil de l'épée et autres écrits*, pp. 327–500. This little known work, though never published in the United States, was published in England at the end of the Second World War in an inadequate translation that is little more than an effort at elegant paraphrase. See de Gaulle, *France and Her Army* (London: Hutchinson, 1945). It has never been published in the United States. This work makes clear de Gaulle's admiration for the "classicism" of the Old Regime and corrects the impression of the hurried reader that the individualism of the "man of character" highlighted in *The Edge of the Sword* is to be understood as a Nietzschean or quasi-Nietzschean affirmation of the unrestrained human will. See our detailed analysis of the neoclassicism of de Gaulle in Chapter 2 of this book.

13. Shennan, *De Gaulle*, pp. 1–2.

14. Lacouture, *The Rebel*, pp. 1–2.

15. On de Gaulle's break with Pétain in 1938, which precedes and foreshadows their complete and total divergence of paths in June of 1940, see Lacouture, *The Rebel*, pp. 157–165.

16. Shennan, *De Gaulle*, p. 7.

17. Lacouture, *The Rebel*, pp. 166–178.

18. See de Gaulle's "Mémorandum" of January 26, 1940 in *Le Fil de l'épée et autres écrits*, pp. 797–810. See also his discussion of the "Memorandum" in *The Complete War Memoirs of Charles de Gaulle* (New York: Simon and Schuster, 1967), pp. 29–30. Throughout these notes, I will cite this widely available edition of the three volumes of de Gaulle's *Mémoires de Guerre: L'Appel, L'Unité, Salut* (Paris: Plon, 1989).

19. Lacouture, *The Rebel*, pp. 42–54.

20. *The Edge of the Sword*, pp. 41–53, and *The Army of the Future*, pp. 173–174. The phrase "man of character" is not explicitly used in *The Army of the Future*, where he is instead called the "man made for great deeds" (*The Army of the Future*, p. 173) ("hautes actions" in the French).

21. See Claude Mauriac's account of André Malraux's discussion of the portrait of the "man of character" in Mauriac, *The Other de Gaulle* (New York: John Day, 1973), p. 137.

22. *The Army of the Future*, p. 173.

23. *The Edge of the Sword*, p. 22.

24. Stanley Hoffmann, *Decline or Renewal? France Since the 1930's* (New York: Viking, 1974), p. 231. This work is indebted to Hoffmann's eloquent and consistently thoughtful analyses of de Gaulle's writings, character, and statesmanship. See especially his remarkable analysis of de Gaulle's *War Memoirs*, "The Hero as History: De Gaulle's *War Memoirs*," in *Decline or Renewal*, pp. 187–201.

25. Mauriac, *The Other de Gaulle*, p. 261.

26. Ibid.

27. *The Army of the Future*, p. 174.

28. *The Edge of the Sword*, p. 64. (I have modified the translation.)

29. For de Gaulle's sympathetic account of the opportunistic and "realistic" but measured statecraft of the Old Regime, see *La France et son armeé* in *Le Fil de l'épée et autres écrits*, pp. 368, 372–373.

30. For de Gaulle's sometimes nostalgic evocation of an older European order where the "sensible" principle of the "balance of power" reigned, see Mauriac, *The Other de Gaulle*, pp. 231, 313–314.

31. *La France et son armeé* in *Le Fil de l'épée et autres écrits*, p. 421.

32. The quotations in this paragraph are drawn from the "Avant-Propos" to the first edition of *La Discorde chez l'ennemi* in *Le Fil de l'épée et autres écrits*, p. 12.

33. See Chapter 1 of *La Discorde chez l'ennemi* entitled "The Disobedience of General von Kluck" in ibid., pp. 17–26.

34. Ibid., pp. 27–50. On the possibility of Wilson's mediation, see pp. 27, 49.

35. The word "Principles" in this context suggests a recognition of natural limits or an "order of human things" that cannot be finally "conquered" or willfully ignored. See de Gaulle's reference to "the natural order of things" in the concluding paragraph of *The Army of the Future*, p. 179. The "natural order of things" provides the contour or context within which the political condition of man operates and unfolds. De Gaulle shares the classical sentiment that nature, despite the most powerful efforts of the human will, always returns. Discussing the reversal of German fortunes in the summer of 1918, de Gaulle writes: "L'effondrement soudain d'une peuple fort et vaillant allait servir de témoinage à la vengeance des Principes outragés" (ibid., p. 112).

36. *La France et son armée* in ibid., p. 421.

37. Ibid., p. 422.

38. Jean Lacouture, *The Rebel*, pp. 164, 227.

39. Raymond Aron, *Memoirs: Fifty Years of Political Reflection* (New York: Holmes and Meier), pp. 256–257.

40. Charles de Gaulle, "Discours Prononcé à Bayeux 16 Juin 1946," in *L'esprit de la Ve République*, pp. 309–317. The English-language text can be found in *The War Memoirs of Charles de Gaulle: Salvation. Documents 1944–1946* (New York: Simon and Schuster, 1960), pp. 384–390. See Lacouture's analysis of the Bayeux address, *The Ruler*, pp. 129–31.

41. *War Memoirs: Salvation*, p. 387.

42. Ibid., p. 387.

43. On Maurras and de Gaulle, see Lacouture, *The Rebel*, pp. 168–169 and Raymond Aron, "Maurrassisme et Gaullisme," in *Commentaire* 68 (Winter 1994–1995): 927–928. See de Gaulle's revealing criticism of Maurras as being "against France, too. Against the France of his time." See Mauriac, *The Other de Gaulle*, p. 170.

44. *The Army of the Future*, pp. 30–31.

45. Lacouture, *The Rebel*, p. 166.

46. Ibid., pp. 168–169.

47. *The Army of the Future*, pp. 177–179.

48. *The Complete War Memoirs*, p. 727.

49. Malraux, *Felled Oaks: Conversation with de Gaulle* (New York: Holt, Rinehart and Winston, 1971), p. 29.

50. See Charles Williams, *The Last Great Frenchman: A Life of General de Gaulle* (New York: John Wiley and Sons, 1993), pp. 209–219, especially pp. 217–218.

CHAPTER 2

1. *The Complete War Memoirs of Charles de Gaulle* (New York: Simon and Schuster, 1967), p. 1. I have corrected the English translation. For a convenient one-volume French edition of the *War Memoirs*, see Charles de Gaulle, *Mémoires de Guerre: L'Appel, L'Unité, Le Salut* (Paris: Plon, 1989), p. 9. *The War Memoirs of Charles de Gaulle* originally appeared in translation in three separate volumes with the subtitles *The Call to Honor 1940–1942, Unity 1942–1944,* and *Salvation 1944–1946* (New York: Simon and Schuster, 1955, 1959, and 1960). Throughout this book I will cite the one-volume, unabridged edition cited above. In the one-volume edition of the book, Vol. I covers pp. 1–302, Vol. II, pp. 303–666, and Vol. III, pp. 667–998.

2. See Charles Péguy, *Notre jeunesse* (Paris: Gallimard-Folio, 1993), pp. 102–116 and *Basic Verities: Prose and Poetry* (New York: Pantheon, 1943), pp. 103–111. For an introduction to Péguy's analysis of the theological-political problem and his critique of modern historical and sociological consciousness, see Pierre Manent, "Charles Péguy: Between Political Faith and Faith," in John A. Hall, ed., *Rediscoveries: Some Neglected Modern European Political Thinkers* (Oxford: Clarendon Press, 1986), pp. 104–121. On de Gaulle and Péguy, see Stanley Hoffmann, *Decline or Renewal? France Since the 1930's* (New York: Viking, 1974), p. 215.

3. Péguy, *Notre jeunesse*, pp. 102–103, and *Basic Verities*, pp. 103–105.

4. *The Complete War Memoirs*, p. 3.

5. Péguy, *Notre jeunesse*, pp. 140–142.

6. Charles de Gaulle, *The Army of the Future* (Philadelphia: Lippincott, 1941), pp. 15-21.

7. Cited in Will Morrisey, *Reflections on de Gaulle: Political Founding in Modernity* (Lanham, Md.: University Press of America, 1984), p. 113.

8. Ibid.

9. Ibid., p. 114.

10. "Speech delivered by General de Gaulle at the meeting of the 'Français de Grand-Bretagne,' at the Albert Hall, London, 18th June 1942," in *The War Memoirs of Charles de Gaulle: The Call to Honor Documents 1940–1942*. (New York: Simon and Schuster, 1955), p. 427.

11. Ibid.

12. Ibid.

13. Charles de Gaulle, "Allocution Radiodiffusé d'Alger, 27 Juillet 1943," in *Discours et Messages*, vol. 1, *Pendant la Guerre 1940–1946* (Paris: Plon, 1970), p. 314.

14. Charles de Gaulle, *La France et son armée* in *Le Fil de l'épée et autres écrits* (Paris: Plon, 1990), pp. 327–500. The only existing English-language translation of this book is woefully inadequate for the serious student of de Gaulle; it is more of a paraphrase in free verse than anything resembling a reasonably accurate translation. For the convenience of the reader, I will cite the English-language edition, but I have revised the translation in order to accurately render de Gaulle's text.

15. See Péguy, *Notre jeunesse*, p. 103.

16. *The Complete War Memoirs*, pp. 3–4.

17. For the account of de Gaulle's family, see ibid., p. 4.

18. *The Army of the Future*, pp. 94–95.

19. Ibid., pp. 30–32.

20. Ibid., p. 31.

21. *France and Her Army*, p. 7.

22. See Carl von Clausewitz, *On War*, edited and translated by Michael Howard and Peter Paret (Princeton, N.J.: Princeton University Press, 1976).

23. Hoffmann, *Decline or Renewal?*, pp. 228–229.

24. *La France et son armée* in *Le Fil de l'épée et autres écrits*, p. 470; *France and Her Army*, p. 87.

25. Péguy, *Notre jeunesse*, pp. 115–116 and *Basic Verities*, pp. 107, 109.

26. Charles de Gaulle, "Avant-Propos" to *La Discorde chez l'ennemi* in *Le Fil de l'épée et autres écrits*, p. 13.

27. Ibid.

28. *France and Her Army*, p. 6.

29. See Manent, "Charles Péguy: Between Political Faith and Faith," pp. 120–121.

30. See note 10 and *The Complete War Memoirs*, pp. 300–302.

31. *The Complete War Memoirs*, p. 302.

32. *France and Her Army*, pp. 7–23.

33. Ibid., p. 7.

34. Ibid.

35. *The Army of the Future*, p. 34.

36. Ibid., p. 12.

37. Ibid.

38. Ibid., p. 22.

39. Pierre Manent, "De Gaulle's Destiny: The Modern Nation as an Object of Thought and Action" (unpublished speech delivered in Munich in November 1993).

40. *France and Her Army*, pp. 23–33. See "Ancien Régime" in *La France et son armée* in *Le Fil de l'épée et autres écrits*, pp. 359–375.

41. Ibid., p. 23.

42. Manent, "De Gaulle's Destiny."

43. *France and Her Army*, p. 23.

44. Ibid.

45. Ibid.

46. Ibid.

47. Ibid.

48. Quotations in this paragraph are drawn from ibid.

49. Morrisey, *Reflections on de Gaulle*, p. 67.

50. *France and Her Army*, pp. 23–24.

51. Quotations are drawn from de Gaulle's portrait of Louvois, ibid., pp. 25–27.

52. Morrisey, *Reflections on de Gaulle*, pp. 67–68.

53. *France and Her Army*, pp. 27–30.

54. Ibid., p. 28.

55. Ibid.

56. Ibid, p. 30.

57. Ibid, p. 28.

58. Ibid.

59. Ibid.

60. Montesquieu, *The Spirit of the Laws*, Book 9, Chapter 7, translated by A. Cohler, B. Miller, and H. Stone (Cambridge, U.K.: Cambridge University Press, 1989), p. 136.

61. *France and Her Army*, pp. 31–32.

62. Bertrand de Jouvenel, *On Power* (Indianapolis, Ind.: Liberty Fund, 1993).

63. Academic international relation theory aims to give a "scientific" account of the universal laws of international action, and hence tends to be both ahistorical and remarkably abstract and unpolitical.

64. Pierre Manent, "Raymond Aron-Political Educator," in D. Mahoney, ed., *In Defense of Political Reason: Essays by Raymond Aron* (Lanham, Md.: Rowman and Littlefield, 1994), p. 15.

65. "Address by Premier Charles de Gaulle Outlining the Draft Constitution on September 4, 1948," in *Major Addresses, Statements and Press Conferences of General Charles de Gaulle: May 19, 1958–January 31, 1964* (New York: French Embassy, Press and Information Division), p. 13.

66. For the French text of the chapter of *La France et son armée* entitled "Révolution," see *Le Fil de l'épée et autres écrits*, pp. 380–396. For this quotation, see *France and Her Army*, p. 33.

67. Ibid., p. 34.

68. Ibid.

69. Ibid.

70. Ibid.

71. Ibid., pp. 34–44.

72. Ibid., pp. 38–39.

73. Ibid., p. 38.

74. Ibid., p. 45.

75. Ibid., p. 37.

76. Ibid., p. 44.

77. *The Army of the Future*, pp. 35–36.

78. Péguy, *Notre jeunesse*, p. 112.

79. Alexis de Tocqueville, "Preface" to *The Ancien Régime* (London: J. M. Dent and Sons, 1988), p. xxiv.

80. *The Army of the Future*, pp. 177–178.

81. *The Complete War Memoirs*, p. 996.

82. Manent, "De Gaulle's Destiny."

83. *France and Her Army*, p. 45. The French text of the chapter "Napoléon" of *La France et son armée* can be found in *Le Fil de l'épée et autres écrits*, pp. 399–422.

84. *France and Her Army*, p. 45.

85. Ibid.

86. Ibid., p. 55.

87. De Jouvenel, *On Power*, p. 164.

88. *La France et son armée* in *Le Fil de l'épée et autres écrits*, p. 421; *France and Her Army*, p. 60. In the English translation the crucial word "limits," which is so central to de Gaulle's political intention, simply disappears. The translators' aversion to literalism obscures the fundamental lesson of the chapter and therefore the profundity of de Gaulle's thought.

89. *Le Fil de l'épée et autres écrits*, p. 422; *France and Her Army*, p. 60.

90. André Malraux, *Felled Oaks: Conservation with de Gaulle* (New York: Holt, Rinehart and Winston, 1971), pp. 63, 67.

91. *France and Her Army*, p. 60.

92. *Le Fil de l'épée et autres écrits*, p. 470 and *France and Her Army*, p. 87.

93. *France and Her Army*, pp. 93, 102–103.

94. Ibid., pp. 100–101, 103.

95. *The Complete War Memoirs*, pp. 72–73.

96. Malraux, *Felled Oaks*, p. 49.

CHAPTER 3

1. See in particular the excellent, detailed summary and discussion of *The Edge of the Sword* by Will Morrisey in *Reflections on de Gaulle: Political Founding in Modernity* (Lanham, Md.: University Press of America, 1983), pp. 25-39.

2. Interpreters have not been aided by the felicitous but rather loose and often inaccurate English translation of *The Edge of the Sword* (New York: Criterion Books, 1960). In the crucial discussion of the man of character, references to "justice," "nature," and the man of character as "good prince" disappear in the translation. For an illustration, compare the French edition of *Le Fil de l'épée* in *Le Fil de l'épée et autres écrits* (Paris: Plon, 1990), pp. 168–171, with the English edition, pp. 41–46. I have corrected the English translation throughout to more accurately render de Gaulle's language and intention.

3. *Le Fil de l'épée*, p. 170. The reference is missing in the English-language edition, p. 44.

4. Letter of Charles de Gaulle to Raymond Aron, quoted in Raymond Aron, *Memoirs: Fifty Years of Political Reflection* (New York: Holmes and Meier, 1990), p. 370.

5. *The Edge of the Sword*, p. 20.

6. Ibid., p. 22.

7. Ibid.

8. Ibid., pp. 15–16.

9. Charles de Gaulle, *The Army of the Future* (Philadelphia: Lippincott, 1941), pp. 95–153.

10. Cf. de Gaulle, "Mémorandum" of January 26, 1940, in *Le Fil de l'épée et autres écrits*, pp. 799–810, especially pp. 809–810.

11. *The Complete War Memoirs of Charles de Gaulle* (New York: Simon and Schuster, 1963), p. 19.

12. Ibid., p. 9.

13. *The Army of the Future*, pp. 177–179.

14. *The Complete War Memoirs*, p. 8.

15. *The Edge of the Sword*, p. 34.

16. Ibid.

17. Ibid., pp. 44–45.

18. *The Complete War Memoirs*, pp. 8–9.

19. Cf. Pierre Manent's penetrating analysis of magnanimity and humility as the two contradictory poles or "spiritual masses" whose rivalry and coexistence animated the moral, spiritual, intellectual, and political life of the Christian West in *La Cité de l'homme* (Paris: Fayard, 1994), Chapter 1, esp. pp. 39–43. For a discussion of the possibilities and limits of Christian magnanimity, see Manent, pp. 286–291 and Manent, "De la causalité historique" in *Commentaire* 67 (Fall 1994): 705–14, especially 711–14. Compare Thomas Aquinas, *Summa Theologica*, IIa, IIae, Q. 129, articles 3 and 6.

20. *The Complete War Memoirs*, p. 27.

21. *The Edge of the Sword*, p. 63.

22. Raymond Aron, "Maurrassisme et gaullisme" in *Commentaire* 68 (Winter 1994–1995): 927–928.

23. *The Edge of the Sword*, p. 40.

24. Ibid.

25. Ibid., pp. 40–41.

26. Ibid., pp. 8, 71–72.

27. Ibid., p. 41.

28. Aristotle, *Politics*, Book I, Chapter 2.

29. *The Edge of the Sword*, p. 41.

30. Ibid., p. 41.

31. Aristotle, *Nichomachean Ethics*, Book 4, Chapter 3, W. R. Ross, trans. (Oxford, U.K.: Oxford University Press, 1992), pp. 89–94. I have replaced references in the quotation to "pride" and the "proud man" with "magnanimity" and "magnanimous man," which better capture Aristotle's notion of great souledness, or *megalopsychia*.

32. *The Edge of the Sword*, p. 41.

33. Friedrich Nietzsche, *Thus Spake Zarathustra*, "Prologue," in *The Portable Nietzsche Reader*, ed. and trans. by W. Kaufmann (New York: Penguin Viking, 1968), pp. 128–131.

34. Friedrich Nietzsche, *Beyond Good and Evil*, Section 258 (New York: Vintage, 1966), p. 202.

35. Ibid.

36. *The Edge of the Sword*, p. 43.

37. Ibid., p. 41.

38. Ibid., p. 58.

39. Aristotle, *Politics*, Book 1, Chapter 2.

40. *The Edge of the Sword*, p. 56.

41. Ibid., p. 64.

42. Ibid., p. 42.

43. Ibid.

44. On Malraux's relationship with de Gaulle, see Will Morrisey, *Malraux: Cultural Founding in Modernity* (Lanham, Md.: University Press of America, 1984), pp. 220–235 and Raymond Aron, *Memoirs*, pp. 63–65.

45. For a lively expression of de Gaulle's spiritual and intellectual affinities, see Claude Mauriac, *The Other de Gaulle 1944–1954* (New York: John Day, 1973), pp. 230–235.

46. *The Edge of the Sword*, p. 42.

47. Ibid.

48. Ibid., p. 58.

49. Ibid., p. 42.

50. Ibid.

51. Ibid.

52. Ibid.

53. Ibid., p. 44.

54. Ibid., pp. 43–44. Because of the inadequacy of the existing translation, it is necessary to consult the original *Le Fil de l'épée*, pp. 169–170.

55. See Max Weber, "Politics as a Vocation" and "Science as a Vocation" in H. H. Gerth and C. Wright Mills, trans. and eds., *From Max Weber: Essays on Sociology* (New York: Oxford University Press, 1946), pp. 77–156. See also Leo Strauss, *Natural Right and History* (Chicago: University of Chicago Press, 1953), Chapter 2, pp. 35–80.

56. Cf. Abraham Lincoln, "Address to the Young Men's Lyceum of Springfield Illinois: January 27, 1938," in *Lincoln: Speeches and Writings, 1832–1858* (New York: Library of America, 1989), p. 34.

57. *The Edge of the Sword*, p. 44.

58. Ibid., p. 63. This sentence with its explicit reference to "justice" is mutilated in the translation. See *Le Fil de l'épée et autres écrits*, p. 169.

59. Ibid., p. 44.

60. Ibid., p. 43.

61. I owe this insight to Mary P. Nichols.

62. Charles de Gaulle, Preface to *La Discorde chez l'ennemi* in *Le Fil de l'épée et autres écrits* (Paris: Plon, 1990), p. 13.

63. Pierre Manent, "De Gaulle as Hero" in *Perspectives on Political Science* (Fall 1992): 204.

64. *The Complete War Memoirs*, p. 88.

65. The sentence disappears in the English language translation. See *The Edge of the Sword*, p. 44. Compare *Le Fil de l'épée*, p. 170.

66. Cited in Stanley Hoffmann, *Decline and Renewal: France Since the 1930's* (New York: Viking, 1974), p. 236.

67. Niccolo Machiavelli, *The Prince*, Chapter 9, H. Mansfield, trans. (Chicago: University of Chicago Press, 1985).

68. For a rich articulation of the antinaturalism of modern "social science," see Pierre Manent, *La Cité de l'homme*, esp. Chapter 2, pp. 73–124.

69. *The Edge of the Sword*, p. 43.

70. Ibid., p. 44. Compare *Le Fil de l'épée*, p. 170.

71. *Major Addresses, Statements and Press Conferences of General de Gaulle: May 19, 1958–January 31, 1964* (New York: French Embassy, Press and Information Division), p. 6.

72. Raymond Aron, *France: Steadfast and Changing* (Cambridge, Mass.: Harvard University Press, 1960), p. 106.

73. *The Edge of the Sword*, p. 58.

74. Ibid., p. 56.

75. Ibid., p. 57.

76. Ibid. See also de Gaulle's letter to Jean Auburtin dated November 13, 1937 in *Lettres, Notes et Carnets*, Vol. I, 1919–June 1940 (Paris: Plon, 1970), pp. 457–458.

77. Ibid., p. 56.

78. Ibid.

79. Ibid., pp. 59–66.

80. Ibid., pp. 58–59.

81. Ibid., p. 42.

82. Emmanuel d'Astier, "Great, Cold Prelate," in F. Roy Willis, ed., *De Gaulle: Anachronism, Realist or Prophet?* (New York: Holt, Rinehart and Winston, 1967), p. 108.

83. *The Edge of the Sword*, p. 66.

84. Ibid., p. 58.

85. *The Complete War Memoirs*, p. 866.

86. *The Edge of the Sword*, p. 62.

87. Ibid., p. 63.

88. Ibid., p. 64.

89. Ibid., p. 65.

90. *The Complete War Memoirs*, pp. 228–229, 736–737.

91. Cf. our discussion in Chapter 2.

92. Machiavelli, *The Prince*, Chapter 18, p. 70.

93. *The Edge of the Sword*, p. 65.

94. Nora Beloff, "Enigma," in F. Roy Willis, ed., *De Gaulle: Anachronism, Realist or Prophet?* p. 111.

95. *The Edge of the Sword*, p. 64.

96. Ibid., p. 100.

97. See Jean-Marie Mayeux, "De Gaulle as Politician and Christian," in Hugh Gough and John Horne, eds., *De Gaulle and Twentieth Century France* (London: Edward Arnold, 1994), pp. 95–107. This article provides anecdotal evidence and testimony from a diversity of sources and witnesses to the "authenticity" of de Gaulle's Catholic faith. Of course, dogmatists who believe that no thoughtful or self-conscious philosopher or statesman can be a believer will remain unconvinced. I have suggested throughout this book that de Gaulle's affinity for the work of Péguy helps account for the theological resonances of his patriotism and the "national" or "political" character of his Catholicism.

98. André Malraux, *Felled Oaks: Conversation with de Gaulle* (New York: Holt, Rinehart and Winston, 1971), pp. 101–102.

99. See Chapter 5 of this work.

100. *The Complete War Memoirs*, p. 727.

101. Alain Peyrefitte, *C'était de Gaulle* (Paris: Éditions de Fallois/Fayard, 1994), pp. 84–94, 124, 191–192, and 196.

102. Cf. Aron, *Memoirs*, pp. 253–262.

103. Elie Kedourie, "De Gaulle," in *Commentary*, January 1993, pp. 47–48.

104. De Gaulle, *Memoirs of Hope: Renewal and Endeavor* (New York: Simon and Schuster, 1971), pp. 35–36; *The Complete War Memoirs*, pp. 871, 931–932.

105. Mauriac, *The Other de Gaulle*, p. 235.

106. Ibid.

107. Ibid.

108. Charles Péguy, *Notre jeunesse* (Paris: Gallimard-Folio, 1993), p. 149. See Charles Péguy, *Basic Verities—Prose and Poetry* (New York: Pantheon Books, 1943), p. 109.

CHAPTER 4

1. See Raymond Aron, *Memoirs: Fifty Years of Political Reflection* (New York: Holmes and Meier, 1990), pp. 123–124, 259; Jean-François Revel, *Le Style du Général* (Brussels: Editions Complexe, 1988); Alain Peyrefitte, *C'était de Gaulle* (Paris: Editions de Fallois-Fayard, 1994), pp. 433–434.

2. Peyrefitte, *C'était de Gaulle*, pp. 434–435. All quotations in this paragraph are drawn from these pages.

3. Father Gaston Fessard, S.J., was the author of a remarkable polemic warning Christians and all men of goodwill of the corruption inherent in political and spiritual collaboration with Nazism, entitled *France, Beware of Losing Your Soul*. This work appeared clandestinely in *Cahiers du Témoignage Chrétien* in 1941. He followed that work with a warning against the temptation of Christian collaboration with communism in *France, Beware of Losing Your Freedom*, published in 1946. See Gaston Fessard, S.J., *Au temps du Prince-esclave*, edited and introduced by Jacques Prévotat (Limoges, France: Criterion, 1989). See also Jean Chaunu, S.J., "Le Prince et le Jesuite: Un inédit du Pére Fessard, in *Commentaire* 67 (Fall 1994): 563–566, followed by Gaston Fessard, S.J., "De la legitimité du gouvernement provisoire du général de Gaulle: Consultation pour Mgr. Theas (8 Septembre 1944)," pp. 567–569.

4. Peyrefitte, *C'était de Gaulle*, p. 435.

5. *The Complete War Memoirs of Charles de Gaulle* (New York: Simon and Schuster, 1967) p. 49.

6. Ibid.
7. Ibid.
8. Ibid.
9. Ibid., p. 50.
10. Ibid., p. 51.
11. Ibid.
12. Ibid., pp. 51–52.
13. Ibid., p. 52.
14. Ibid.
15. Ibid.
16. Ibid., pp. 53–80.
17. Ibid., pp. 72–73.
18. Ibid., p. 73.
19. Ibid.
20. Ibid., p. 78.
21. Ibid., pp. 78–79.

22. Ibid., p. 79.

23. Ibid., pp. 57–58.

24. Ibid., p. 57.

25. Ibid., pp. 57–58.

26. Ibid., p. 58.

27. Ibid., p. 900.

28. Ibid.

29. Stanley Hoffmann, *Decline or Renewal? France Since the 1930's* (New York: Viking, 1974), p. 264.

30. *The Complete War Memoirs*, p. 58.

31. Ibid., p. 79.

32. Ibid., p. 80.

33. Ibid.

34. Ibid., p. 81.

35. Ibid.

36. Ibid.

37. Ibid., p. 88.

38. Ibid., p. 98.

39. Ibid., pp. 81–82.

40. Ibid., p. 951.

41. Ibid.

42. Ibid.

43. I am indebted to Pierre Manent's remarkable reflection on the moral foundation of the Gaullist enterprise, "De Gaulle as Hero," *Perspectives on Political Science* 21, no. 4 (Fall 1992): 201–206.

44. Ibid., p. 202.

45. *The Complete War Memoirs*, p. 82.

46. Ibid.

47. Charles de Gaulle, "Speech Delivered at Bayeux, June 16, 1946," in *The War Memoirs of Charles de Gaulle: Salvation. Documents 1944–1946* (New York: Simon and Schuster, 1960), p. 385.

48. *The Complete War Memoirs*, p. 82.

49. Ibid., p. 760. See pp. 759–763 for the whole of this dialogue which reveals the profound political and spiritual chasm dividing Roosevelt and the U.S. government from their Free French allies.

50. Ibid., p. 576. Roosevelt's obstinate and unabated opposition to de Gaulle, reinforced by de Gaulle's intransigence and haughtiness, is chronicled in Charles Williams, *The Last Great Frenchman* (New York: John Wiley and Sons, 1993), pp. 162–163, 213–214, 216–218, 230–231, 263–265, 339–340.

51. Williams, *The Last Great Frenchman*, p. 291.

52. This eloquent and measured letter is the best short apologia for the Gaullist enterprise. It also reveals the extent to which de Gaulle recognized the importance of an alliance and genuine political understanding and accommoda-

tion between the United States and Free France. It is impossible to read this letter and to continue to believe that de Gaulle was in any fundamental sense "anti-American." See "Letter from General de Gaulle to President F. D. Roosevelt in Washington, October 26, 1942," in *The War Memoirs of Charles de Gaulle: Unity. Documents 1942–1944* (New York: Simon and Schuster, 1959), pp. 66–71.

53. Ibid., p. 67.

54. *The Complete War Memoirs*, p. 82.

55. Ibid., pp. 82–83.

56. Williams, *The Last Great Frenchman*, pp. 180–181.

57. *The Complete War Memoirs*, p. 900.

58. Williams, *The Last Great Frenchman*, pp. 154–156, 189, 220–221.

59. *The Complete War Memoirs*, p. 83.

60. Williams, *The Last Great Frenchman*, p. 217.

61. *The Complete War Memoirs*, p. 576.

62. Ibid.

63. Ibid., pp. 85–87.

64. Ibid., pp. 87–88.

65. Ibid., p. 87.

66. Ibid., p. 88.

67. Manent, "De Gaulle as Hero," p. 203.

68. For the French text of the "Appeal," see "Discours Prononcé a la Radio de Londres, 18 Juin 1940," in Charles de Gaulle, *Discours et Messages*, Vol. 1: *Pendant la Guerre (Juin 1940–Janvier 1946)* (Paris: Plon, 1970), pp. 3–4. The English-language text can be found on pp. 83–84 of *The Complete War Memoirs*. The following quotations from "Appeal" are all drawn from that text.

69. Raymond Aron, *The Dawn of Universal History*, in D. Mahoney, ed., *In Defense of Political Reason: Essays by Raymond Aron* (Lanham, Md.: Rowman and Littlefield, 1994), p. 142.

70. Ibid., p. 142.

71. *The Complete War Memoirs*, p. 84.

72. Quoted in Jean-François Revel, "La résurrection d'une voix. Le de Gaulle d'Alain Peyrefitte," in *Commentaire* 69 (Spring 1995): 159.

73. See note 3 above.

74. See Gaston Fessard, S.J., "De la legitimité du gouvernement provisoire du général de Gaulle," p. 568.

75. Ibid.

76. Ibid.

77. Gabriel Marcel, "Sketch of a Phenomenology and a Metaphysic of Hope," in *Homo Viator: Introduction to a Metaphysic of Hope* (New York: Harper and Brothers, 1962), p. 48. I was alerted to Marcel's essay by the illuminating discussion of Marcel in H. Stuart Hughes, *Between Commitment and Disillusion: The Obstructed Path and the Sea Change 1930–1965*, part 1, *The Obstructed Path* (Middletown, Conn.: Wesleyan University Press, 1987), pp. 87–89.

CHAPTER 5

1. *The Complete War Memoirs of Charles de Gaulle* (New York: Simon and Schuster, 1967), p. 939.

2. Alexis de Tocqueville, *Democracy in America*, ed. J. P. Mayer (New York: Doubleday, 1965), pp. 703–704.

3. Pierre Manent, *Tocqueville and the Nature of Democracy* (Lanham, Md.: Rowman and Littlefield, 1996), pp. 77–81.

4. Tocqueville, *Democracy*, p. 704.

5. Ibid., pp. 695–702.

6. Raymond Aron, "On Tocqueville," in D. Mahoney, ed., *In Defense of Political Reason: Essays by Raymond Aron* (Lanham, Md.: Rowman and Littlefield, 1994), p. 176.

7. Alexis de Tocqueville, *Selected Letters on Politics and Society*, ed. Roger Boesche (Berkeley: University of California Press, 1985), pp. 150–151.

8. Alexis de Tocqueville, *The Ancien Régime* (London: J. M. Dent and Sons, 1988), pp. 166–169.

9. Tocqueville, *Democracy*, p. 705. See the concluding two paragraphs of Tocqueville's work.

10. Charles de Gaulle, *The Edge of the Sword* (New York: Criterion, 1960), pp. 15–34. The epigram to Chapter 1 of *The Edge of the Sword*, a quotation from Goethe's *Faust*, powerfully suggests the existential primacy of action over thought: "In the beginning was the Word? No! In the beginning was the Act." (*The Edge of the Sword*, p. 15).

11. *The Complete War Memoirs*, p. 8.

12. The speech is anthologized in several recent French volumes of readings in the history of political thought. See the remarks of the ex-Maoist Roland Castro that the Oxford speech is "one of the finest texts against Nazism ever written," quoted in Julian Jackson, "De Gaulle and May 1968," in Hugh Gough and John Horne, eds., *De Gaulle and Twentieth Century France* (London: Edward Arnold, 1994), p. 146.

13. I will cite from the English-language translation of the November 25, 1941 address to the Oxford French Club at Oxford University in *The Call to Honor. Documents 1940–1942* (New York: Simon and Schuster, 1955), pp. 313–320. The French text can be found in Charles de Gaulle, *Discours et Messages*, Vol. 1: *Pendant la Guerre (Juin 1940–Janvier 1946)* (Paris: Plon, 1970), pp. 138–146. The quotation is from *The Call to Honor*, p. 313. (Future citations in this chapter to the speech will read *Oxford Speech*, followed by the page reference in the English-language edition.)

14. *Oxford Speech*, p. 313.

15. Ibid.

16. Ibid., p. 314.

17. Ibid.

18. Ibid.

19. Ibid., pp. 314–315.
20. Ibid., p. 315.
21. Ibid.
22. Ibid.
23. Ibid., p. 316.
24. Ibid., p. 317.
25. Ibid.
26. Ibid.
27. See the illuminating discussion of this concept in Stanley Hoffmann, *Decline or Renewal? France Since the 1930's* (New York: Viking, 1974), p. 190.
28. *The Complete War Memoirs*, p. 27.
29. Ibid., p. 317.
30. Ibid.
31. Ibid., p. 318.
32. Ibid.
33. Ibid.
34. Ibid.
35. Ibid.
36. See Tocqueville's "Preface" to *The Ancien Régime*, p. xxiv and Bertrand de Jouvenel, *On Power* (Indianapolis, Ind.: Liberty Classics, 1993).
37. See Robert Nisbet, *The Quest for Community* (New York: Oxford University Press, 1953) and Pierre Manent, *An Intellectual History of Liberalism* (Princeton, N.J.: Princeton University Press, 1994). Analyzing the movement of modern politics through the lenses of sociology and political philosophy, respectively, Nisbet and Manent arrive at remarkably complementary conclusions concerning the erosion, intrinsic to modern individualism, of those communities or spiritual bodies that connect and enlarge human beings.
38. See Charles de Gaulle, *France and Her Army* (London: Hutchinson, 1945), pp. 23–33.
39. *The Edge of the Sword*, p. 56.
40. Ibid., p. 70.
41. *Oxford Speech*, pp. 318–319.
42. Ibid., p. 319.
43. *The Complete War Memoirs*, p. 721.
44. Michael Oakeshott, "The Masses in Representative Democracy," in *Rationalism in Politics and Other Essays*, augmented edition (Indianapolis, Ind.: Liberty Press, 1991), pp. 363–383.
45. Tocqueville, *The Ancien Régime*, p. 134.
46. *Oxford Speech*, p. 319.
47. Ibid.
48. Ibid.
49. Ibid.
50. Ibid.

51. Ibid., p. 320.

52. Winston Churchill, "Mass Effects in Modern Life," in Churchill, *Thoughts and Adventures* (New York: Scribner's, 1932), pp. 23–30.

53. *Oxford Speech*, p. 320.

54. Ibid.

55. Ibid.

56. Charles de Gaulle, *Memoirs of Hope: Renewal and Endeavor* (New York: Simon and Schuster, 1971), p. 343.

57. Ibid., p. 343. See also André Malraux, *Felled Oaks: Conversation with de Gaulle* (New York: Holt, Rinehart and Winston, 1971), pp. 21–22.

58. *Oxford Speech*, p. 320.

59. Ibid.

60. Cf. note 43.

61. *The Complete War Memoirs*, p. 58.

62. See Churchill's and de Gaulle's dialogue on Franco-British relations and the future of Europe, in ibid., pp 725–728.

63. See "Text of the Address Delivered by General de Gaulle at Westminster Hall, April 7, 1960," in *Major Addresses and Statements of General de Gaulle Delivered Outside France, April 7, 1960–October 17, 1963* (New York: French Embassy, Press and Information Division).

64. Ibid., p. 1.

65. This is drawn from an unpublished address by Pierre Manent, delivered in Munich in November 1993, entitled "De Gaulle's Destiny: The Modern Nation as an Object and Thought and Action."

CHAPTER 6

1. *The Complete War Memoirs of Charles de Gaulle* (New York: Simon and Schuster, 1967), p. 936.

2. For a profound analysis of postrevolutionary French history as an ongoing effort to put an end to the Revolution, see François Furet, *Revolutionary France 1770–1870* (Oxford, U.K.: Blackwell, 1992).

3. *The Complete War Memoirs*, p. 936.

4. The French text of the Bayeux address can be found in Charles de Gaulle, *L'ésprit de la Ve République: Memoirs d'espoir suivi d'un choix d'allocutions et Messages 1946–1969* (Paris: Plon, 1994). As with earlier chapters, I will cite the English-language translation of the text in *The War Memoirs of Charles de Gaulle: Salvation. Documents 1944–1946* (New York: Simon and Schuster, 1960), pp. 384–390. This passage is from p. 385. Hereafter this reference will be cited as *Bayeux Address*.

5. *Bayeux Address*, p. 385.

6. Ibid.

7. Ibid., p. 386.

8. Charles de Gaulle, "Discours Prononcé a Épinal, 29 Septembre, 1946," in *L'ésprit de la Ve République*, pp. 317–323.

9. See Raymond Aron, *Chroniques de Guerre: La France Libre, 1940–1945* (Paris: Gallimard, 1990), esp. pp. 975–985.

10. *The Complete War Memoirs*, pp. 938–939. De Gaulle uses the words "monarchy" and "despotism" interchangeably in this context.

11. Ibid., p. 938.

12. Ibid., p. 939.

13. Ibid.

14. *Bayeux Address*, p. 388.

15. Montesquieu, *The Spirit of the Laws*, Book 11, Chapters 4 and 6, trans. and ed. by A. Cohler, B. Miller, and H. Stone (Cambridge, U.K.: Cambridge University Press, 1989), pp. 154, 157.

16. *Bayeux Address*, p. 388.

17. Montesquieu, *The Spirit of the Laws*, Book 11, Chapter 6, p. 164. On the power of necessity in Montesquieu's doctrine of the separation of powers, see Pierre Manent, *An Intellectual History of Liberalism* (Princeton, N.J.: Princeton University Press, 1994), pp. 57–62.

18. Montesquieu, *The Spirit of the Laws*, Book 19, Chapter 27, pp. 325–327.

19. See John A. Rohr, "Executive Power and Republican Principles at the Founding of the Fifth Republic," *Governance: An International Journal of Policy and Administration* 7, no. 2 (April 1994): 113–134. I am indebted to Rohr's article for its discussion of the tension between the constitutional practice of the Fifth Republic with its clear recognition of presidential primacy and the intentions of the framers of the Fifth Republic's Constitution, who seemed to give broad executive power to the prime minister and to shield him from removal by the president of the Republic. Perhaps, however, Rohr takes his bearings too much from the constitutional discussions and debates of the Advisory Committee on the Constitution of August 1958 and the testimony of Michel Debré or even de Gaulle before that committee, and not enough from de Gaulle's own broader constitutional reflection. The more parliamentary focus of discussion of executive power within the Advisory Committee on the Constitution has much to do with the parliamentary sympathies of its members. Perhaps de Gaulle did not unnecessarily challenge that prejudice when he testified before the Committee in August of 1958—hence, the greater discrepancy between founding intentions and constitutional practice than de Gaulle himself ever openly recognized or affirmed.

20. *Bayeux Address*, pp. 389–390.

21. Ibid., p. 389.

22. See Charles de Gaulle, *Memoirs of Hope: Renewal and Endeavor* (New York: Simon and Schuster, 1971), pp. 306–307, 311–334, 340, 377. See also Charles Williams, *The Last Great Frenchman: A Life of Charles de Gaulle* (New York: John Wiley and Sons, 1993), pp. 422–423.

23. *Memoirs of Hope*, pp. 306–307.

24. See Harvey C. Mansfield, *The Taming of the Prince* (New York: Free Press, 1989), esp. pp. 1–20.

25. Charles de Gaulle, "Ninth Press Conference held by General de Gaulle as President of the French Republic January 31, 1964," in *Major Addresses, Statements and Press Conferences of Charles de Gaulle May 19, 1958–January 31, 1964* (New York: French Embassy, Press and Information Division, 19), p. 248. De Gaulle's discourse on the French Constitution on the occasion of this press conference contains his most grandiloquent defense of presidential authority and an argument against the applicability of an American-style presidential system in the French context.

26. Ibid., p. 248.

27. John Rohr has interesting things to say about Michel Debré's rhetorical strategy for defending the truly popular and even "parliamentary" character of the Fifth Republic's Constitution in a forthcoming comparative study of the founding of the American Republic and the French Fifth Republic entitled *Founding Republics in France and America: A Study in Constitutional Governance*, to be published by University Press of Kansas in 1996.

28. *Bayeux Address*, p. 388.

29. Ibid.

30. *Memoirs of Hope*, p. 31.

31. See the helpful discussions in William Safran, *The French Polity*, 4th ed. (White Plains, N.Y.: Longman USA, 1995), pp. 9–21, 162–200.

32. *The Complete War Memoirs*, pp. 960–966.

33. *Bayeux Address*, p. 390.

34. Montesquieu, *The Spirit of the Laws*, Book 11, Chapter 6, p. 158.

35. See Safran, *The French Polity*, pp. 217–218.

36. *Bayeux Address*, pp. 388–389.

37. Ibid., p. 389.

38. Ibid.

39. Ibid. The Constitution of the Fifth Republic can be found in Safran, *The French Polity*, pp. 331–345.

40. *Bayeux Address*, p. 389.

41. Manent, *An Intellectual History of Liberalism*, p. 51.

42. Ibid.

43. Ibid., p. 52.

44. Mansfield, *The Taming of the Prince*, p. 256.

45. *Bayeux Address*, p. 389.

46. See Wolfgang Mommsen, *Max Weber and German Politics—1870–1920* (Chicago: University of Chicago Press, 1984), pp. 411–414; Allan Bloom, *The Closing of the American Mind* (New York: Simon and Schuster, 1987), pp. 212–214; Raymond Aron, *Main Currents in Sociological Thought*, Volume II (New York: Doubleday Anchor, 1970), p. 299.

47. Max Weber, "The President of the Reich," in P. Lassman and D. Speirs, eds., *Weber: Political Writings* (Cambridge, U.K.: Cambridge University Press, 1994), p. 307.

48. *Bayeux Address*, p. 389.

49. See the thoughtful discussion of the classical dimensions of de Gaulle's "founding" in Will Morrisey, *Reflections on de Gaulle* (Lanham, Md.: University Press of America, 1983), pp. 159–170, esp. p. 165.

50. Jean-François Revel, *L'Absolutisme Inefficace* (Paris: Plon, 1992).

CHAPTER 7

1. Sir Winston Churchill, Speech at Zurich, September 19, 1946, "Something That Will Astonish You," in *Blood, Toil, Tears and Sweat*, ed. David Cannadine (Boston: Houghton Mifflin, 1989), pp. 309–314.

2. This outline of the history of the European project draws broadly on the concise and informative account of Geoffrey Smith, "Euro-what?" in *World Monitor* (December 1992): pp. 44–49.

3. Ibid., pp. 46–47.

4. Ibid., p. 48 and Jean Monnet, *Mémoires* (Paris: Fayard, 1976).

5. Monnet, *Mémoires*, pp. 420–430, 464, 427–430, and 510–515, and Ghita Ionesco, *Leadership in an Interdependent World: The Statesmanship of Adenauer, De Gaulle, Thatcher, Reagan and Gorbachev* (Boulder, Colo.: Westview, 1991), pp. 123–136, esp. p. 123.

6. Friedrich Nietzsche, *Beyond Good and Evil*, Aphorism 241 (New York: Vintage, 1966), p. 174.

7. Cited in Jean Lacouture, *De Gaulle: The Ruler 1945–1970* (New York: W. W. Norton, 1991), p. 345.

8. Charles de Gaulle, *Discours et Messages: Vol. III; Avec le renouveau 1958–1962* (Paris: Plon, 1970), pp. 244–245. The English translation is taken from *Major Addresses, Statements and Press Conferences of General de Gaulle May 19, 1958–January 31, 1964* (New York: French Embassy, Press and Information Division), pp. 92–93.

9. Charles de Gaulle, *Memoirs of Hope: Renewal and Endeavor* (New York: Simon and Schuster, 1971), p. 3.

10. *Discours et Messages: Vol. III*, pp. 406–407 and *Major Addresses*, p. 175.

11. Nietzsche, *Beyond Good and Evil*, Aphorism 242, p. 176.

12. *Major Addresses*, p. 176.

13. On the details of, different versions of, and controversies engendered by the Fouchet Plan, see Lacouture, *The Ruler*, pp. 345–350.

14. *Memoirs of Hope*, p. 171.

15. Charles de Gaulle, Press Conference of December 21, 1951, *Discours et Messages: Vol. II. Dans l'Attente 1946–1958* (Paris: Plon, 1970), p. 482.

16. De Gaulle, "Notes au sujet de l'Europe, 17 juillet 1961," *Lettres, Notes et Carnets* 1961–1963 (Paris: Plon, 1986), p. 107.

17. Ibid.

18. *Memoirs of Hope*, p. 11.

19. This characterization of America as Europe's cousin does not fit the stereotype of de Gaulle as a reflexive and emotional anti-American. For a reasoned discussion of de Gaulle's views of his American "cousins," see Lacouture, *The Ruler*, pp. 363–386.

20. Cf. note 16.

21. On de Gaulle's behavior during the Berlin and Cuban crises, see Lacouture, *The Ruler*, pp. 339–340, 369, and 375–376. At a meeting of the four leading Western powers on November 10, 1960, Macmillan and Eisenhower were in favor of reaching an accommodation with Moscow after Khrushchev demanded a Western withdrawal from Berlin. Only de Gaulle stood adamantly behind Adenauer and the cause of a free Berlin. In October of 1962, de Gaulle, though annoyed that he had not been consulted by President Kennedy in the matter of the Cuban missile crisis, informed Kennedy's emissary Dean Acheson that France supported the United States "unreservedly." (He did not need to see the aerial photographs of the Soviet missiles that Acheson had brought with him. The word of the president of the United States was sufficient, he announced.) During that same crisis, when rudely hounded during a meeting with Khrushchev's ambassador to France, Serge Vinogradov, who warned de Gaulle of France's possible, impending nuclear destruction, de Gaulle stretched out his hand to Vinogradov and ironically replied, "Helas, Monsieur l'Ambassadeur, nous mourrirons ensemble! Au revoir, Monsieur l'Ambassadeur." As Will Morrisey has well observed, de Gaulle was possibly the greatest statesman of modern times to oppose the dispiritedness endemic to democratic psychology and practice. The self-respect of free peoples forbade appeasement or even equivocation before totalitarian blackmail and intimidation. De Gaulle's support of détente with the East must be located within that larger context. Cf. Will Morrisey, "De Gaulle: Man with a Chest," *Chronicles of Culture* (March 1985): 11–12.

22. Raymond Aron, *Memoirs: Fifty Years of Political Reflections* (New York: Holmes and Meier, 1990), p. 286.

23. Ibid., p. 289.

24. *Memoirs of Hope*, p. 171.

25. De Gaulle, "Speech Made to the Oxford French Club, November 25, 1941" in *The Call to Honor. Documents 1940–1942* (New York: Simon and Schuster, 1955), p. 318.

26. De Gaulle, *The Edge of the Sword*, Part III: "Prestige" (New York: Criterion, 1950), p. 70.

27. An excellent example of this can be found in the wartime synthesis of traditionalist and republican discourses and themes in de Gaulle's speech to a meeting of *Les Français de Grande-Bretagne*, London, November 15, 1941, in *The*

Call to Honor. Documents 1940–1942, pp. 378–384. The following excerpt is characteristic of de Gaulle's efforts to transcend the conflict between the Old Regime and the Revolution and the Left and the Right in the name of liberty and grandeur of the French nation:

We believe that the foundations of the future institutions of France can best be defined by the three mottoes of the Free French. We say: "Honor and Country," meaning thereby that the nation can live again only through victory and endure only through the cult of her own greatness. We say: "Liberty, Equality, Fraternity," because we are resolved to remain faithful to the democratic principles established by our forbears and drawn from the genius of our race—those very principles now at stake in this life and death struggle. We say "Liberation," and we use the term in its widest sense, for if our efforts must not cease until the enemy has been defeated and punished, it is equally necessary that they should result in the establishment of conditions in which every Frenchman may live, think, work, and act in dignity and security (pp. 383–384).

28. Memoirs of Hope, p. 36.
29. Ionesco, Leadership in an Interdependent World, p. 94.
30. Charles Péguy, Notre jeunesse (Paris: Gallimard-Folio, 1993), pp. 141–142.
31. The Complete War Memoirs of Charles de Gaulle (New York: Simon and Schuster, 1967), pp. 753–769.
32. André Malraux, Felled Oaks: Conversation with de Gaulle (New York: Holt, Rinehart and Winston, 1972), p. 76.
33. The Complete War Memoirs, p. 84.
34. See de Gaulle's Speech of June 18, 1942 in London at the meeting of the Français de Grande-Bretagne, The Call to Honor. Documents 1940–1942, pp. 424–425.
35. For Roosevelt's blind and ungenerous view of de Gaulle, see Ionesco, Leadership in an Interdependent World, pp. 87–89 and 101–103. Compare Churchill's more complex and accurate judgment in The Hinge of Fate, paperback ed. (New York: Bantam, 1962), p. 593. Churchill writes:

In these pages various severe statements, based on events of the moment are set down about General de Gaulle, and certainly I had continuous difficulties and many sharp antagonisms with him. There was however a dominant element in our relationship. I could not regard him as representing captive and prostrate France, nor indeed the France that had a right to decide freely the future for herself. I knew he was no friend of England. But I always recognized in him the spirit and conception which, across the pages of history, the word "France" would ever proclaim. I understood and admired, while I resented, his arrogant demeanour. Here he was a refugee, an exile from his country under sentence of death, in a position entirely dependent upon the good will of the British Government, and also now of the United States. The Germans had conquered his country. He had no real foothold anywhere. Never mind, he defied all. Always, even when he was behaving worst, he seemed to express the personality of France—a great nation, with all its pride, authority, and ambition. It was said in mockery that he thought himself the living representative of Joan of Arc, with whom it is said one of his ancestors served as a faithful adherent. This did not seem to me as absurd as it looked. Clemenceau, with whom it was said he also compared himself, was a far wiser and more experienced statesman. But they both gave the same impression of being unconquerable Frenchmen.

36. *The Complete War Memoirs*, p. 721.

37. Ibid.

38. De Gaulle, "Third Press Conference as President of the Fifth Republic, September 5, 1960," in *Major Addresses*, p. 84.

39. Ibid.

40. De Gaulle, "Eighth Press Conference as President of the Fifth Republic, July 29, 1963," in *Major Addresses*, p. 237.

41. See de Gaulle's portrait of Stalin in *The Complete War Memoirs*, pp. 736–739 and 741–759, esp. pp. 736–737.

42. Charles Williams, *The Last Great Frenchman: A Life of General de Gaulle* (New York: John Wiley and Sons, 1993), p. 456.

43. See the self-serving analysis of Régis Débray in *Charles de Gaulle: Futurist of a Nation* (London: Veno, 1994), pp. 57–74. Débray continues to suffer from a juvenile anti-anticommunism.

44. For a devastating attack on the fraudulent and contrived notions of "Great Soviet Patriotism," see Alexander Solzhenitsyn, *Rebuilding Russia* (New York: Farrar, Straus and Giroux, 1991), pp. 1–14, esp. pp. 10–11.

45. Cf. *The Memoirs of Hope*, pp. 174–181, 223–224, and Lacouture, *The Ruler*, pp. 212, 215–216, 333–345, 376–377, 480–481.

46. Churchill, *Blood, Toil, Tears and Sweat*, p. 312.

47. For de Gaulle's profound, if equivocal, admiration for Churchill, see *The Complete War Memoirs*, pp. 57–58; for his sympathetic judgment of British political institutions and life, see his address of April 7, 1960 to the House of Commons, the most important parts of which are reproduced in *Memoirs of Hope*, pp. 235–237; for his suspicions of the "Anglo-Saxons," see ibid., pp. 216–220.

48. Ionesco, *Leadership in an Interdependent World*, p. 4.

49. Ibid., p. 5.

50. Ibid., Chapters 2 and 3, esp. pp. 144–146 and 206–207.

51. Ibid., pp. 112, 115–116.

52. Ibid., p. 146.

53. Ibid., pp. 144–145.

54. Ibid., p. 145.

55. This illuminating formulation is derived from an unpublished address of Pierre Manent, "De Gaulle's Destiny: The Modern Nation as an Object of Thought and Action," delivered in Munich in November 1993.

56. Ionesco, *Leadership in an Interdependent World*, pp. 79, 81, 144.

57. Manent, "De Gaulle's Destiny."

58. See Pierre Manent, "Modern Individualism," in *Crisis*, October 1995, pp. 35–38.

59. Malraux, *Felled Oaks*, pp. 123–124.

60. Ibid., p. 17.

Selected Bibliography

The following is a very selected listing of the major writings of Charles de Gaulle and of those secondary sources that were found to be most helpful for reflecting on de Gaulle and the problem of democratic statesmanship. Full bibliographical information is provided for all other sources in the notes.

De Gaulle, Charles. *The Army of the Future*. Philadelphia: Lippincott, 1941.
————. *The Complete War Memoirs of Charles de Gaulle*. New York: Simon and Schuster, 1967.
————. *Discours et messages: Pendant la Guerre (Juin 1940–Janvier 1946), Dans l'Attente (Février 1946–Avril 1958), Avec le Renouveau (Mai 1958–Juillet 1962), Pour l'Effort (Août 1962–Décembre 1965), Vers le Terme (Janvier 1966–Avril 1969)* Paris: Librairie Plon, 1970.
————. *The Edge of the Sword*. New York: Criterion, 1960.
————. *France and Her Army*. London: Hutchinson, 1945.
————. *Le Fil de l'épée et autres écrits*. Paris: Plon, 1990.
————. *L'ésprit de la Ve République: Mémoires d'espoir suivi d'un choix d'Allocutions et messages 1946–1969*. Paris: Plon, 1994.
————. *Major Addresses, Statements and Press Conferences of General Charles de Gaulle: May 19, 1958–January 31, 1964*. New York: French Embassy, Press and Information Division.
————. *Mémoires de Guerre: L'Appel, L'Unité, Salut*. Paris: Plon, 1989.
————. *Memoirs of Hope: Renewal and Endeavor*. New York: Simon and Schuster, 1971.
————. *The War Memoirs of Charles de Gaulle: The Call to Honor. Documents 1940–1942*. New York: Simon and Schuster, 1955.

————. *The War Memoirs of Charles de Gaulle: Unity. Documents 1942–1944*. New York: Simon and Schuster, 1959.

————. *The War Memoirs of Charles de Gaulle: Salvation. Documents 1944–1946*. New York: Simon and Schuster, 1960.

OTHER WRITINGS

Aron, Raymond. *Memoirs: Fifty Years of Political Reflection*. New York: Holmes and Meier, 1990.

Hoffman, Stanley. *Decline or Renewal? France Since the 1930's*. New York: Viking, 1974.

Ionesco, Ghita. *Leadership in an Interdependent World: The Statesmanship of Adenauer, De Gaulle, Thatcher, Reagan and Gorbachev*. Boulder, Colo.: Westview, 1991.

Lacouture, Jean. *De Gaulle: The Rebel 1890–1944*. New York: W. W. Norton, 1991.

————. *De Gaulle: The Ruler 1945–1970*. New York: W. W. Norton, 1991.

Malraux, André. *Felled Oaks: Conversation with de Gaulle*. New York: Holt, Rinehart and Winston, 1971.

Manent, Pierre. "De Gaulle as Hero." *Perspectives on Political Science* 21, no. 4 (Fall 1992): 201–206.

Mauriac, Claude. *The Other de Gaulle 1944–1954*. New York: John Day, 1973.

Montesquieu. *The Spirit of the Laws*. Translated and edited by A. Cohler, B. Miller, and H. Stone. Cambridge, U.K.: Cambridge University Press, 1989.

Morrisey, Will. *Reflections on de Gaulle: Political Founding in Modernity*. Lanham, Md.: University Press of America, 1983.

Péguy, Charles. *Notre jeunesse*. Paris: Gallimard-Folio, 1993.

Peyrifitte, Alain. *C'était de Gaulle*. Paris: Éditions de Fallois/Fayard, 1994.

Rohr, John A. "Executive Power and Republican Principles at the Founding of the Fifth Republic." *Governance: An International Journal of Policy and Administration* 7, no. 2 (April 1994): 113–114.

Tocqueville, Alexis de. *The Ancien Régime*. London: J. M. Dent and Sons, 1988.

Williams, Charles. *The Last Great Frenchman: A Life of Charles de Gaulle*. New York: John Wiley and Sons, 1993.

Index

About the Author

DANIEL J. MAHONEY teaches political science at Assumption College, Worcester, MA. He is the author of *The Liberal Political Science of Raymond Aron* (1992), and the editor of *In Defense of Political Reason* (1994).